European Union and its Neighbours in a Globalized World

Volume 28

The series publishes monographs and edited volumes in the field of European and international law and policy. A special focus is put on the European neighbourhood policy, current problems in European and international law and policy as well as the role of the European Union as a global actor. The series supports the publishing and distribution of research results of cross-border research consortia. Besides renowned scientists the series is also open for publication projects of young academics. The series emphasizes the interplay of the European Union and its neighbouring countries as well as the important role of the European Union as a key player in the international context of law, economics and politics.

Cătălin-Silviu Săraru • Cristina Elena Popa Tache
Editors

AI, Sustainability and Solidarity in Advancing European Values in a Globalized Age

Springer

Editors
Cătălin-Silviu Săraru
Faculty of Law
Bucharest University of Economic Studies
Bucharest, Bucuresti, Romania

Cristina Elena Popa Tache
Faculty of Law and International Governance
Danubius International University
Galati, Romania

ISSN 2524-8928 ISSN 2524-8936 (electronic)
European Union and its Neighbours in a Globalized World
ISBN 978-3-032-06507-0 ISBN 978-3-032-06508-7 (eBook)
https://doi.org/10.1007/978-3-032-06508-7

This Springer imprint is published by the registered company Springer Nature Switzerland AG
The registered company address is: Gewerbestrasse 11, 6330 Cham, Switzerland

Preface

This volume contains the scientific papers presented at the 14th International Conference "Perspectives of Business Law in the Third Millennium" that was held on 15 November 2024 in online format on Zoom. The conference is organized each year by the *Society of Juridical and Administrative Sciences*. More information about the conference can be found on the official website: www.businesslawconference.ro.

The scientific studies included in this volume are grouped into four parts:

Artificial Intelligence and Digital Transformation Dealing with Problems and Opportunities The papers in this chapter refer to: looking to the future with confidence: towards the "AI Act" implementation; the new challenges of artificial intelligence legal framework in European Union cyberspace; the legal influence of artificial intelligence on intellectual property rights: a comparative approach; artificial intelligence and civil justice.

Sustainable Development and Solidarity in the European Context This chapter includes papers on: deposit-return system—One year of operation; the principle of solidarity in European Union law: solidarity and energy security; European sustainability reporting standards in the Slovak accounting legislation; shaping the future of shipping: legal and policy impacts of EU emissions trading and fuel EU maritime regulations.

Public Property and Governance in the Cyber Age The papers in this chapter refer to: public property rights: origins and developments in the cyber age; towards a public domain of cybernetic space-time as a challenge for international law: about the cybercommons; legal foundations of the digital transformation of administrative proceedings.

Human Resources and Cooperative Structures in the Global Economy This chapter includes papers on: the power of scale: how European large corporations' HR practices drive global workforce standards; opportunities of digital transformation in local autonomy: successful examples and learnings; European cooperative society in creating a community—a current issue.

This volume is aimed at practitioners, researchers, students and PhD candidates in juridical sciences, who are interested in recent developments and prospects for development in the field of business law at international and national level.

We thank all contributors and partners and are confident that this volume will meet the needs for growing documentation and information of readers in the context of globalization and the rise of dynamic elements in contemporary business law.

Bucharest, Romania — Cătălin-Silviu Săraru
Galati, Romania — Cristina Elena Popa Tache

Contents

About the Editors

Cătălin-Silviu Săraru Activity Cătălin-Silviu Săraru is Associate Professor Habilitated at the Faculty of Law, Bucharest University of Economic Studies, Romania, where he specializes in administrative law and comparative public law. He is an associate member of the Academy of Scientists in Romania, PhD supervisor in the field of administrative law at Bucharest University of Economic Studies, arbitrator at the Vienna International Arbitral CentreCourt (VIAC), Editor in Chief of the *Juridical Tribune—Review of Comparative and International Law* (indexed in Clarivate Analytics and Scopus) and *Perspectives of Law and Public Administration*; President of the *Society of Juridical and Administrative Sciences* and member in *Société de législation comparée*, *Research Network on EU Administrative Law (ReNEUAL)*; organizer of numerous international conferences: *Perspectives of Business Law in the Third Millennium, Contemporary Challenges in Administrative Law from an Interdisciplinary Perspective, Contemporary Approaches in Banking and Financial Law, Conference on Comparative and International Law*.

Publications Cătălin-Silviu Săraru is the editor of numerous volumes, among which we mention: *Le droit international en transition*, L'Harmattan, 2024; *Current Issues in Administrative Law,* Cambridge Scholars Publishing, 2020; *Contemporary Challenges in the Business Law*, ADJURIS—International Academic Publisher, 2016; *Studies of Business Law—Recent Developments and Perspectives*, Peter Lang International Academic Publishers, 2013; 15 books as sole author among which: *Le droit administratif en Roumanie*, L'Harmattan, Paris, 2022; *Tratat de contencios administrativ (Treatise on administrative litigation),* Universul Juridic, Bucharest, 2022; *Drept administrativ. Probleme fundamentale ale dreptului public (Administrative law. Fundamental issues of public law)*, C.H. Beck Publishing House, Bucharest, 2016, *Legea contenciosului administrativ nr. 554/2004. Examen critic al Deciziilor Curtii Constitutionale (Administrative Litigation Law no. 554/2004. Critical examination of the Constitutional Court Decisions)*, C.H. Beck Publishing House, Bucharest, 2015;

Contractele administrative. Reglementare, doctrină, jurisprudență (*Administrative agreements. Regulatory, doctrine, jurisprudence*), C.H. Beck Publishing House, Bucharest, 2009; 2 books as coauthor among which: *Drept administrativ European* (*European Administrative Law*), Lumina Lex Publishing House, Bucharest, 2005; author of over 100 articles published in journals: *Cogent Social Sciences, Lex Humana, Precedente Revista Jurídica, Journal of Knowledge Dynamics, International Investment Law Journal, Access to Justice in Eastern Europe Juridical Tribune—Tribuna Juridica, European Review of Public Law, Transylvanian Review of Administrative Sciences, Acta Juridica Hungarica, Dreptul, Juridical Current, Acta Universitatis Danubius. Juridica, Revista de Drept Public, Pandectele române, Curierul Judiciar, Notebooks of international law, Tribuna Economică, Economie și Administrație locală*, etc.

Prizes He is the laureate of the following prizes:"Tudor Popescu" Prize awarded by the Romanian Academy of Scientists in 2024 for the work *Tratat de contencios administrativ* (*Treatise on administrative litigation*), Universul Juridic Publishing House, Bucharest 2022."Anibal Teodorescu" Prize awarded by the Union of Jurists of Romania in 2014 for the work "Cartea de contracte administrative—modele, comentarii, explicații" ("The Book of administrative contracts—models, comments, explanations"), C.H. Beck Publishing House, Bucharest, 2013.

Cristina Elena Popa Tache **Activity** Cristina Elena Popa Tache is associate professor of public international law and communications and new technologies law, Co-Chair in European Society of International Law—IG International Business and Human Rights, expert member in COST Actions-European Cooperation in Science and Technology and project member recommended by Institut national supérieur du professorat et de l'éducation de l'académie de Paris and Sorbonne Université. She continues to be a promoter of multi and transdisciplinarity in law, researcher promoter for international investment law in Romania, and also scientific researcher at the International Center for Transdisciplinary Research (CIRET) Paris.

Publications At the same time, she carries out an intense scientific research activity in the field of international law, as well as a publishing and editing activity, being the author of more than 100 legal publications, editor-in-chief of several specialized publications high indexed, including the International Investment Law Journal. Cristina Elena Popa Tache is co-editor of several co-authored volumes with international scientific personalities such as Professor Jin Banggui, Professor Thierry Bonneau, Federica Cristani, Professor Cătălin-Silviu Săraru, and Professor Dalvinder Singh. She is associate editor at Taylor & Francis and Routledge, arbitrator and mediator at the Vienna International Arbitral Centre and member of the Board of Directors in AEDBF Europe. Her scientific activity is extended to participation as a member in the scientific committees and speaker of prestigious international conferences. Recent monographs and works: *Le* *dynamisme du droit international public contemporain et la transdisciplinarité*, L'Harmattan Paris, Collection "Le droit aujourd'hui", 2023; *Introduction to International Investment Law*, ed. Adjuris International Academic Publisher, 2020, translated edition of the monograph Introduction to International Investment Law, Ed. Universul Juridic, 2018; *Legal treatment standards for international investments. Heuristic aspects*, Ed. Adjuris International Academic Publisher, 2021; *Vers un droit de l'âme et des bioénergies du vivant*, Ed. L Harmattan, Collection: Logiques Juridiques, 2022, preface by Jean-Luc MartinLagardette; *Report Chapter, Specific Threats to Human Rights Protection from the Digital Reality. International Responses and Recommendations to Core Threats from the Digitalized World*, Tina Pajuste (ed.), Tallinn University, 2022 or contribution to *Report about the comparative content analysis of instruments adopted by international and European organizations/countries regarding human rights protection online* (Deliverable No. 11), published by The Global Digital Human Rights Network (GDHRNet), 2023.

Artificial Intelligence and Digital Transformation Dealing with Problems and Opportunities

Looking to the Future with Confidence: Towards the "AI Act" Implementation

Elena Emilia Ştefan

Abstract The development of modern society brings to the forefront new challenges for the legislator, namely to be constantly in touch with the society's needs and to create new legal rules. We are currently witnessing the unprecedented expansion of modern technology involving artificial intelligence. At the European level, the Artificial Intelligence Act was adopted in the summer of 2024, by representing a normative act that will have an impact on society in the near future in ways that we cannot predict at the moment, but the implications of which will be felt by both economic operators and state administration. From this perspective, this paper will explore what business environment and public authorities need to know about the European legislation in order to comply with it. The proposed scope is to know as much as possible about the Artificial Intelligence Act and to find out how our country is prepared to implement this European act. The results of the research show that while the huge potential that artificial intelligence brings to everyday work cannot be denied, caution is required in the use of modern technologies, with public authorities constantly having to assess their impact on fundamental rights and freedoms in order to avoid harming individuals.

1 Introduction

Regulation (EU) 2024/1689 of the European Parliament and of the Council of 13 June 2024 laying down harmonized rules of artificial intelligence and amending Regulations (EU) no.300/2008, (EU) no.167/2013, (EU) no.168/2013, (EU) 2018/858, (EU) 2018/1139 and (EU) 2019/1144 and Directives 2014/90/ EU, (EU) 2016/797 and (EU) 2020/1828.[1] The European Act is generally known as the

[1] Published in OJEU L 2024/1689, 12.7.2024.

E. E. Ştefan (✉)
"Nicolae Titulescu" University of Bucharest, Bucharest, Romania

C.-S. Săraru, C. E. Popa Tache (eds.), *AI, Sustainability and Solidarity in Advancing European Values in a Globalized Age*, European Union and its Neighbours in a Globalized World 28, https://doi.org/10.1007/978-3-032-06508-7_1

Artificial Intelligence Act - "AI Act" and it comes after the adoption on 25 May 2018 of another European Act that changed the public perception of data privacy, namely the G.D.P.R.

In this background, we emphasize the novelty of the topic, so that the issue of artificial intelligence must be permanently in the attention of the scientific community.[2] The topic is also relevant for the general public, which is invited to reflect on the opportunities and risks of modern technology in everyday life. For the legislator, the regulation of social needs must be carried out in compliance with the principle of legality because "the stakes for leaders at the highest level in states today are huge and on the long-term (…): the identification of solutions and mechanisms to increase public trust in state authorities (…)".[3]

The AI Act, being adopted by an European Regulation, we note that it is binding on the Member States, the document being of general application. According to the Constitution, Romania is bound to harmonize its legislation with the acquis communautaire. Furthermore, "national actors are particularly important as they are mainly responsible for the day-to-day implementation of EU legislation".[4]

Researching the correspondence between legislation and academic environment, we note a subject dealing with modern technologies in the curricula of universities: *Communications and new technologies law.*[5] At the international level, on the one hand, in the major university centers "sub-branches of this discipline are studied separately, such as the law of technology, which is an individual discipline for Harvard University (...) and on the other hand there are publications under this name: European Journal of Law and Technology (OUP), Berkeley Technology Law Journal (appeared since 1985) (...)".[6] It seems that globally, "international organizations such as OECD, UNESCO and WHO have promoted ethical development of the A.I., proposing principles of governance that are non-binding but inspire future practice and regulation."[7]

Methodologically, the paper is structured in three parts: one part is dedicated to the AI Act, the second part presents information on the national plan on artificial intelligence and the third part presents brief perspectives on the use of artificial intelligence in public and private environments.

[2] Popa Tache and Săraru (2024).

[3] Ştefan (2017).

[4] Petric (2023).

[5] See for example the work issued by Popa Tache (2023).

[6] Popa Tache (2023), pp. 7–12.

[7] Voicu (2024).

2 The AI Act: Several Theoretical References

2.1 Views on Artificial Intelligence and Its Imminent Application in Society at Large

The discussions held on the need and advisability of normative regulation of a technology to support citizens, the business environment and public authorities[8] took the form of the publication in the Official Journal of the European Union of the AI Act. The Doctrine emphasized that "thanks to this new and unprecedented regulation, Europe becomes the first model continent to have adopted a legal and technical corpus that creates an environment favorable to its affirmation in conditions of security for man and society."[9]

Comparative law researchers note that "European public administration increasingly relies on personal data to deliver their public services, which implies that they must comply with the rules contained in the General Data Protection Regulation. These rules are especially important in the advent of new artificial intelligence (AI) technologies, which increase the public administration's capability to make informed decisions in order to provide public services and to support their decision-making."[10] Furthermore, another author emphasized that "the stakes involved in the legal framing of AI are fundamental, especially when its applications are interwoven in all sectors of activity and sometimes with radical consequences."[11]

From another perspective, a research paper presents the principle of good governance—transparency and reasoning for AI decisions.[12] With regard to the recognition of the practical importance of new technologies, it has been pointed out in an expert study that "the evolution of social behavior under the pressure of the digitized conversion of society will determine the most important evolution of electronic agent services through the intelligent integration of several services of the information society and by increasing the complexity and the level of autonomy of their functioning, leading to the emergence of the personoid/virtual person service as a complete information assistance service."[13]

---

[8] More information on public authorities in paperwork Cliza and Ulariu (2021), pp. 7–22.

[9] Duțu (2024).

[10] Tombal et al. (2022).

[11] Duțu (2024).

[12] Pedro (2023).

[13] Acsinte (2010).

2.2 *Brief Description of the Artificial Intelligence Act: Conceptual Delimitations*

In terms of the rules of legislative technique, the AI Act has a very elaborate Preamble, with 170 paragraphs.

The scope of the AI Act is regulated in art. 1, where we find out what the Regulation lays down, namely: "harmonized rules for the placing on the market, the putting into service, and the use of AI systems in the Union; prohibitions of certain AI practices; specific requirements for high-risk AI systems and obligations for operators of such systems; harmonized transparency rules for certain AI systems; harmonized rules for the placing on the market of general-purpose AI models; rules on market monitoring, market surveillance, governance and enforcement; measures to support innovation, with a particular focus on SMEs, including start-ups".

Furthermore, in what concerns *the scope,* AI act applies to: "providers placing on the market or putting into service AI systems or placing on the market general-purpose AI models in the Union, irrespective of whether those providers are established or located within the Union or in a third country; deployers of AI systems that have their place of establishment or are located within the Union; providers and deployers of AI systems that have their place of establishment or are located in a third country, where the output produced by the AI system is used in the Union; importers and distributors of AI systems; product manufacturers placing on the market or putting into service an AI system together with their product and under their own name or trademark; authorized representatives of providers, which are not established in the Union; affected persons that are located in the Union" [art. 2 para. (1)].

The provisions of the Preamble to the European legislative act expressly state, and we have in mind paragraph 58, that "another area in which the use of AI systems deserves special consideration is the access to and enjoyment of certain essential private and public services and benefits necessary for people to fully participate in society or to improve one's standard of living". The *essential public services* covered by AI Act are detailed: "In particular, natural persons applying for or receiving essential public assistance benefits and services from public authorities namely healthcare services, social security benefits, social services providing protection in cases such as maternity, illness, industrial accidents (...) as well as housing assistance, are typically dependent on those benefits and services and in a vulnerable position in relation to the responsible authorities."[14]

One of the most important concepts with which the AI Act operates is the "*AI system*"*:* "AI system' means a machine-based system that is designed to operate with varying levels of autonomy and that may exhibit adaptiveness after deployment, and that, for explicit or implicit objectives, infers, from the input it receives,

[14] Preamble AI Act, para. 58.

how to generate outputs such as predictions, content, recommendations, or decisions that can influence physical or virtual environments"[15] [art. 3 para. 1)].

Article 3 of the AI Act defines six targeted actors:

- "*'provider'* means a natural or legal person, public authority, agency or other body that develops an AI system or a general-purpose AI model or that has an AI system or a general-purpose AI model developed and places it on the market or puts the AI system into service under its own name or trademark, whether for payment or free of charge" [art. 3 para. 3)].
- "*'deployer'* means a natural or legal person, public authority, agency or other body using an AI system under its authority except where the AI system is used in the course of a personal non-professional activity" [art. 3 para. 4)];
- "*'authorized representative'* means a natural or legal person located or established in the Union who has received and accepted a written mandate from a provider of an AI system or a general-purpose AI model to, respectively, perform and carry out on its behalf the obligations and procedures established by this Regulation" [art. 3 para. 5)];
- "*'importer'* means a natural or legal person located or established in the Union that places on the market an AI system that bears the name or trademark of a natural or legal person established in a third country" [art. 3 para. 6)];
- "*'distributor'* means a natural or legal person in the supply chain, other than the provider or the importer, that makes an AI system available on the Union market" [art. 3 para. 7)];
- "*'operator'* means a provider, product manufacturer, deployer, authorized representative, importer or distributor" [art. 3 para. 8)].

The doctrine noted that "the European Enterprises Alliance stressed that there was general uncertainty about the roles and responsibilities of the different actors in the AI value chain (developers, providers, and users of AI systems)."[16] Notwithstanding, it is clear from the AI Act that all these actors concerned have clearly defined obligations that they have to fulfill in order to ensure compliance with the relevant European legislation, ranging from technical requirements to patterns of behavior, such as the obligation to cooperate with the competent authorities, the obligation of data confidentiality, etc. In the same vein, another concept covered by the normative act is the idea of *risk*. Therefore, on the one hand, prohibited AI practices are expressly mentioned and, on the other hand, high-risk AI systems are classified.

In addition, the section on requirements for high-risk AI systems sets out mandatory requirements to be fulfilled. Therefore, a risk management system is established (art. 9), governance and data management practices that are fit for purpose are defined (art. 10), the technical documentation of a high-risk AI system which is to be drawn up before that system is placed on the market or put into service and kept up-to date

[15] Public information, online: https://eur-lex.europa.eu/legal-content/RO/TXT/?uri=OJ%3AL_202401689.

[16] Popa Tache (2023), p. 79.

is specified (art. 11), the obligation to allow for the automatic recording of events (logs) over the lifetime of the system is established (art. 12). Furthermore, the obligation of transparency and provision of information to deployers (art. 13) but also human oversight (art. 14) is emphasized. Furthermore, the AI Act establishes that providers of high-risk AI systems shall put a quality management system in place that ensures compliance with this Regulation (art. 17) and describes the responsibilities along the AI value chain (art. 25). Furthermore, deployers that are bodies governed by public law, or are private entities providing public services, and deployers of high-risk AI systems, shall perform an assessment of the impact on fundamental rights that the use of such system may produce (art. 27).

AI Act regulates *the rights of persons affected by AI systems*. Therefore, we talk about "the right to be informed (art. 26 and art. 50); the right to complain to the relevant market surveillance authority (Preamble 170 and art. 85); the right to explanation of individual decision-making (Preamble 171 and art. 86)".[17]

Furthermore, the AI Act provides for a regime of "*sanctions for operators of AI systems* that do not comply with the obligations set out in the regulation: administrative sanctions (fines), corrective measures (withdrawal or recall of the AI system from the market, etc.), other sanctions (civil - damages; criminal: disciplinary, contractual liability)".[18] At the European level, the European Office for Artificial Intelligence was established on 24 January 2024[19] which was officially inaugurated on 29 May 2024.[20] The AI Act provides in art.28 that "Each Member State shall designate or establish at least one notifying authority responsible for setting up and carrying out the necessary procedures for the assessment, designation and notification of conformity assessment bodies and for their monitoring".

Regarding the time period within which states must implement the AI Act, there are several different points in time. Thus, although it entered into force on 1 August 2024, the regulatory act will be applied in stages, the duration of this period extending until 2 August 2030. According to the provisions of art.69, para. (2) AI Act: "Member States shall make publicly available information on how competent authorities and single points of contact can be contacted, through electronic communication means by 2 August 2025".

3 National Background on Artificial Intelligence

The specialized literature has noted that "in the accelerated context of digitalization of public institutions in Romania and technological advancement, the government faces significant opportunities to improve the efficiency, transparency and quality of

[17] Popescu (2024), pp. 256–257.

[18] Popescu (2024), pp. 258–260.

[19] Commission Decision of 24 January 2024 establishing the European Artificial Intelligence Office (C 2024/1459), https://eur-lex.europa.eu/eli/C/2024/1459/oj.

[20] https://ec.europa.eu/commission/presscorner/detail/en/ip_24_2982.

services provided to citizens."[21] The National Strategy in the field of artificial intelligence 2024–2027 was approved by means of G.R. no. 832/2024.[22] The Romanian Committee for Artificial Intelligence, established by Order no. 20.484/2023 of the Minister of Research, Innovation and Digitalization is also operating in Romania.[23] This is an advisory body without legal personality of the Ministry of Research, Innovation and Digitalization—MRID. The role of the Committee is to support the Ministry in the exercise of its duties as state authority in the field of research and development, innovation and digitalization, through proposals on the regulation, coordination, monitoring and evaluation of activities related to artificial intelligence (AI) and its development in Romania. At the same time, the Authority for the Digitalization of Romania was established in our country by means of G.R. no.89/2020.[24]

The Interministerial Commission for coordinating the implementation of NS-AI (the Commission) was established by G.R. no. 832/2024, body without legal personality, the meetings of which are chaired by the MRID representative. Subsequent action plans/ Roadmaps will be developed to follow up actions. The public authorities and institutions responsible for implementing the actions set out in the Roadmap will report on progress every 6 months. According to the law, the Romanian Committee for Artificial Intelligence shall support the work of the Commission.

According to the NS-AI, several *specific objectives* are established: "increasing the training capacity and level of training of artificial intelligence experts; increasing people's basic understanding of the benefits; use and regulation of AI technologies, the development of AI-specific hardware infrastructure and transparent and equitable access to it, in order to facilitate R&D&I and production processes in this field; the development of fundamental and applied scientific research specific to the field of AI, as well as at interdisciplinary level (...)". Furthermore, the five *general objectives* shall be: "supporting education and skills training in AI; developing the necessary infrastructure and datasets; strengthening the AI R&D&I system; facilitate technology transfer through partnerships; society-wide adoption of AI; creation of an appropriate governance and regulatory framework[25]":

From another perspective, in the draft Code of administrative procedure,[26] a normative act that has not yet been adopted, the emphasis is placed on changing the usual way of interaction of citizens with the authorities from going to a desk to communicating via computer and the internet, i.e. digitalization of the administrative procedure.

---

[21] Vrabie (2024), p. 9.

[22] Published in the Official Journal no. 730 of 25 July 2024.

[23] Published in the Official Journal no. 382 of 4 May 2023.

[24] Published in the Official Journal no.113 of 13 February 2020.

[25] Public information, online: https://www.asro.ro/ue-si-romania-fac-pasi-importanti-in-reglementarea-inteligentei-artificiale/.

[26] Public information, online: https://www.mdlpa.ro/pages/proiectlegecodadministrati8v21112023.

4 News and Perspectives on the Use of Artificial Intelligence

At international level, the concept of the smart city is increasingly gaining ground in modern administrations anchored in the technologies of the future. According to the European Commission, "a smart city is a place where traditional networks and services are made more efficient with the use of digital solutions for the benefit of its inhabitants and business.[27] This means smarter urban transport networks, upgraded water supply and waste disposal facilities and more efficient ways to light and heat buildings."[28] Furthermore, "the interests of the local community are specified in the process in which the municipal authorities, which are responsible for creating the city's policies (the transport, urban, economic, educational, environmental and municipal waste management policy etc.) in a specified area, set objectives, after which they implement and enforce them."[29]

The doctrine shows that, "digital technologies are making transport and mobility smarter, safer and greener, according to the European Commission."[30] Furthermore, "information systems can also act as managers, coordinating and optimizing a range of complex processes. A noteworthy example is the intelligent traffic light system that manages urban traffic flow. These systems not only manage the movements of vehicles (and therefore drivers) and pedestrians, but optimize them with the aim of reducing congestion and improving road safety".[31] Also, "(smart city) means a more interactive and responsive city administration, safer public spaces and meeting the needs of an ageing population."[32] It seems that "cities around the world are at different stages of developing and implementing smart technology, such as: Barcelona, Spain; New York City, New York, USA; Melbourne, Australia, London, England, etc."[33]

Well-known authors emphasize that "the impact of digitalization on the work of public administration, the main form of which is the administrative act, an activity traditionally governed by bureaucratic rules and procedures, requires an in-depth analysis, as the general interest mission of public administration requires the work of public institutions and authorities to be carried out electronically in complete security, distinct from the speed required by an increasingly demanding daily life".[34] Furthermore, "throughout history, how a nation is governed has consistently sparked lively disputes."[35]

---

[27] Public information, online: https://commission.europa.eu/eu-regional-and-urban-development/topics/cities-and-urban-development/city-initiatives/smart-cities_en.

[28] Idem.

[29] Chrisidu-Budnik and Przedanska (2019), p. 25.

[30] Stănilă (2020), p. 131.

[31] Vrabie (2024), p. 9.

[32] Public information, online: https://commission.europa.eu/eu-regional-and-urban-development/topics/cities-and-urban-development/city-initiatives/smart-cities_en.

[33] Public information, online: https://smartcityblog.ro/conceptul-smart-city/.

[34] Cătană (2022).

[35] Săraru (2023).

Another use of the artificial intelligence is in the legal system. In this regard, it was pointed out that <the need for the involvement of the judiciary in AI-related issues was recognized by the Round Table on “AI and the Rule of Law”, Athens 2022, organized by UNESCO in the framework of the Internet Governance Forum sessions on “Rule of Law as a Key Concept in the Digital Ecosystem”>.[36] Furthermore, artificial intelligence is used in “medicine most often in surgery, but also as a means of diagnosis and treatment in most branches of medicine”.[37]

5 Conclusions

The research carried out was based on a documentation that included both national and comparative law. Most of the data was collected from sources that were documented by consulting internet sites, which facilitated the realization of the work in optimal conditions.

The adoption of the AI Act by the legislator at EU level signifies, in our opinion, a leap into the future. This is a piece of legislation with multiple practical implications at Member State level, we estimate that it will go beyond the General Data Protection Regulation 679/2016 in terms of impact. From this perspective, the present paper has brought to the fore the most important provisions of the European Act in the idea that it is necessary that this act is known both by the business environment and by the public system, the state authorities.

In our opinion, at the EU level the AI Act brings a paradigm shift for all sectors of the national economy, i.e. it will change the way people think and recreate new patterns of behavior adapted to the future. In this context, there are national doctrinal but also comparative law concerns analyzing the impact of new technologies on people’s lives, with the main categories of areas in which artificial intelligence could operate. For example, one of these concepts that is becoming more and more common internationally is the concept of the smart city, where artificial intelligence is already operating in the judicial system or medicine.

Our country is building the legal framework for the future implementation of the AI Act in Romania. One of the most important documents presented in the paper is the National Strategy for Artificial Intelligence 2024–2027. The analysis shows that the Interministerial Commission for coordinating the implementation of NS-AI has recently been set up.

In our opinion, modern technologies are necessary for life in general and business in particular. Artificial intelligence is a factor of progress that will force mankind to adapt to the demands of knowing how it works, which even involves attending courses on the subject in order to acquire new knowledge in this field. Of course, not all the questions about the AI Act will be clarified, but like any new piece of legislation, the test of time will show how ready we, the ordinary people and

[36] Voicu (2024).

[37] Nanu (2024), p. 16.

public authorities, are to embrace artificial intelligence. The analyzed topic is far from being exhausted in the present work, so we intend to extend the research through a future analysis that will consider the deepening of the AI Act in terms of compliance with it.

References

Books and Articles

Acsinte M (2010) Personoidul - perspective tehnice şi juridice. Curierul Judiciar 9
Cătană EL (2022) Impactul digitalizării activităţii administraţiei publice asupra actului administrativ. Aspecte normative, jurisprudenţiale şi din perspectiva codificării procedurii administrative. Revista de Drept Public 3
Chrisidu-Budnik A, Przedanska J (2019) Smart city: from concept to implementation. Wroclaw Rev Law Admin Econ 9(2). https://doi.org/10.2478/wrlae-2019-0009
Cliza MC, Ulariu CC (2021) Drept administrativ. Ediţie revizuită conform modificărilor Codului administrativ. Pro Universitaria Publishing House, Bucharest
Duţu M (2024) *Inteligenţa artificială: obiect şi/sau subiect de drept? Aceasta-i întrebarea!*, https://www.juridice.ro/essentials/7440/inteligenta-artificiala-obiect-si-sau-subiect-de-drept-aceasta-i-intrebarea
Nanu RM (2024) Ghid practic privind răspunderea pentru malpraxis a medicilor în cazul folosirii roboţilor cu inteligenţă artificială. Universul Juridic, Bucharest
Pedro R (2023) Artificial intelligence on public sector in Portugal: first legal approach. Juridical Tribune - Tribuna Juridica 13(2). https://doi.org/10.24818/TBJ/2023/13/2.01
Petric D (2023) The Court of Justice of the E.U.: a Contextualist Court, in University of Bologna Law Review, 8(2), 44. https://doi.org/10.6092/issn.2531-6133/v8-n2-2023, visited on 24.09.2024
Popa Tache CE (2023) Dreptul comunicaţiilor şi al noilor tehnologii. Pro Universitaria, Bucharest
Popa Tache CE, Săraru CS (2024) Evaluating today's multi-dependencies in digital transformation, corporate governance and public international law triad. Cogent Soc Sci 10(1). https://doi.org/10.1080/23311886.2024.2370945
Popescu A (2024) Viitorul deciziilor noastre AI Act. Reguli explicate, studii de caz şi exemple practice pe înţelesul tuturor. Universul Juridic, Bucharest
Săraru C-S (2023) A cross - country examination: administrative litigation in China and Romania, access to justice in eastern. Europe 6(3). https://doi.org/10.33327/AJEE-18-6.3-a000313
Stănilă LM (2020) Inteligenţa artificială, Dreptul penal şi sistemul de justiţie penală. Amintiri despre viitor. Universul Juridic, Bucharest
Ştefan EE (2017) Legalitate şi moralitate în activitatea autorităţilor publice. Revista de Drept Public 4
Tombal T, Willem P, de Terwangne C (2022) Legal framework for the use of artificial intelligence and automated decision-making in public governance. In: Tan E, Crompvoets J (eds) The new digital era governance. Brill. https://doi.org/10.3920/978-90-8686-930-5_5
Voicu M (2024) Inteligenţa artificială (IA) Statul de drept şi drepturile fundamentale în programele de master din universităţile europene, https://www.juridice.ro/essentials/7520/inteligenta-artificiala-ia-statul-de-drept-si-drepturile-fundamentale-in-programele-de-master-din-universitatile-europene
Vrabie C (2024) Elemente de e-guvernare, 2nd edn. Pro Universitaria, Bucharest

Legislation

Commission Decision of 24 January 2024 establishing The European Artificial Intelligence Office (C/2024/1459), https://eur-lex.europa.eu/eli/C/2024/1459/oj

G.R. no. 832/2024 approving the National Strategy in the field of artificial intelligence 2024-2027, published in the Official Journal no. 730 of 25 July 2024

G.R. no. 89/2020 on the organization and operation of the Authority for the Digitalization of Romania, published in the Official Journal no. 113 of 13 February 2020

Order no. 20.484/2023 of the Minister of Research, Innovation and Digitalization on the establishment, organization and operation of the Romanian Committee for Artificial Intelligence, published in the Official Journal no. 382 of 4 May 2023

Regulation (EU) 2024/1689 of The European Parliament European and of The Council of 13 June 2024 laying down harmonized rules on artificial intelligence and amending Regulations (EC) no.300/2008, (EU) no.167/2013, (EU) no.168/2013, (EU) 2018/858, (EU) 2018/1139 and (EU) 2019/1144 and Directives 2014/90/UE, (EU) 2016/797 and (EU) 2020/1828, published in Official Journal of The European Union L 2024/1689, 12.7.2024

The New Challenges of Artificial Intelligence Legal Framework in European Union Cyberspace

Constantin-Marius Arădan

Abstract The new challenges of Artificial Intelligence legal framework in the European Union cyberspace. The galloping rise of Artificial Intelligence technologies has created a large variety of opportunities across all of industries and sectors, and also, it is going to reshape the European Union cyberspace. On the other hand, it has raised significant challenges in the context of legal framework, doctrine and jurisprudence, beginning with the concepts of accountability and liability, data privacy to cybersecurity. This paper analyzes and makes *lex ferenda* proposals for the suitable legal solutions according to these new challenges. The EU's approach to AI legal framework will need to be more proactive, comprehensive, multi-faceted and balanced in the context of this dynamic landscape of evolving the cyberspace. One of the biggest challenges analyzed in this paper is the methods to establish a solid framework that ensures respecting human and fundamental rights according to the European and international treaties and conventions and also, to guarantee that the use of AI is safe, uphold the rule of law, remain ethical, and align with European principles and values. Finally, the innovation of this paper consists in how the EU regulators should adapt to the new paradigm of evolving Artificial Intelligence in the new shape of EU cyberspace.

1 Introduction

In the context of this dynamic landscape of evolving the cyberspace, the objective of this paper is to analyse the EU's approach to the AI legal framework in comparison with international AI jurisdiction like superpowers country United States of America and China. Also, another main objective is to promote the implementation of a trustworthy AI through the *lex ferenda* proposals for the suitable legal solutions according to these new challenges. In this direction, the author makes efforts to find

C.-M. Arădan (✉)
"Aurel Vlaicu" University of Arad, Arad, Romania

C.-S. Săraru, C. E. Popa Tache (eds.), *AI, Sustainability and Solidarity in Advancing European Values in a Globalized Age*, European Union and its Neighbours in a Globalized World 28, https://doi.org/10.1007/978-3-032-06508-7_2

the methods to establish a solid framework to ensure respecting the human and fundamental rights according to the European and international treaties and conventions and also, to guarantee that the use of AI is safe, uphold the rule of law, ethical, transparent and aligned with European principles and values.

In the White Paper on Artificial Intelligence—an European approach to excellence and trust of 19 February 2020, European Commission stated at point 5, an ecosystem of trust: regulatory framework for AI,"... *Under the Partnership Instrument, the Commission will finance a €2.5 million project that will facilitate cooperation with like-minded partners, in order to promote the EU AI ethical guidelines and to adopt common principles and operational conclusions. Such a regulatory framework should be consistent with other actions to promote Europe's innovation capacity and competitiveness in this field. In addition, it must ensure socially, environmentally and economically optimal outcomes and compliance with EU legislation, principles and values. This is particularly relevant in areas where citizens' rights may be most directly affected, for example in the case of AI applications for law enforcement and the judiciary."*[1] As a result, the *European Artificial Intelligence Act (AI Act)*[2] was proposed by the Commission in April 2021 and agreed by the European Parliament and the Council in December 2023. Later, on 1 August 2024, the AI Act entered into force in order to provide an united legal framework across all EU countries, based on a forward-looking definition of AI and a risk-based approach: *minimal risk, specific transparency risk, High risk, Unacceptable risk.*

Regarding to the AI Act, Mathieu Michel, Belgian secretary of state for digitisation, administrative simplification, privacy protection, and the building regulation, stated that *"The adoption of the AI act is a significant milestone for the European Union. This landmark law, the first of its kind in the world, addresses a global technological challenge that also creates opportunities for our societies and economies. With the AI act, Europe emphasizes the importance of trust, transparency and accountability when dealing with new technologies while at the same time ensuring this fast-changing technology can flourish and boost European innovation."*[3]

On the other hand, Max von Thun, Europe director of the Open Markets Institute said *"While Brussels deserves "real credit" for being the first jurisdiction globally to pass regulation mitigating AI's many risks, there are several problems with the final agreement. There are "significant loopholes for public authorities" and*

---

[1] https://commission.europa.eu/document/download/d2ec4039-c5be-423a-81efb9e44e79825b_en?filename=commission-white-paper-artificial-intelligence-feb2020_en.pdf.

[2] Was published in the Official Journal of the European Union (EU), Regulation (EU) 2024/1689 of the European Parliament and of the Council of 13 June 2024 laying down harmonised rules on artificial intelligence and amending Regulations (EC) No 300/2008, (EU) No 167/2013, (EU) No 168/2013, (EU) 2018/858, (EU) 2018/1139 and (EU) 2019/2144 and Directives 2014/90/EU, (EU) 2016/797 and (EU) 2020/1828 (Artificial Intelligence Act) (Text with EEA relevance) PE/24/2024/REV/1, *OJ L, 2024/1689, 12.7.2024.*

[3] https://www.consilium.europa.eu/en/press/press-releases/2024/05/21/artificial-intelligence-ai-act-council-gives-final-green-light-to-the-first-worldwide-rules-on-ai/.

"relatively weak regulation of the largest foundation models that pose the greatest harm". In addition, he stated *"The AI Act is incapable of addressing the number one threat AI currently poses: its role in increasing and entrenching the extreme power a few dominant tech firms already have in our personal lives, our economies, and our democracies,"*[4]

From the tech experts, Alex Combessie, co-founder and CEO of French open source AI company Giskard, stated *"The EU Parliament's final adoption of the EU AI Act is both a historic moment and a relief. While the Act imposes additional constraints and rules on developers of high-risk AI systems and foundation models, deemed as 'systemic risks,' we're confident that these checks and balances can be effectively implemented. This historic moment paves the way for a future where AI is harnessed responsibly, fostering trust and ensuring the safety of all."*[5]

In our opinion, the AI Act is the first complex and comprehensive legal framework in the EU cyberspace and is structured around two pillars' approach:

- Pillar I: concerns the gathering and exchange of knowledge through the AI Pact network. Pillar I is addressed to all stakeholders (including, but not limited to, companies, non-for-profit organisations, academics, civil servants, etc). In this direction *"participants contribute to the creation of a collaborative community, sharing their experiences and knowledge. This includes webinars organised by the AI Office which provide participants with a better understanding of the AI Act, their responsibilities and how to prepare for its implementation. In turn, the AI Office gathers insights into best practices and challenges faced by the participants."*[6]
- Pillar II: represent the facilitating and communicating company pledges. The goal of this pillar is to provide a framework to foster the early implementation of some of the measures of the AI Act. *"This initiative encourages organisations to proactively disclose the processes and practices they are implementing to anticipate compliance. Specifically, companies providing or deploying AI systems can demonstrate and share their voluntary commitments towards transparency and high-risk requirements and prepare early on for their implementation."*[7]

Moreover, the AI Act is aligned with OECD's principles (The Organisation for Economic Co-operation and Development), as both frameworks pursue similar goals, including fairness, transparency, and accountability. Also, the AI Act takes into consideration *Principles for responsible stewardship of trustworthy AI* of OECD, in special, the principle *1.2. Respect for the rule of law, human rights and democratic values, including fairness and privacy,* which states: *"a) AI actors should respect the rule of law, human rights, democratic and human-centred values*

[4] https://www.euronews.com/next/2024/03/16/eu-ai-act-reaction-tech-experts-say-the-worlds-first-ai-law-is-historic-but-bittersweet.

[5] https://www.msn.com/en-xl/news/other/eu-ai-act-reaction-tech-experts-say-the-world-s-first-ai-law-is-historic-but-bittersweet/ar-BB1jZrWw.

[6] See https://digital-strategy.ec.europa.eu/en/policies/ai-pact.

[7] Ibid.

throughout the AI system lifecycle. These include non-discrimination and equality, freedom, dignity, autonomy of individuals, privacy and data protection, diversity, fairness, social justice, and internationally recognised labour rights. This also includes addressing misinformation and disinformation amplified by AI, while respecting freedom of expression and other rights and freedoms protected by applicable international law. b) To this end, AI actors should implement mechanisms and safeguards, such as capacity for human agency and oversight, including to address risks arising from uses outside of intended purpose, intentional misuse, or unintentional misuse in a manner appropriate to the context and consistent with the state of the art."[8]

The author Anu Bradford considers that the "Brussels Effect"[9] will set up a global standard and values in AI governance, aligned with the legal framework of the EU AI Act.[10] Already, the EU AI strategy turned the EU into a *"world-class AI hub"*[11] to ensure the safety and trustworthiness of AI systems used within the Union. In other opinion, "*the risk of a Brussels Side Effect maps an internal tension within EU digital policy because promoting the AI Act as a global standard is likely to also spread many of the shortcomings associated with the EU regulatory approach. On the theoretical side, our argument complicates one of the Brussels Effect's tenets: that the EU can set global regulatory agendas because EU regulation is strict.*"[12]

Professor John McGinnis from Northwestern University Pritzker, School of Law, stated that "*artificial intelligence research is done by institutions no richer than colleges and perhaps would require even less substantial resources.*"[13] So, he try to show that the combined with strong tort rules that penalize AI developers who ignore the results of that safety research. If more data on AI behavior is strongly correlated with AI safety, then subsidizing such research might have a significant positive impact on the development of safer AI.[14]

2 International AI Jurisdictions

2.1 The Case of United States of America

Related to the role of standards. The US Government implements the NIST AI Risk Management Framework (RMF) which is a voluntary resource for different stakeholders to manage risks across the lifecycle of AI systems. While it does not

[8] See OECD, Recommendation of the Council on Artificial Intelligence, OECD/LEGAL/0449, p. 8.

[9] See Bradford (2023), p. 67.

[10] See Bradford (2020), p. 211.

[11] See European Commission, *Fostering a European Approach to Artificial Intelligence,* No. COM/2021/205 final 2021.

[12] See Almada and Radu (2024).

[13] See McGinnis (2010).

[14] Scherer (2016).

propose standards *per se*, it recommends that its risk management approaches should align with existing sector - or application - specific guidelines or standards. It aims to take advantage of and foster greater awareness of existing standards, guidelines, and tools for managing AI risks as well as illustrate the need for additional, improved resources. The RMF follows NIST's US Leadership in AI Plan for Federal Engagement in Developing Technical Standards (2019) which promotes research on AI standards, coordination among agencies, public-private partnerships, and international engagements.[15]

Related to role of impact assessments. The RMF aims to foster the development of innovative approaches to the management of AI risks, including the use of impact assessments. While it does not propose an impact assessment procedure or template, it underlines the importance of impact assessments to understand the potential impacts or harms of AI systems within specific contexts. Furthermore, it states that actors, including impact assessors and evaluators are expected to provide technical, human factor, socio-cultural, and legal expertise to carry out impact assessments of AI systems, including evaluating the requirements for AI system accountability, combating bias, examining the impacts of AI systems, product safety, liability, and security, among others.[16]

Related to role of audits. Similar to impact assessments, the NIST AI RMF underlines the role of audits in the identification and evaluation of potential risks or impacts that may emerge during the life cycle of AI systems. It aims to foster the development of innovative approaches, including audits, to address various characteristics of trustworthy AI systems, including accuracy, explainability, privacy, robustness, safety, and mitigation of harmful biases. It states that audits that confirm that a system is performing as intended will be an important part of making impact assessments.[17]

2.2 *The Case of China*

Based on China's Internet Information Service Algorithmic Recommendation Management Provisions, which take into force by 1 March 2022, is designed to manage and regulate, the use of algorithmic recommendation systems by cyberspace. These provisions have the main goals:

- *Support National Security and Social Order:* correlate algorithmic practices with national security priorities and social stability.
- *Regulate Algorithmic Influences:* establish the guidelines for how recommendation algorithms should operate.
- *Enhance Transparency and Accountability:* require IoT platforms to disclose their algorithmic recommendation methods and provide transparency.

[15] See Roberts et al. (2023), p. 44.

[16] Ibid.

[17] Ibid.

- *Ensure User Privacy and Safety:* protect users' personal data and safeguard them from harmful content by setting clear guidelines on the collection, use, collection and securing of users' information.
- *Promote Fair and Non-Discriminatory Practices:* combating and preventing algorithms from increasing harmful behaviors such as disinformation, intoxication, addiction, or content that promotes illegal or moral activities.

Begin with 2021, a set of regulations related to artificial intelligence was adopted and entered into force, primarily the following:

- Data Security Law of the People's Republic of China, dated June 10, 2021, effective from September 1[18];
- Personal Information Protection Law of the People's Republic of China, dated August 20, 2021, effective from November 1[19];
- Critical Information Infrastructure Security Protection Regulations, dated August 17, 2021, effective from September 1.[20]

2.2.1 The Case of the Nanshan District Court in Shenzhen, China

Professor Banggui Jin, explain very clearly, a case-law if AI-generated can works be protected by copyright law under Chinese law and highlight the affirmative answer given by the Chinese court.

> In December 24, 2019, the Nanshan District Court in Shenzhen affirming that AI-generated objects can constitute works. The plaintiff in this case is the Chinese internet giant Tencent, which developed a writing robot called "Dreamwriter" in 2015. Since its inception, the software "Dreamwriter" has generated approximately 300,000 articles per year. On August 20, 2018, Tencent published a financial report completed by "Dreamwriter" on its website. On the same day, the Yingxun company copied and published the whole article on its website. Thus, a copyright dispute between Tencent and Yingxun arose.[21]

On the other hand, in April 2018, the Beijing High People's Court issued the "Guideline for the Trial of Copyright Infringement Cases", which clearly defined "creation by natural persons" as a condition for the identification of works subject to copyright law.[22]

---

[18] See Data Security Law of the People's Republic of China. (2021, June 29), https://goo.su/yUFiOA.

[19] See Creemers and Webster (2021).

[20] Creemers et al. (2021).

[21] Dai and Jin (2023), p. 248.

[22] See article 2.1 of the Guideline for the Trial of Copyright Infringement Cases rules: "To examine whether the object of copyright claimed by the plaintiff constitutes a work, the following factors are generally considered: (1) Whether it is a creation by natural persons within the scope of literature, art and science; (2) Whether it is original; (3) Whether it has a certain form of expression; (4) Whether it can be copied".

The Professor Wang Yan said that "*owing to the mobility of data, one of AI's pillars, regulations based on territoriality cannot strictly cover all the problems caused by AI. In the absence of international governance, EU legislators have endowed the EU's AI legislation with extraterritorial effects. That is also true in the case of China*".[23]

3 Conclusions

In conclusion, the main challenges of EU AI Legal Framework are:

1. Technological Innovation Outpacing Regulation. One of the most significant challenges is the rapid pace of technological innovation in AI. As new AI methodologies, such as deep learning, machine learning, and quantum computing evolve, the regulatory landscape risks becoming outdated. For example, AI systems that utilize deep learning techniques often operate as "black boxes," meaning it is difficult to explain their decision-making processes.[24]
2. Cross-Border Jurisdiction and Enforcement. Cyberspace is inherently global, and AI technologies often function across borders. For instance, a company based in one EU member state could deploy an AI system used by individuals or organizations worldwide. This creates jurisdictional challenges for enforcement. AI systems, especially in critical infrastructure or security-related fields, may operate outside the EU's borders, and it is unclear how the EU will regulate such systems that do not fall within its jurisdiction.[25]
3. Data Privacy and Protection. The General Data Protection Regulation (GDPR) has been one of the EU's flagship regulations to protect individuals' data privacy, but as AI becomes more integrated into everyday life, the intersection of AI and data protection law becomes more complex. Many AI systems, particularly those in high-risk areas such as healthcare, finance, and law enforcement, require vast amounts of personal data to operate effectively.[26]
4. Ethical Considerations and Bias. The ethical risks associated with AI, such as algorithmic bias and discrimination, have garnered widespread attention. The AI Act seeks to address these risks by implementing risk assessments for AI systems and requiring that high-risk AI be designed to avoid bias. However, algorithmic bias remains a major and critical concern in AI applications that influence decisions in critical areas like hiring, criminal justice, or healthcare.

---

[23] See Wang (2024).

[24] See https://op.europa.eu/en/publication-detail/-/publication/359880c1-a4dc-11ec-83e1-01aa75ed71a1/language-en.

[25] See https://edri.org/our-work/eu-ai-act-fails-to-set-gold-standard-for-human-rights/.

[26] See European Data Protection Supervisor. EDPS Annual Activity Report 2022, https://www.edps.europa.eu/system/files/2023-05/edps_aar_2022_en.pdf.

5. Accountability and Liability. Determining accountability for harms caused by AI systems is one of the most pressing issues in the regulation of AI. In the event of an accident or legal dispute involving AI, the question arises: who should be held liable—the developer, the operator, or the user of the AI system? This issue is compounded by the autonomous nature of many AI systems, which can make decisions without direct human input.

References

Almada M, Radu A (2024) The Brussels side-effect: how the AI act can reduce the global reach of EU policy. German Law J 25(4):646–663. https://doi.org/10.1017/glj.2023.108

Bradford A (2020) The Brussels effect: how the European Union rules the world. Oxford University Press

Bradford A (2023) Digital empires: the global battle to regulate technology. Oxford University Press, New York

Creemers R, Webster G (2021) Personal information protection law of the People's Republic of China. Stanford University. https://goo.su/Fkeic

Creemers R, Sacks S, Webster G (2021) Critical information infrastructure security protection regulations. Stanford University. https://goo.su/DS6o

Dai Z, Jin B (2023) The copyright protection of AI-generated works under Chinese law. Juridical Tribune - Tribuna Juridica 13(2)

Data Security Law of the People's Republic of China (29 June 2021) Stanford University. https://goo.su/yUFiOA

European Data Protection Supervisor. EDPS Annual Activity Report 2022., https://www.edps.europa.eu/system/files/2023-05/edps_aar_2022_en.pdf

McGinnis JO (2010) Accelerating AI. Northwest Univ Law Rev 104:366–381

Regulation (EU) 2024/1689 of the European Parliament and of the Council of 13 June 2024 laying down harmonised rules on artificial intelligence and amending Regulations (EC) No 300/2008, (EU) No 167/2013, (EU) No 168/2013, (EU) 2018/858, (EU) 2018/1139 and (EU) 2019/2144 and Directives 2014/90/EU, (EU) 2016/797 and (EU) 2020/1828 (Artificial Intelligence Act) (Text with EEA relevance) PE/24/2024/REV/1, *OJ L, 2024/1689, 12.7.2024*

Roberts H, Ziosi M, Osborne C, Saouma L (2023) A Comparative Framework for AI Regulatory Policy, The International Centre of Expertise on Artificial Intelligence in Montreal

Scherer MU (2016) Regulating artificial intelligence systems: risks, challenges, competencies, and strategies. Harv J Law Technol 29(2)

Wang Y (2024) Do not go gentle into that good night: the European Union's and China's different approaches to the extraterritorial application of artificial intelligence laws and regulations. Comp Law Secur Rev 53. https://doi.org/10.1016/j.clsr.2024.105965

The Legal Influence of Artificial Intelligence on Intellectual Property Rights: A Comparative Approach

Adnan Jashari, Albana Metaj-Stojanova, and Stefani Stojchevska

Abstract This paper analyzes the influence of artificial intelligence (AI) on intellectual property rights (IPRs), as well as the evolutionary effects which occur as a result of such influence. This paper begins by exploring the historical development of IPRs and the evolution of AI, with particular reference to AI-influenced growing copyrighted works, its role in patent innovation, and its impact on trademarks. The comparative evaluation of international jurisprudence regarding some of the most relevant and contemporary cases which include Thaler v. Hirshfeld, the copyright lawsuits of major record labels in the music industry and the controversy with Google's Project Nightingale, simultaneously tend to reveal a range of legal responses to these increasing challenges. The paper similarly addresses the ethical implications and issues which occur from the influence of AI in the field of IP, based on which there is a need for reforms in the legal framework for the protection of IPRs. Through this comprehensive analysis, looking forward to future legal trends, recommendations are proposed.

1 Introduction

The introduction of artificial intelligence (AI) has revolutionized everyday life by creating certain opportunities, but also difficult situations and problems in the field of intellectual property rights (IPRs) protection. The adaptation of the IP system to AI-generated creativity is a topic of critical interest. On one side, existing IP regimes, including copyright law, trade secrets, and patent law, can protect software on which AI technology is based. On the other side, however, the protection afforded

A. Jashari · A. Metaj-Stojanova (✉) · S. Stojchevska
South East European University (SEEU), Faculty of Law,
Tetovo, Republic of North Macedonia
e-mail: a.jashari@seeu.edu.mk; a.metaj@seeu.edu.mk; s.stojchevska@seeu.edu.mk

C.-S. Săraru, C. E. Popa Tache (eds.), *AI, Sustainability and Solidarity in Advancing European Values in a Globalized Age*, European Union and its Neighbours in a Globalized World 28, https://doi.org/10.1007/978-3-032-06508-7_3

to the software does not extend to the output possibly generated by the AI.[1] At the moment, scholars are discussing the open question about whether AI could be the subject of IPR, as well as whether AI could bear responsibility for the consequences of the influence of the product of its creativity on society, with the ensuing legal consequences. From a legal standpoint, AI cannot claim IPRs since it does not physically exist.[2] However, the reality is that IPRs, being designed to protect human creativity and innovation, are currently being challenged by inventions generated by AI assets. This raises fundamental questions concerning the nature of (human) authorship, copyright, patents and trademarks. For copyright and human authorship, the issue revolves around whether AI-generated works — ranging from art and music to literary works—can be protected, and if so, who owns the rights. In the area of patents, the debate centers on whether AI could be recognized as an inventor and how the standard applies the concepts of novelty and non-obviousness to AI-generated inventions. Trademarks also face new challenges as AI systems begin to create and use brand names and logos autonomously.

2 The Historical Perspective of Artificial Intelligence and Intellectual Property Rights

IPRs have advanced over the centuries by reflecting the development of society's creativity and innovation. The IP, as we are defining it, is ancient in origin[3]; many of our ideas about property—ideas that have provided the foundations for modern IP—come ultimately from Rome. More precisely, those ideas come from Roman legal thinkers knows as *jurists*. Between the first and sixth centuries of our era, Roman jurists built an elaborate legal edifice, one that included abstract and systemized ideas about property and legal obligation.[4] The first general IP laws were created by the City States of Italy in the Middle Ages. From the fifteenth until the nineteenth centuries, technological developments such as the invention of the printing press ushered in a new industrial and social climate that increased the value for states of rights in respect of printed materials and manufacturing methods.[5] The landmarks in its history include the Venetian Patent Act of 1474, the English Statute of Monopolies of 1624, the petition of the English Stationers' Company to Parliament in 1643, the English Copyright Act of 1710 (a.k.a. the Statute of Anne), the patent and copyright clause of the U.S. Constitution of 1787, the U.S. patent and copyright statutes of 1790, and the French Patent Act of 1791.[6] Moreover, the for-

[1] Frosio (2024), p. 228.

[2] Gribincea (2020).

[3] Landes and Posner (2009), p. 1.

[4] Ford (2021), p. 5.

[5] Dreyfuss and Pila (2018), p. 9.

[6] Landes and Posner (2009), p. 1.

malized system of IPRs began to take shape during the Renaissance. This era witnessed the first legal act, the Copyright Directive, aimed at encouraging authors and publishers by granting exclusive rights to reproduce works.[7] The industrial revolution spurred the development of IP legislation, faced with the need to protect and preserve innovation. Patents were introduced as legal mechanisms to encourage inventiveness by granting inventors exclusive rights to their inventions for a specified period of time. Similarly, trademarks have emerged to protect trademark names. Over time, international treaties and organizations, such as the World Intellectual Property Organization (WIPO) and the Agreement on Trade-Related Aspects of Intellectual Property (TRIPS), have been established to harmonize IPRs across borders, reflecting the increasing globalization of exchange and trade. Along similar lines, the WIPO and the World Trade Organization (WTO) are no longer the only international organizations involved in international IP law making. As IP rights have expanded, other international organizations including the World Health Organization (WHO) and the United Nations Conference on Trade and Development (UNCTAD) have begun to appreciate the role that IP can play in the economy, development, and culture, and they, too, have sought to influence the shape and implementation of international obligations.[8]

By contrast, the concept of AI has its roots in the beginning of and the mid-twentieth century, as a result of the development and advancement of computing power, algorithms and data available that catapulted AI from theory to a pervasive reality. Although it is difficult to pinpoint, the roots of AI can probably be traced back to the 1940s, specifically 1942, with the publication of *Runaround*, a short story written by the American science fiction writer Isaac Asimov explaining the *Three Laws on Robotics* and the English mathematician Alan Turner developing a code-breaking machine called *The Bombe* for the British Government.[9] The word "Artificial Intelligence" was officially coined in 1956 at Dartmouth College, New Hampshire, where a workshop was held by computer scientists Marvin Minsky and John McCarthy: the objective of the workshop was to develop machines with the ability to simulate human intelligence.[10]

Although most histories of the field of AI emphasize the Dartmouth workshop, there were several earlier meetings that played a critical role in the evolution of the concept of AI, including the 1942 Cerebral Inhibition Meeting, the ten Macy Conferences held between 1946 and 1953, and the Hixon Symposium held in 1948.[11] The journey of AI began with simple programmed computers and has progressed to today's complex machine learning and deep learning models capable of processing and learning from vast amounts of data. This evolution has led to the proliferation of AI in various sectors, from autonomous vehicles and smart home

[7] Sully (1997), https://www.dlib.org/dlib/january97/01sully.html.

[8] Dreyfuss and Pila (2018), p. 13.

[9] Haenlein and Kaplan (2019), p. 2.

[10] Kar et al. (2021), p. 329.

[11] Chrisley (2000), p. 19.

devices to sophisticated medical diagnostics and personalized learning systems.[12] The development and growth of AI is not only a technological phenomenon, but also a socio-economic one, affecting the labor market, privacy, and even cultural products.

3 Legal Definitions Addressing the Concepts of Artificial Intelligence and Intellectual Property

The creations of the human mind—*intellect*, are an object of IP protection. Perceived most comprehensively, IP represents the rights arising from intellectual activities in industry, science, as well as other fields relevant to human society. In shedding light on the issue of IP, it is necessary to explain the concept of ownership. Theorists believe that the most important feature of ownership consists in the fact that the owner can basically use, that is, exploit the ownership, unlimitedly in accordance with his will and needs and that no one can maliciously use his or her ownership. Of course, there are legal restrictions on the utilization of the right of ownership. More importantly, it is emphasized that the concept of ownership, in general, could be appropriately categorized into three groups of ownership, by primarily taking into account the object of ownership: (1) *ownership of movables*, (2) *ownership of immovable objects*, and (3) *IP*. Furthermore, the Convention Establishing the World Intellectual Property Organization of July 14th 1967, establishes that IP includes rights relating to: literary, artistic and scientific works; the performances of artists-performers, phonograms and radio-television stations; inventions from all fields of human activity; scientific discoveries; industrial design; trade and service marks, commercial names and marks; protection against unfair competition, as well as all other rights related to IP in the industrial, scientific, literary and artistic fields. By the same token, IP is also usually divided into two large groups, namely: Industrial property and Copyright and related (neighboring) rights. Nevertheless, what is considered critical to such analysis lies in the question of how AI challenges and reshapes traditional notions of IPRs. For that matter, the following sections of this paper will delve into specific issues and cases where AI intersects with these IP categories by simultaneously highlighting both the legal complexities and the need for potential reform. Legal scholars must grasp the gravity of this question in our contemporary and dynamic society, given that the emergence of AI as creators of artistic and literary works represents a paradigm shift in copyright. Works generated by AI, such as images, musical compositions and literary texts, challenge the fundamental notion of "authorship" and "ownership" as the key legal issues determining who owns the copyright for AI-generated works: would it be the AI machine or program itself, the developer or the user who commissioned the work? Earlier, there was no dispute pertaining to copyright over works in question because the program/

[12] Becker (2017).

machine used to create said work merely served as a tool, similar to using a pen and paper, where the idea of said work belonged to the programmer. With the advancement of AI, however, when we are creating machines with human intelligence which are capable of creating original work on their own, then the question shifts as to who will own the copyright is being raised in the sense of whether the copyright will belong to the programmer or the AI machine/program.[13]

Assessing whether AI creations meet the set standards of originality and creativity is established under copyright rules. Namely, unlike physical goods, digital content is intangible by raising intricate questions about ownership, distribution, as well as the application of copyright doctrines whose scope must be redefined within this new context.[14] And intangible assets are unique in terms of their characteristics, their composition, and the level of influence on the results of economic activity and the financial condition of enterprises.[15] On the other hand, we question whether AI should be granted moral rights, including the right of attribution and the right of integrity.[16] The ability of AI to invent or at least contribute to the process of invention raises significant uncertainties in patent law, particularly regarding the legal concepts of both invention and ownership. Namely, can AI systems be legally recognized as inventors? This challenges the traditional view that only humans may be regarded as inventors. Or when regarding the ownership of patents invented by AI under the circumstance that AI may be regarded as an inventor, then who would own the patent?—Would that be the developer of the AI machine/program, the user of the AI machine/program or the AI machine/program itself? To a greater extent, the utilization of AI in the creation and management of brands introduces new considerations in trademark law. By considering issues of distinctiveness and the potential for AI to analyze market trends, highly effective AI-generated trademarks may be created, whereas the utilization of such AI-generated trademarks in online environments (for example, in digital marketing) would examine how AI affects some important legal issues related to the protection of trademarks, generally speaking.

4 Significant Legal Cases Involving Artificial Intelligence and Intellectual Property Rights

In this segment of the paper, we look at some key legal cases, precedents and comparative case law on understanding how exclusive legal structures are in practice. In determining what is the position of legislative practice in the relationship between AI and IPRs, several cases are analyzed in which the complex interaction between

[13] Upadhyay and Rathee (2020), p. 370.

[14] Zakir et al. (2020).

[15] Gruzdova (2011).

[16] Andreotta (2021).

AI and IPRs is seen. These cases offer insight into how courts grapple with situations posed by AI:

1. *Thaler v. United States Patent and Trademark Office (USPTO)*: Given the immense potential of AI, this raises the question whether an "invention" conceived solely by an AI machine can be patented and becoming an important aspect to interpret under patent law.[17] In this case, the United States Patent and Trademark Office (USPTO) denied patents for an innovation created through an AI machine knows as the Device for the Autonomous Bootstrapping of Unified Sentience (DABUS) created and owned by Dr. Stephen Thaler. Namely, the USPTO argued that AIs cannot be inventors. The decision was upheld by the U.S. District Court, emphasizing the human-centric nature of the current patent system.[18] On December 17th, 2019, the USPTO in *Thaler v. Hirshfeld* issued a written decision dismissing the plaintiff's petition, explaining that the explicit statutory language used by Congress defined the term 'inventor" – e.g., "individual" and "himself or herself"—was uniquely trained on human beings. The USPTO also explained that the Federal Circuit had twice held that an inventor could only be a natural person.[19] On appeal, in September 2021 Judge Leonie Brinkema in the U.S. District Court for the Eastern District of Virginia upheld the decision of the USPTO that an AI machine cannot be an inventor under the U.S. patent law.[20] Concluding, the Court said: *"As technology evolves, there may come a time when artificial intelligence reaches a level of sophistication such that it might satisfy accepted meanings of inventorship. But that time has not yet arrived, and, if it does, it will be up to Congress to decide how, if at all, it wants to expand the scope of patent law"*[21]

In reaching this decision, Brinkema J pointed out that the language used in the Patent Act (35 U.S. Code) and the America Invents Act 2011 refers to a human quality, especially in terms such as 'individual', 'himself or herself'. According to Brinkema J, this implies that an inventor must be a human being. The decision was appealed by Thaler, but the Supreme Court of the U.S. declined to hear the appeal in April 2023.[22] This is not to assert that computers, including AI systems, cannot contribute to a natural person's conception of a patentable invention, but an "invention" without conception by a natural person is not patentable in the U.S.[23] Be that as it may, patent offices and courts have here reached opposite decisions, with the European Patent Office (EPO) and the U.K. Intellectual Property Office (UKIPO) concluding that machines cannot be designated as inventors, whereas courts in

[17] Giovannini and Pasha (2022), p. 398.

[18] Fleming (2007).

[19] Scott (2019), pp. 8–40.

[20] Klobucnik (2024), p. 104.

[21] Scott (2019), pp. 8–40.

[22] Klobucnik (2024), p. 104.

[23] Giovannini and Pasha (2022), p. 398.

South Africa and (previously) Australia find the opposite.[24] Perhaps the reasoning behind the majority of patent offices and courts refusing to accept inventorship belonging to AI machines lies in the fact that AI-generated inventions do not have the notion of a natural person. In this legal case, by supposing that DABUS independently developed the innovative technologies that are new and there was no human involvement, then the application of an objective standard of inventorship would mean that DABUS is the inventor.[25] Moreover, the WIPO also rejected the decision for DABUS as the applicant for patent protection. That decision was confirmed by the Court as well. Namely, the Court emphasized that an "inventor" must be a person, which was previously confirmed by the Court of Appeal.[26] Finally, even though this case explains the current patentability of AI inventions in the U.S., the approach can be changed by Congress or case law as this, or other cases work their way through the judicial process in the coming years.[27]

2. *Copyright of Warner Music Group on AI-Generated Music*: With regards to the utilization of AI systems for training purposes, it is widely acknowledged that there are no explicit limitations within the law that could prevent the use of any type of source material.[28] Hence the reason why AI has recently been a heated topic of conversation in the music industry, with debates ranging from the creative possibilities of the new technology to concerns about its legality.[29] Warner Music Group (WMG) has tackled AI-generated music creations by citing commercial interest in AI-generated works and invoking copyright for such creations: *"Warner Music Group believes that machine learning and AI technologies have creative potential for artists and songwriters. However, it is imperative that all uses and implementations of machine learning and AI technologies respect the rights of all those involved in the creation, marketing, promotion and distribution of music"*.[30]

Similarly enough, Sony Music Group (SMG) also sent a letter to some 700 AI developers and digital service providers (DSPs) in May 2024 warning them not to use its content to train AI.[31] Concerning the cases of both WMG and SMG, such letters are a reaction to a European Union (EU) regulation which the EU passed into law in 2019, was recently adopted as part of the EU's AI Act, the democratic world's first comprehensive set of laws regulating the development and use of AI technology that allows *"reproductions and extractions of lawfully accessible works"* for

[24] Bonadio and Contardi (2023), p. 195.

[25] Sharma and Manchikanti (2024), p. 37.

[26] The latest news on the DABUS patent case, IP STARS, https://www.ipstars.com/NewsAndAnalysis/The-latest-news-on-the-DABUS-patent-case/Index/7366.

[27] Giovannini and Pasha (2022), p. 398.

[28] Noshokaty (2023), p. 40.

[29] Mouriquand (2024).

[30] Wodecki (2024).

[31] Aswad (2024).

data mining, unless the owners of those works explicitly state they are opting out of having their content used in that way.[32] Moreover, other major record labels including Universal Music Group (UMG) are taking an aggressive stance to protect their IP by filing lawsuits against AI startups by claiming that such companies are unlawfully training their AI models on massive amounts of copyrighted sound recordings.[33] Namely, in lawsuits filed against Suno, Inc., and Udio AI, the record labels—including UMG, SMG and WMG—accused the companies of *"massive and ongoing infringement,"* alleging that they copied sound recordings from the labels *"en masse and ingested them into its AI model,"* which the plaintiffs say violate copyright laws.[34]

In the past, AI companies have argued that their use of the material is legitimate under the fair use doctrine, which allows copyrighted works to be used without a license under certain conditions, such as for satire and news.[35] Nevertheless, the fact that AI systems are highly dependent on input material has been emphasized.[36] To the extent this training requires reproducing source music in order to assemble datasets, it is *prima facie* infringement. Moreover, because such a use of data harnesses expressive works for expressive purposes, it is possible that even the U.S.'s relatively permissive fair use doctrine would not excuse it.[37] Therefore, it is suggested that using copyright-protected material for the purposes of AI learning, development and creation could be copyright infringement, if done without permission. As such, licensing solutions need to be considered to enable this type of permission to use works for AI purposes, unless a copyright exception applies.[38] At the same time, it is presumed that the judiciary's patience and musicology acuity will be tested as copyright owners turn to the courts for redress. In the short term, the court system will be overwhelmed by countless infringement actions—reasons enough to question the utility of applying case-by-case, fact-specific copyright doctrines to generative AI.[39]

When policymakers are deciding whether AI infringes copyright, they will need to be specific about the use of the input material for AI learning and AI generation of new content. Whether the AI output material is substantially similar to the input material and therefore constitutes copyright infringement is another question altogether.[40] Once AI music generators evolve to the point that their outputs sound less like their inputs, and more likely intelligently composed original works, traditional notions of infringement that focus on an appropriation's substantiality will become

[32] Tencer (2024).

[33] Carman and Metz-Bloomberg (2024).

[34] Bohannon (2024).

[35] Sherman (June 25, 2024), https://www.bbc.com/news/articles/ckrrr8yelzvo.

[36] Bosher (2021), p. 222.

[37] Sobel (2021), p. 233.

[38] Bosher (2021), p. 222.

[39] Sunray (2021).

[40] Bosher (2021), pp. 223–224.

insufficient to hold accountable those who make undetected—but no less violative—use of others' works.[41]

3. *Google's "Project Nightingale" and Privacy Data*: Although not representing a direct legal case of AI and IP, Google's healthcare data collection project raises questions about data ownership and use, a key component of AI development, relevant to IP considerations.[42] Namely, AI systems elicit worries about the security and privacy of data, where due to the progress of AI, individuals may erroneously see artificial systems as human and grant permission for surreptitious data collection, resulting in significant privacy problems.[43] An examination of the privacy of patient data was conducted in the U.S. regarding Google's Project Nightingale, which was meant to *"[...] store patient information in Google's cloud, then apply machine-learning technology to deliver recommendations or predictions to clinicians and administrators at Ascension."*[44] In 2019, *The Wall Street Journal* revealed details of Google's secret Project Nightingale. In this project, Google secretly harvested medical data on 50 million Americans, including lab results, diagnoses, hospitalization records and prescriptions, from more than 2000 hospitals belonging to Ascension, a large U.S. healthcare provider.[45] Being discovered in an anonymously uploaded video by a whistleblower, this partnership aims to build AI and machine-learning products to help Ascension better manage its clinical care and financial operations.[46] For its part, Google's aim was to build machine-learning algorithms able to make recommendations about diagnoses and treatment.[47] In an effort to assuage any public concern or mistrust of the company's use of patient data, the president of Google's Industry Solutions and Products division, Tariq Skahaut, issued a statement explaining that Google has a *"Business Associate Agreement (BAA) with Ascension, which governs access to Protected Health Information (PHI) for the purpose of helping providers support patient care ... under this arrangement, Ascension's data cannot be used for any other purpose than for providing these services we're offering under the agreement, and patient data cannot and will not be combined with any Google consumer data"*.[48]

With the 1996 Health Insurance Portability and Accountability Act (HIPAA) being the primary federal statute that governs the use and disclosure of health-related data, it restricts the ability of covered entities to freely disclose, transfer, and

[41] Sunray (2021), p. 213.

[42] Schneble et al. (2020).

[43] Dadwal et al. (2024), p. 50.

[44] Nguyen (2023), p. 21.

[45] Haggart and Tusikov (2023), p. 164.

[46] Ebeling (2022), p. 75.

[47] Haggart and Tusikov (2023), p. 164.

[48] Ebeling (2022), p. 77.

sell protected health-related data.[49] However, HIPAA presents a significant legal loophole which allows companies to obtain third-party access to patient data through the use of a BAA.[50] Such circumstance is additionally explained by Wachter and Cassel that *"this form of data sharing is entirely legal"* because *"virtually all hospitals and clinics enter into what are commonly known as BAA to share certain data with outside vendors who agree to keep data secure as they analyze it for various purposes [...]."*[51] Data privacy, also known as *information privacy*, is the right of individuals to control how their personal information is used, which mandates third parties to handle, process, store, and use such information properly in accordance with the law.[52] Although these organizations are technically safe under these laws, the trust between patients and their respective healthcare organizations is heavily tested regarding the collection and usage of big data, especially given in the absence of informed consent.[53] Scholars suggest that the most ethical approach to selling data involved full awareness and approval of all parties affected by the data transaction.[54] Since AI systems frequently handle substantial volumes of personal data, it is therefore critical to enforce robust data protection protocols, while Google's Project Nightingale should serve as a cautionary tale[55] regarding this specific legal aspect of litigation.

5 Comparative Analysis of the Approach of Legal Systems Towards Artificial Intelligence

Different jurisdictions have different approaches to the challenges that AI poses for IP. By way of illustration, the U.S. leans towards a traditional approach, emphasizing human involvement in the creative and inventive processes for IP. The EU's approach is also conservative, similar to the U.S., focusing on human creators and inventors.[56] Japan and South Korea are actively exploring legal reforms to address the impacts of AI on IPRs. Some jurisdictions maintain a conventional stance, while others are exploring more modern tactics, signaling a dynamic and evolving legal landscape. The outcomes of these cases and the different procedures from different jurisdictions will drastically affect future legal frameworks relating to AI and IPRs.

[49] Elvy (2021), p. 104.

[50] Motsi-Omoijiade and Kharlamov (2021), p. 186.

[51] Nguyen (2023), p. 21.

[52] Nakayama and Jeno (2022), p. 5.

[53] Nguyen (2023), p. 21.

[54] Charles and Delgado (2022), p. 154.

[55] Joshi (2024), p. 211.

[56] At the beginning of December 2023, the European Union reached an agreement on the legal regulation of artificial intelligence. The President of the European Commission, Ursula von der Leyen on December ninth 2023 welcomed the political agreement of the European Parliament with the Council on the Law on Artificial Intelligence.

AI-generated works call into question who or if anyone at all for that matter, should be considered the author of said work. Would that be the AI developer, the user who inputs data into the AI, or AI itself? This question challenges the conventional understanding of creativity and originality. If AI cannot legally possess authorship rights or copyright, then determining the rightful authorship or copyright owner becomes a complex legal issue. The ownership could potentially be contributed to the AI developer or user or be treated under a work-for-hire arrangement. These frameworks usually require human authorship with the exception of works being entirely generated by AI. This exclusion raises further concerns about the protection and commercial exploitation of such works, which could stifle innovation and investment in AI-driven creative industries. Hence, in order to address these challenges, various reforms and theoretical models have been proposed:

- *First*, extension of AI copyright: Some proposals have suggested changing copyright laws to recognize AI as authors or creators, although this raises philosophical and practical questions about the nature of creativity and the purpose of copyright;
- *Second,* alternative ownership models, such as assigning rights to the AI operator or developer, or creating a new category of rights specifically generated by AI;
- *Third,* compulsory licensing which could provide schemes for AI-generated works as a way to exploit these works and ensure fair compensation to rights holders; and.
- *Fourth,* the use of existing doctrines—the exploitation of existing legal doctrines, such as joint authorship or works for hire, may offer temporary solutions, although they do not fully resolve all issues revolving around the subject-matter in question.

The concept of inventory and ownership in the context of AI is complex—by considering AI as an inventor, current patent laws are based on the premise that only humans can be inventors. Recognizing AI as an inventor would require significant legislative changes. Determining the patent owner of an AI-generated invention involves complex considerations, including the roles of the AI developer,[57] the user and potentially AI itself. In the U.S., the USPTO currently requires human invention, not recognizing AI as an inventor. The EPO takes a similar view, having rejected patent applications naming AI as an inventor.[58] Striking a balance between fostering innovation and protecting IPRs in the age of AI is of crucial importance, where IP law should encourage the development of AI and AI-generated technologies all while ensuring fair competition and preventing monopolies. Another legal issue concerns the protection of human creators, where policies must ensure that the rights of human creators are not overshadowed by AI-generated works. In that respect, several policy proposals could help regulate AI in the context of IP: (1) *first*, revising and updating statutory legal definitions to include or specifically address

[57] Kazim and Koshiyama (2021).

[58] Verbandt and Vadot (2018).

the role of AI in creation and invention processes; (2) *second*, creating new IP address categories is considered given the establishment of new IP categories or rights specifically tailored to creations generated by artificial intelligence; and (3) *third*, encouraging international cooperation for the development of harmonized standards and approaches to the regulation of AI and IP law, as well as future trends and predictions. Such policy proposals explore the potential future trajectory of AI in the field of IP regarding its evolving role which is expected to grow with the increased utilization in creative processes, data analysis for IP strategies and enforcement mechanisms. By anticipating future legal challenges and opportunities, the legal system will in all likelihood face ongoing challenges in adapting to rapid technological advances, which require continuous reassessment and reform of IP laws.[59]

6 Conclusions and Recommendations

Guarenteeing the protection of IPRs in the digital era relies on the combined endeavors of stakeholders worldwide, where it is important for legal frameworks to be flexible and encourage innovation while simultaneously ensuring the marketplace being fair and secure for everyone.[60] The development and consequential impact of AI on IP has created corresponding legal challenges. As AI continues to advance, it will undoubtedly test the limits of current IP frameworks, requiring ongoing legal adaptation and reform. On that account, future IP laws need to balance the promotion of innovation with the protection of IPRs in a manner that is both ethically sound and economically viable. However, there are genuine concerns that the potential circumstance of granting AI more favorable treatment may have a negative impact on human creativity in the long run. Indeed, if creative AI benefits from more lenient fair use rules, this could contribute to a gradual automation of 'roboticisation' of entire industries, ultimately displacing humans as creators or at least diminishing their involvement to a significant extent.[61]

IP systems are continuously called on to accommodate new forms of technology, such as AI, whereas scholars such as Robert M. Sherwood have proposed a uniform, high-stimulation world system where countries would learn from each other, as traditional forms of protection are adjusted to accommodate new technology.[62] At the international level, WIPO launched a public consultation process on AI and IP policy in order to identify the most pressing questions likely to be faced by IP policymakers in this specific area of study, especially taking into account that international coordination could benefit from the considerable WIPO groundwork

[59] Hsieh et al. (2023) and Hartley et al. (2023).

[60] Zakir et al. (2023).

[61] Bonadio et al. (2022), p. 250.

[62] Sherwood (1993), p. 70.

on AI that reaches back as far as the early 1990s.[63] Unfortunately, the current international legal system fails to timely modernize the legal aspects of AI as an emerging technology due to the possibility of the product of intellectual activity not being produced by an individual, but by something else—a subject which cannot be regarded as a natural person in any possible manner. Therefore, modern international legislation does not yet contain a specific definition of the owner of the rights to the product generated by an AI machine or program,[64] which is why the need for international cooperation in developing harmonized standards and regulations will become increasingly important to deal with the global nature of AI technology and IPRs.

References

Andreotta AJ (2021) The hard problem of AI rights. AI & Soc 36(1). https://doi.org/10.1007/s00146-020-00997-x

Aswad J (2024) Sony music warns AI developers not to use its content for training, variety, https://variety.com/2024/digital/news/sony-music-warns-ai-developers-training-1236006557/

Becker M (2017) Rights in Data—Industry 4.0 and the IP Rights of the Future, Zeitschrift für geistiges Eigentum (ZGE). Intellect Prop J 9(3). https://doi.org/10.1628/186723717X15069451170847

Bohannon M (2024) Major record labels sue AI music startups for allegedly copying songs to train AI, Forbes, https://www.forbes.com/sites/mollybohannon/2024/06/24/major-record-labels-sue-ai-music-startups-for-allegedly-copyi ng-songs-to-train-ai/

Bonadio E, Contardi M (2023) Artificial intelligence, patents and health innovation. In: Pihlajarinne T, Mähönen J, Upreti PN (eds) Intellectual property rights in the post pandemic world: an integrated framework of sustainability, innovation and global justice. Edward Elgar, Cheltenham

Bonadio E, Dinev P, McDonagh L (2022) Can artificial intelligence infringe copyright? Some reflections. In: Abbott R (ed) Research handbook on intellectual property and artificial intelligence. Edward Elgar Publishing, Cheltenham

Bosher H (2021) Copyright in the music industry: a practical guide to exploiting and reinforcing rights. Edward Elgar, Cheltenham

Carman A, Metz-Bloomberg R (2024) Major Record Labels Sue AI Music Generators, Time, https://time.com/6991466/record-labels-sue-ai-music-generator-startups/

Charles WM, Delgado BM (2022) Valuing research data: Blockchain-based management methods. In: Charles W (ed) Blockchain in life sciences. Springer, Cham

Chrisley R (2000) Introduction: the development of the concept of artificial intelligence—historical overviews and milestones. In: Chrisley R (ed) Artificial Intelligence: Critical Concepts, vol I. Routledge, London

Dadwal S et al (2024) Demystifying the dark side of AI in business. IGI Global

Dreyfuss RC, Pila J (2018) Intellectual property law: an anatomical overview. In: Dreyfuss RC, Pila J (eds) The Oxford handbook on intellectual property law. Oxford University Press

Ebeling MFE (2022) Afterlives of data: life and dept under capitalist surveillance. University of California Press

Elvy S-A (2021) A commercial law of privacy and security for the internet of things. Cambridge University Press, Cambridge

[63] Meier-Ewert and Gutierrez (2022), p. 161.

[64] Gribincea (2020), p. 236.

Fleming DS (2007) US patent and trademark office refuses registration of flavor trade mark. J Intellectual Property Law Practice 2(5). https://doi.org/10.1093/jiplp/jpm044
Ford LR (2021) The intellectual property of nations: sociological and historical perspectives on a modern legal institution. Cambridge University Press
Frosio G (2024) The artificial creatives: the rise of combinatorial creativity from DALL-E to ChatGPT. In: Garcia-Murillo M, MacInnes I, Renda A (eds) Handbook of artificial intelligence at work: interconnections and policy implications. Edward Elgar
Giovannini A, Pasha AS (2022) Artificial Intelligence: A Legal Landscape. In: Pasha AS (ed) Laws of medicine: Core legal aspects for the healthcare professional. Springer, Cham
Gribincea A (2020) Intellectual property rights to an artificial intelligence product. J Natl Acad Legal Sci Ukraine 27(4). https://doi.org/10.37635/JNALSU.27(4)
Gruzdova TV (2011) Definition and evaluation of intangible assets (of objects of intellectual property). Ukrainian Soc 3. https://doi.org/10.15407/socium2011.03.099
Haenlein M, Kaplan A (2019) A brief history of artificial intelligence: on the past, present, and future of artificial intelligence. Calif Manag Rev 61(4):2. https://doi.org/10.1177/0008125619864925
Haggart B, Tusikov N (2023) The new knowledge: information, data and the remaking of global power. Rowman & Littlefield
Hartley S et al (2023) More on AI-generated content. Curr Psychiatr Ther 22(6). https://doi.org/10.12788/cp.0371
Hsieh T et al (2023) Intellectual property in the era of AI, Blockchain and web 3.0. SSRN Electron J. https://doi.org/10.2139/ssrn.4392895
Joshi R (2024) Ethical conundrums and privacy concerns in new innovations: a systematic review. In: Abouhawwash M, Rosak-Szyrocka J, Gupta SK (eds) Aspects of quality Management in Value Creating in the industry 5.0 way. CRC Press
Kar SK et al (2021) Artificial intelligence in mental healthcare during COVID-19 pandemic. In: Mohanty SN, Saxena SK, Satpathy S, Chatterjee JM (eds) Applications of artificial intelligence in COVID-19. Springer
Kazim E, Koshiyama A (2021) The interrelation between data and AI ethics in the context of impact assessments. AI Ethics 1(4). https://doi.org/10.1007/s43681-020-00029-w
Klobucnik L (2024) Intellectual property regulation of artificial intelligence: a matter of time or a step too far? In: Naim N (ed) Developments in intellectual property strategy: the impact of artificial intelligence, robotics and new technologies. Palgrave Macmillan
Landes WM, Posner RS (2009) The economic structure of intellectual property law. Harvard University Press
Meier-Ewert WR, Gutierrez J (2022) Intellectual property and digital trade—mapping international regulatory responses to emerging issues. In: Taubman A, Watal J (eds) Trade in knowledge: intellectual property, trade and development in a transformed global economy. Cambridge University Press
Motsi-Omoijiade I, Kharlamov A (2021) Blockchain for healthcare applications and use cases. In: Pollicino O, Gregorio G (eds) Blockchain and public law: global challenges in the era of decentralisation. Edward Elgar Publishing
Mouriquand D (2024) World's biggest musical labels sue AI song-generators for copyright infringement, Euro News, https://www.euronews.com/culture/2024/06/25/worlds-biggest-music-labels-sue-ai-song-generators-for-copyright-infringement
Nakayama K, Jeno G (2022) Federated learning with python: design and implement a federated learning system and develop applications using existing frameworks. Packt Publishing
Nguyen T (2023) The ethical governance of artificial intelligence and machine learning in healthcare. Ethics International Press
Noshokaty IE (2023) Consciousness genesis in artificial intelligence. Enosh Science Center
Schneble CO, Elger BS, Shaw DM (2020) Google's project nightingale highlights the necessity of data science ethics review. EMBO Mol Med 12(3). https://doi.org/10.15252/emmm.202012053
Scott MD (2019) Scott on multimedia law, 4th edn. Wolter Kluwers

Sharma K, Manchikanti P (2024) Artificial intelligence in drug development: patenting and regulatory aspects. Springer

Sherman N (25 June 2024) World's biggest music labels sue over AI copyright, BBC, https://www.bbc.com/news/articles/ckrrr8yelzvo

Sherwood RM (1993) Why a uniform intellectual property system makes sense for the world. In: Wallerstein MB, Mogee ME, Schoen RA (eds) Global dimensions of intellectual property rights in science and technology. The National Academies Press

Sobel B (2021) A taxonomy of training data: disentangling the mismatched rights, remedies, and rationales for restricting machine learning. In: Lee J-A, Hilty R, Liu K-C (eds) Artificial intelligence and intellectual property. Oxford University Press

Sully SE (January 1997) An IP Practitioner's Perspective, D-lib Magazine, https://www.dlib.org/dlib/january97/01sully.html

Sunray E (2021) Sounds of science: copyright infringement in AI music generator outputs. Catholic Univ J Law Technol 29(2)

Tencer D (2024) Warner music notifies tech firms that they need permission to use WMG content to train their AI models. Music Business Worldwide. https://www.musicbusinessworldwide.com/warner-music-group-ai-developers-they-need-permission-to-use-its-content1/

Upadhyay NK, Rathee M (2020) Impact of Artificial Intelligence on Intellectual Property Rights, Proceedings of 2020 International Young Scholars Workshop Vol. 9, https://doi.org/10.47344/iysw.v9i0.192

Verbandt Y, Vadot E (2018) Non-patent literature search at the European patent office. World Patent Inf 54. https://doi.org/10.1016/j.wpi.2017.07.001

Wodecki B (2024) Warner Music Group Cracks Down on Unauthorized AI Use, AI Business, https://aibusiness.com/data/warner-music-group-cracks-down-on-unauthorized-ai-use#close-modal

Zakir MH, Rasha AS (2023) Cross-border trademark infringement in the digital age: jurisdictional challenges and harmonization efforts. Pakistan Islamicus (Int J Islamic Social Sci) 3(2)

Zakir MH, Gul R, Begum M (2020) Digital exhaustion: navigating copyright and distribution challenges in the digital marketplace. Int Rev Soc Sci 8

Artificial Intelligence and Civil Justice

Konstantinos Kouroupis and George Christofides

Abstract The integration of artificial intelligence (AI) into various sectors has revolutionized traditional practices, and the justice system is no exception. This paper examines the integration of artificial intelligence (AI) within the justice system, highlighting its applications, implications, and the evolving legal frameworks that govern its use. The study employs a dogmatic methodology that includes a comprehensive review of current literature, case law analysis, and comparative studies across jurisdictions such as the USA, UK, Canada, and Australia. The primary research question guiding this investigation is: How does the implementation of AI technologies in legal processes enhance efficiency while navigating ethical and procedural challenges? By exploring specific instances of AI applications, including e-discovery and predictive coding, the paper elucidates both the benefits and potential pitfalls of AI in legal contexts. The structure of the paper is organized into key sections detailing various AI applications, relevant case law, the forecasting of judicial decisions, and the acceptance of AI as evidence in court proceedings. Ultimately, the paper discusses institutional reactions to AI advancements and concludes with recommendations for future legal frameworks to ensure the ethical and effective use of AI in the judiciary, fostering a balanced approach to technological integration in the legal landscape.

1 Introduction

The integration of artificial intelligence (AI) into the justice system marks a transformative shift in how legal processes are conducted and managed. As jurisdictions around the world embrace AI technologies, the potential for enhanced efficiency, accuracy, and accessibility in legal services becomes increasingly evident. From

K. Kouroupis (✉) · G. Christofides
Department of Law, Frederick University, Limassol, Cyprus
e-mail: law.ck@frederick.ac.cy; gio@legalpartners.cy.net

C.-S. Săraru, C. E. Popa Tache (eds.), *AI, Sustainability and Solidarity in Advancing European Values in a Globalized Age*, European Union and its Neighbours in a Globalized World 28, https://doi.org/10.1007/978-3-032-06508-7_4

advanced legal research engines to electronic dispute resolution platforms, AI applications are redefining traditional practices and offering innovative solutions to long-standing challenges within the legal framework. This evolution not only streamlines operations but also raises important questions about the ethical implications, procedural integrity, and the future role of human judgment in an increasingly automated landscape. As we navigate this complex interplay between technology and law, it is essential to critically assess both the benefits and potential pitfalls of AI integration in the justice system.

This paper explores the integration of artificial intelligence (AI) within the justice system, focusing on its applications, implications, and the evolving legal frameworks that govern its use. The dogmatic methodology employed includes a comprehensive review of current literature, case law analysis, and comparative studies across jurisdictions such as the USA, UK, Canada, and Australia. The primary research question guiding this study is: How does the implementation of AI technologies in legal processes enhance efficiency while navigating ethical and procedural challenges? By examining specific instances of AI applications, such as e-discovery and predictive coding, this paper aims to elucidate the benefits and potential pitfalls of AI in legal contexts.

The structure of the paper is organized into several key sections. Following this introduction, the paper will detail the various categories of AI applications in the justice system, followed by an in-depth analysis of relevant case law that illustrates the practical implications of AI technologies. Subsequent sections will address the forecasting of judicial decisions and the acceptance of AI as evidence in court proceedings. Finally, the paper will discuss the reactions of institutional bodies to AI advancements and conclude with recommendations for future legal frameworks to ensure ethical and effective use of AI in the judiciary.

2 Applications of AI in the Justice System

2.1 *The Integration of Artificial Intelligence in the Justice System: Applications and Implications*

In the justice system in general, there are categorizations according to the services provided, and the degree of use of AI varies significantly depending on the applications. Indicatively, the main categories are[1]:

- Advanced legal research engines.
- Online or electronic dispute resolution.
- Assistance in drafting decision drafts (anonymized or pseudonymized decisions).

[1] For a detailed presentation of AI tools and methods used in justice see Ashley (2017), p. 10 et seq.; Negnevitsky (2020), p. 25 et seq.; Custers and Fosch-Villaronga (2022), p. 30 et seq.

- Analysis (Predictive Justice).
- Categorization of contracts according to various criteria and detection of non-standard clauses.
- Chatbots (conversation applications with users) for informing litigants or assisting them in the judicial process.

The political economy and, consequently, the political trial are compatible with applications of artificial intelligence. The presence of artificial intelligence in civil justice is already noticeable in various countries such as the USA, UK, Canada, Australia, and EU member states. The justification for the compatibility of artificial intelligence with political trials is primarily due to the fact that the process before civil jurisdiction is generally written and requires a number of written evidence.

The most significant form is e-discovery, known as electronic disclosure:

2.2 *E-discovery: Electronic Disclosure*

The concept of electronic disclosure pertains to part of the broader process of document disclosure, a process and term of common law under which the parties are called to disclose among themselves the documents they intend to use during the hearing to prove their claims and establish their rights. Furthermore, it is imposed to save costs in the process and to avoid surprising the opposing party, facilitating the speed of the procedure.

Artificial intelligence provides the parties with the ability to process large volumes of information and files, as well as access to evidence that would otherwise not be accessible because it is electronically stored in various types of files.

A basic prerequisite of the process is that the parties must agree to their subjection, but cooperation is required throughout the application. It is further agreed between the parties on the location, the type of electronic data that each party will store, the method of data retrieval, and the format in which they will exchange data. Following this, a software is used to assist in identifying and evaluating the critical files, while those deemed irrelevant are stored in accessible spaces for the parties for transparency and to prevent concealment.

2.3 *Case Law*

Special focus shall be given on an English decision due to the similarity of the legal system with Cyprus and also because of Part 31 of the Civil Procedure Rules, which was implemented in the process and has been in effect in Cyprus since September 1, 2023, without, however, the incorporation of the Practice Direction issued specifically for this procedure. In the case of *Pyrrho Investments Ltd a.o. v. MWB*

Property Ltd a.o. (High Court),[2] the dispute concerned claims for breach of fiduciary duty related to the provision of administrative services or services of a fiduciary nature, with a monetary value of GBP 28.5 million. In this case, the parties agreed to use predictive coding through a specialized software tool. Master Mathews, who delivered the case, permitted the use of this tool for electronic disclosure and the review of three million documents, an undertaking that could not have been accomplished under other circumstances or would have required an enormous amount of time, leading to significant delays and unmanageable costs. It should be noted that this decision enabled the issuance of a Practice Direction regarding matters with retroactive effect.

Master Mathews, referencing the decision *Moore v. Publicis Groupe (2014)* from the USA and the decision of the Irish Court *Irish Bank Resolution Corporation Ltd v. Quinn (2015)*, where the use of software (Bail II) for predictive coding was similarly decided, issued his ruling based on specific reasons:

1. Experience in other jurisdictions has shown that predictive coding can be useful in similar cases.
2. There was no evidence indicating that predictive coding software leads to less accurate document disclosure; on the contrary, experience in other countries, such as the USA, demonstrates the opposite, namely greater accuracy.
3. There is greater consistency in using the software by a specific lawyer handling the case compared to distributing the responsibility among dozens of lawyers to review specific documents.
4. There is nothing in the Civil Procedure Rules that prohibits the use of such software.
5. The number of electronic documents that could be considered relevant and potentially subject to disclosure in this case is enormous, exceeding three million.
6. The cost of conventional document review would entail immense expenses, making it unreasonable to decide otherwise.
7. The monetary value of the dispute is significant, and the use of the software to achieve this specific purpose is proportionate.
8. There is available time until the hearing of the case.
9. The parties have agreed on the use of specific software and the manner of its use to achieve the objective.

Master Mathews concludes: "*Whether it would be right for approval to be given in other cases will, of course, depend upon the particular circumstances obtaining in them*".

Meanwhile, in the case of *David Brown v. BCA Trading Ltd,*[3] the High Court ruled that "the cost of non-automated searching would be enormous, amounting to many millions of pounds at least; therefore, a full automated review of every

[2] *Pyrrho Investments v. MWB Property*, OpenText, https://www.opentext.com/file_source/OpenText/en_US/PDF/pyrrho-investments-v-mwb-property-hc2014-000038-uk-feb16–016.pdf.

[3] *David Brown, Petitioner v. BCA Trading Ltd,* VLex, https://vlex.co.uk/vid/david-brown-petitioner-v-793477117.

document would be unreasonable according to paragraph 25 of Practice Direction B in Part 31, at least when there is a suitable automated alternative at a lower cost." In this case, the dispute involved shareholders, with the claimant seeking the recovery of GBP 20,000,000. The volume of documents was approximately 500,000, and testimony was presented by an expert stating that the use of artificial intelligence instead of conventional keyword searching would save significant time and reduce costs from GBP 338,000 to GBP 132,000. The distinction from previous case law was the objection from one of the parties to the application, which was based on the position that this was new technology that might not be as effective as conventional processes. Nevertheless, the request was approved based on the Practice Direction and also within the framework of the previous case law of Pyrrho.

Similarly, the Supreme Court of Ireland decided in the case of *Irish Bank Resolution Corporation Ltd & Others v. Sean Quinn & Others*[4] that the use of artificial intelligence would expedite the process and significantly save on legal costs, based on the testimony of an expert who noted that it would require the cost of 10 reviewers and 113 days of review, with costs amounting to €220,000.

In Canada, following the decision in the case of *Haghshenas v. Canada (Minister of Citizenship and Immigration) 2023,*[5] part of the decision was made with the assistance of artificial intelligence software known as "Chinook." Evaluating the logical and fair approach of the official, the Court noted the following: "*... the Applicant submits that the Decision is based on artificial intelligence generated by Microsoft in the form of Chinook software. However, the evidence is that the Decision was made by a Visa Officer and not by software. I agree that the Decision had input assembled by artificial intelligence, but it seems to me that the Court is to look at the record and the Decision and determine its reasonableness...* ".

Following this decision, Practice Directions were issued by the Manitoba Court in Canada and the Yukon Court, noting the need for transparency regarding the artificial intelligence tools that may have been used, as there are legal reservations concerning the validity and reliability of the information processed in each case. "*Artificial intelligence is rapidly developing. Cases in other jurisdictions have arisen where it has been used for legal research or submission in Court. There are legitimate concerns about the reliability and accuracy of the information generated from the use of artificial intelligence. As a result, if any counsel or party relies on artificial intelligence (such as ChatGPT or any other artificial intelligence platform) for their legal research or submissions in any matter and in any form before the Court, they must advise the Court of the tool used and for what purpose.*"

In Australia, in the case of *McConnell Dowell Constructions (Aust) Pty v. Santam Ltd & Others,*[6] the use of predictive coding was permitted in the discovery process.

---

[4] Irish Bank Resolution Corporation, VLex, https://ie.vlex.com/vid/irish-bank-resolution-corporation-793077145.

[5] Daly (2023) and Falco (2023).

[6] *McConnell Dowell Constructors v. Santam Ltd*, OpenText, https://www.opentext.com/file_source/OpenText/en_US/PDF/mcconnell-dowell-constructors-v-santam-ltd-vsc734-dec2-016.pdf; Macaulay (2018).

2.4 Forecasting Judicial Decisions

A series of studies and research have emerged regarding the European Court of Human Rights (ECHR), particularly due to the large volume of cases submitted annually (approximately 50,000), which creates delays in processing and ultimately in adjudicating them. The research, which began in 2016,[7] with the first being a collective effort, demonstrated that patterns lead judicial decisions to specific outcomes based on qualitative data. Specifically, it showed that from the factual circumstances of these cases, there is a strong possibility of predicting the outcome of the application.

This approach has provoked a reaction from the European Commission for the Efficiency of Justice (CEPEJ) of the Council of Europe,[8] which notes that while the ambitious efforts and capabilities of technologies should not be undermined, and the need for their application is recognized, there must be guarantees regarding ethics, transparency, and fair treatment when using them. This is to ensure that in the future, the contribution of artificial intelligence to decision-making and the prediction of judicial decisions can be realized.

A study from Trinity University followed,[9] which demonstrated that if patterns were used in ECHR decisions, then 30% of cases would be incorrect. However, it noted that these models could be used as an indication of which delayed cases should be prioritized.

2.5 Artificial Intelligence as Evidence

It is now accepted that the capabilities of artificial intelligence are limitless and astonishing. Studies now show that applications tailored to artificial intelligence can be presented as evidence before a Court. Research also indicates that testimony from artificial intelligence machines evaluating witness statements conflicts with the rule of artificial intelligence, while testimony resulting from processing by artificial intelligence machines avoids the hearsay rule and can be assessed as acceptable evidence before Courts.

It is therefore clear that in the coming years, parties in pending litigation will have the opportunity to present testimony related to artificial intelligence machines before Courts. Its evidential value can be evaluated in accordance with existing rules of procedure and evidence and may be treated as having similar characteristics to those of testimony from ordinary fact witnesses or experts.[10]

---

[7] Aletras et al. (2016).

[8] European Ethical Charter on the Use of AI in Judicial Systems, Council of Europe, https://www.coe.int/en/web/cepej/cepej-european-ethical-charter-on-the-use-of-artificial-intelligence-ai-in-judicial-systems-and-their-environment.

[9] O'Sullivan and Beel (2019).

[10] Sokolova (2023).

For better understanding of the above reference, it is important to note that in cases before Courts, data from FitBit[11] (a wristband for data recording) was used in a Canadian Court as evidence in a personal injury case to demonstrate whether the Plaintiff's activities changed after the accident. Furthermore, in 2021, in a Court in the USA (Missouri), a Judge ordered a Plaintiff in a civil personal injury case to present all data recorded on the FitBit worn since the day the device was put on, to demonstrate whether the Plaintiff could cover long distances, contrary to their claim of incapacity.

3 Institutional Responses to AI in Justice

3.1 Reflexes and Reactions of Institutional Bodies

The rapid development of artificial intelligence (AI) and the use of AI systems in the field of legal science facilitate and accelerate the complex work of justice system stakeholders (Judges, Lawyers) as well as the relevant authorities in their need to ensure and guarantee the use of new technologies without jeopardizing fundamental rights, democracy, and the rule of law. These beneficial achievements of AI systems have encouraged many institutions to evaluate them, while simultaneously raising concerns about the threats, risks, and harm they may pose to humanity due to inadequate oversight and erroneous applications.

3.2 Bletchley Declaration[12]

In a symbolic yet unique conference organized by the United Kingdom, 28 countries and the European Union participated, focusing solely on security issues arising from the risks associated with the development of artificial intelligence.The Parties reached an agreement to sign a declaration that records the following important issues:

(a) It is recognized that artificial intelligence presents enormous and universal opportunities and has the potential to transform and enhance peace, prosperity, and its human-centered role. At the same time, the international community acknowledges the need for developing collaborations on AI issues that promote economic development, sustainable growth, innovation, and the protection of fundamental rights and basic freedoms.

---

[11] Olson (2014).

[12] The Bletchley Declaration, UK Government, November 1, 2023, https://www.gov.uk/government/publications/ai-safety-summit-2023-the-bletchley-declaration/the-bletchley-declaration-by-countries-attending-the-ai-safety-summit-1-2-november-2023. Guzik and Sitek (2023).

(b) It is recognized that the conference represents a unique opportunity for the international community to collaborate on the safe development and use of artificial intelligence.
(c) The Parties note that artificial intelligence poses significant risks to humanity: risks to society, risks due to misuse, and risks arising from loss of control. Since many of these risks affect the international community, it recognizes the need for cooperation to ensure that the development of artificial intelligence is human-centered, responsible, and trustworthy.
(d) To this end, the Parties recognize that, because there are AI systems that are unusually powerful and evolutionarily dangerous, conditions must be established to encourage relevant stakeholders to provide transparency of content and accountability regarding their designs to assess the dangerous capabilities that may arise and to prevent the misuse of systems and loss of control.

3.3 European Union

The EU has developed a legislative proposal for harmonized rules in the field of artificial intelligence (AI), namely the regulation on artificial intelligence. The regulation aims to ensure that AI systems available in the European market and used in the Union are safe and respect the fundamental rights and values of the Union. The AI regulation[13] is a landmark legislative initiative and includes:

- Rules for high-impact general-purpose AI models that may entail systemic risk in the future, as well as for high-risk AI systems.
- A revised governance system with certain enforcement powers at the EU level.
- An expansion of the list of prohibitions, but with the possibility of using remote biometric identification by law enforcement authorities in public spaces, subject to certain safeguards.
- Better protection of rights through the obligation of entities implementing high-risk AI systems to conduct impact assessments on fundamental rights before putting an AI system into use.

[13] Regulation (EU) 2024/1689 of the European Parliament and of the Council of June 13, 2024, laying down harmonized rules on artificial intelligence and amending Regulations. Byers (2018), p. 70 et seq.; Mitrou (2019); Barraud (2019), p. 65 et seq.

3.4 *Judicial Authorities*

Judicial authorities in various countries have engaged with artificial intelligence and the justice system or the process before the Courts. Countries such as Australia,[14] the UK,[15] Canada, and others have developed guidelines urging their members to understand artificial intelligence and its applications, safeguard confidentiality and privacy, ensure accountability and data accuracy, maintain impartiality, data security, and be cautious regarding the potential use of artificial intelligence tools by the parties involved.

3.5 *International Bar Association*

The IBA, the global voice of Lawyers, has included artificial intelligence as a top agenda item for the years 2023–2028 in a way that supports, similarly and methodologically to competition rules, the harmonization of rules based on the EU AI Act, continuous consultation with legislative bodies, and the support of common principles, best practices, or guidelines addressing the concerns raised by artificial intelligence.

3.6 *CCBE*[16]

The European Bar Association has issued its own declaration calling on national, European, and international bodies/authorities and organizations to:

- Establish rules regarding the use of artificial intelligence tools in the field of justice, with a focus on safeguarding the right to a fair trial and the right to a natural/human judge.
- The rules for using artificial intelligence systems should take into account ethical principles, respecting fundamental rights, transparency, accountability, and the maintenance of the rule of law and democracy.

---

[14] Artificial Intelligence and Litigation, future possibilities. Handbook for Judicial Officers (2021), https://www.judcom.nsw.gov.au/publications/benchbks/judicial_officers/artificial_intelligence_and_litigation.html#ftn.id-1.5.10.9.1.4.1.1.

[15] Artificial Intelligence Guidance for Judicial Office Holders (2023), https://www.judiciary.uk/guidance-and-resources/artificial-intelligence-ai-judicial-guidance/.

[16] Council of Bars and Law Societies of Europe, Statement on the use of AI in the justice system and law enforcement (22 May 2023). https://www.ccbe.eu/fileadmin/speciality_distribution/public/documents/Statements/2023/EN_ITL_20230525_CCBE-Statement-on-the-use-of-AI-in-the-jus tice-system-and-law-enforcement.pdf.

4 Conclusions

The effort to subject human reasoning to codified thought in order to derive and arrive at correct conclusions in the new information environment is not a recent phenomenon but has been a constant demand since the time of Aristotle concerning human evolution.

The attempt to subject human reasoning to codified "correct" thought for the purpose of drawing accurate conclusions in the new information environment is clearly not easy in a field like justice, where legal reasoning can never be static.[17]

In these challenges, as guardians and operators of Justice, we have the responsibility and obligation to engage with the innovative issues and applications of artificial intelligence without relinquishing its human-centered character, and we certainly have every reason to positively address the benefits and advantages that may arise.

References

Aletras N, Tsarapatsanis D, Preoţiuc-Pietro D, Lampos V (2016) Predicting judicial decisions of the European court of human rights: a natural language processing perspective. Peer J Comp Sci 2:e93. https://doi.org/10.7717/peerj-cs.93
Artificial Intelligence and Litigation, future possibilities (2021) Handbook for Judicial Officers, https://www.judcom.nsw.gov.au/publications/benchbks/judicial_officers/artificial_intelligence_and_litigation.html#ftn.id-1.5.10.9.1.4.1.1
Artificial Intelligence Guidance for Judicial Office Holders (12.12.2023) Courts and Tribunals Judiciary. https://www.judiciary.uk/guidance-and-resources/artificial-intelligence-ai-judicial-guidance/
Ashley K (2017) Artificial intelligence and legal analytics: new tools for law practice in the digital age. Cambridge University Press, Cambridge
Barraud B (2019) L'intelligence artificielle dans toutes les dimensions. L'Harmattan, Paris
Bensoussan A, Bensoussan J (2019) IA, Robots et Droit. Bryulant, Brussels
Byers J (2018) Artificial intelligence: the practical legal issues. Legal Brief Publishing, London
Council of Bars and Law Societies of Europe (22 May 2023) Statement on the use of AI in the justice system and law enforcement, https://www.ccbe.eu/fileadmin/speciality_distribution/public/documents/Statements/2023/EN_ITL_20230525_CCBE-Statement-on-the-use-of-AI-in-the-justice-system-and-law-enforcement.pdf
Custers B, Fosch-Villaronga E (2022) Law and artificial intelligence: regulating AI and applying AI in legal practice. Springer, Berlin
Daly P (2023) Judicial Review of AI-Aided Decisions: Haghshenas v. Canada (Citizenship and Immigration), 2023 FC 464, Administrative Law Matters, https://www.administrativelawmatters.com/blog/2023/04/04/judicial-review-of-ai-aided-decisions-haghshenas-v-canada-citizenship-and-immigration-2023-fc-464judicial-review-of-ai-aided-decisions/

[17] Streel and Jacquemin (2017), p. 35 et seq.; Bensoussan and Bensoussan (2019), p. 121; Susskind (2019), p. 54; Merabet (2020), p. 70 et seq.

European Ethical Charter on the Use of AI in Judicial Systems, Council of Europe, https://www.coe.int/en/web/cepej/cepej-european-ethical-charter-on-the-use-of-artificial-intelligence-ai-in-judicial-systems-and-their-environment

Falco MP (2023) When AI starts making administrative decisions. Rule Law Report 6(3):1–10. https://www.lexisnexis.ca/en-ca/about-us/rule-of-law/rol-report-vol6-issue-3.page#article-1

Guzik TJ, Sitek A (2023) Global accord on the integration of artificial intelligence in medical science publishing: implications of the Bletchley declaration. Cardiovasc Res 119(17):2681–2682. https://doi.org/10.1093/cvr/cvad170

Macaulay C (2018) The First Australian Case to Endorse the Use of Technology Assisted Review for Discovery… and It Won't Be the Last, Kordamentha, https://kordamentha.com/insights/first-australian-case-to-endorse-tar-review

Merabet S (2020) *Vers un droit de l'intelligence artificielle*, Volume 197. Dalloz, Paris

Mitrou L (2019) Data Protection, Artificial Intelligence and Cognitive Services: Is the General Data Protection Regulation (GDPR) 'Artificial Intelligence-Proof'?, https://papers.ssrn.com/sol3/papers.cfm?abstract_id=3386914

Negnevitsky M (2020) Artificial intelligence: a guide to intelligent systems, 3rd edn. Addison-Wesley, Boston

O'Sullivan C, Beel J (2019) Predicting the Outcome of Judicial Decisions Made by the European Court of Human Rights. In: 27th AI Irish Conference on Artificial Intelligence and Cognitive Science, 2019, https://www.researchgate.net/publication/338137407_Predicting_the_Outcome_of_Judicial_Decisions_made_by_the_European_Court_of_Human_Rights

Olson P (2014) FitBit Data Now Being Used in the Courtroom, Forbes, https://www.forbes.com/sites/parmyolson/2014/11/16/fitbit-data-court-room-personal-injury-claim/

Sokolova M (2023) The role and position of AI evidence in civil litigation. Med Law Soc 16(1):169–190

Streel AD, Jacquemin H (2017) L'intelligence artificielle et le droit. Larcier, Brussels

Susskind R (2019) Online courts and the future of justice. Oxford University Press, Oxford

The Bletchley Declaration, UK Government, November 1, 2023, https://www.gov.uk/government/publications/ai-safety-summit-2023-the-bletchley-declaration/the-bletchley-declaration-by-countries-attending-the-ai-safety-summit-1-2-november-2023

Sustainable Development and Solidarity in the European Context

Deposit-Return System: One Year of Operation

Marta-Claudia Cliza

Abstract A clean environment in which you can breathe and enjoy all that nature has to offer is, on the one hand, a quality of life standard and, on the other hand, a necessity of the utmost importance for both economic operators and the authorities. Pollution, on the other hand, is a problem that both the state and the business community need to address and work together in order to solve it. In this background, one way of taking action to reduce pollution, at state level, is the organized collection and disposal of municipal packaging abandoned in public spaces. One of the means that the legislator has made available to society for this purpose is the deposit-return system for non-reusable primary packaging. Therefore, the scope of this paper is to analyze the progress made by our country but also to identify how the collection and return of these packages works, one year after the actual implementation of the deposit-return system in Romania. The results of the research show that the issue of pollution reduction is a matter of public interest that can only be solved by involving all of us in the community. From this perspective, the issue is topical and important for society as a whole.

1 Introduction

The Romanian Constitution has expressly regulated the right to a healthy environment in Article 35. In this regard, according to the provisions of para. (1) "The State shall acknowledge the right of every person to a healthy, well preserved and balanced environment". Nowadays, nature is undergoing a transformation due to climate change and people often abandon packaging in a chaotic way, disturbing the natural balance. Therefore, in order to have access to a healthy environment, it is important not just to pretend that someone else is protecting the environment, but

M.-C. Cliza (✉)
"Nicolae Titulescu" University of Bucharest, Bucharest, Romania
e-mail: office@cliza.ro

C.-S. Săraru, C. E. Popa Tache (eds.), *AI, Sustainability and Solidarity in Advancing European Values in a Globalized Age*, European Union and its Neighbours in a Globalized World 28, https://doi.org/10.1007/978-3-032-06508-7_5

each of us, by personal example, must rally together to reduce pollution, helping the environment to become clean and people-friendly again.

The date of 30 November 2024 has a special significance: it represents the one-year anniversary of the functioning of the DRS in Romania. On this occasion, a dedicated conference was organized and from the media we learn that Mr. Mircea Fechet, Minister of Environment, Water and Forests, declared that: "we have 2 billion less packaging on the roadside and in landfills."[1] Also, according to the Minister: "DRS is the largest public-private partnership in Romania and the biggest circularity project in our country since the Revolution."[2]

According to the specialized literature "DRS deposit-return systems are one of the most efficient methods of collecting beverage packaging."[3] Comparative law researchers state in their works on this topic that "countries with a deposit and repayment system—(Deposit and Return System) have high rates of selective collection of beverage packaging waste, indicating that it is a powerful economic tool for achieving European packaging recycling targets."[4]

Therefore, since we wish to understand the impact of DRS on the public and private environment in our country, this study will analyze the proposed theme, combining theoretical elements with practical, applied ones. From this perspective, we believe that protecting the environment is one of the most topical issues in the attention of states from all continents and it is important to be debated by the academic world in general. Therefore, the paper is organized in two parts: the first part is dedicated to the implementation of the DRS in Romania and the second part proposes a case study discussing the effectiveness of the implementation of the DRS in our country one year after its launch.

2 On the DRS Implementation in Romania

The day-to-day activity should be conducted only in compliance with the law in any state governed by the rule of law. As our doctrine has shown, "the rule of law is often defined as governed by law, and legality is considered the central element of the legal regime of administrative acts".[5] Furthermore, "it is widely known that public administration is guided by the principle of legality, which expresses the idea

[1] https://www.realitatea.net/stiri/politica/mircea-fechet-pnl-despre-sistemul-de-garantie-returnare-la-aproape-un-an-de-la-inaugurare-avem-cu-2-miliarde-mai-putine-ambalaje-pe-marginea-drumului-si-in-gropile-de-gunoi_671a23cb11d8f2f65697453.

[2] https://www.agerpres.ro/economic-intern/2024/10/22/fechet-sistemul-de-garantie-returnare-este-un-proiect-de-succes-spre-deosebire-de-dezastrul-din-sistemul-de-management-al-deseurilor%2D%2D1374808.

[3] Calabrese et al. (2021) and Ştefan (2024).

[4] Martinho et al. (2024).

[5] Lazăr (2004).

that the administration is subject to the law, taking into account the hierarchy and legal force of normative acts."[6]

Therefore, in accordance with the constitutional provision that: "In Romania, the observance of the Constitution, its supremacy and the laws shall be mandatory", DRS has been introduced at national level in compliance with the legislation in force. In this regard, the legal framework that led to the implementation in Romania on 30 November 2023 of the deposit-return system for non-reusable primary packaging was composed of several normative acts.

First of all, according to the provisions of art. 10 para. (5) of Law no. 249/2015 on the management of packaging and packaging waste[7] the authorities were bound to adopt DRS for non-reusable primary packaging of glass, plastic or metal, until 21 January 2022. According to the provisions of art. 1, the scope of this law is "to regulate the management of packaging and packaging waste in order to prevent or reduce the impact on the environment".

In the application of the law, Government Resolution no. 1.074/2021 on the establishment of the deposit-return system for non-reusable primary packaging was adopted.[8] Subsequently, there have been several other administrative acts that have completed the picture that made up the legal framework applicable in this area. For example, the legislation was supplemented by Order no. 459/2022 of the Minister of the Environment, Water and Forests on the approval of the Procedure for the selection of the administrator of the deposit-return system.[9]

According to art. 3 of the normative act (namely the Procedure for the selection of the administrator of the deposit-return system), there are four stages in the selection procedure, as follows:

a) registration for the selection procedure of the administrator and submission of the documentation within the deadline set by art. 18 para. (5) of Government Resolution no. 1074/202;
b) assessment of the fulfillment of the eligibility criterion set out in art. 5;
c) assessment of the submitted documentation and awarding the score;
d) publication of the selection result.

The selection procedure was carried out by the Selection Commission organized at the level of the central public authority for environmental protection and business environment was invited to analyze the legislation and participate in the selection. Furthermore, according to the provisions of art. 13 of the Selection Procedure, the decision made by the Commission can be appealed in court, according to Law no.

[6] Bogasiu (2015).

[7] Law no. 249/2015 on the management of packaging and packaging waste, published in Official Journal no. 809 of 30 October 2015, as further amended and supplemented.

[8] Published in Official Journal no. 1120 of 21 November 2021, as further amended and supplemented by G.R. no. 580/2024, published in the Official Journal no. 510 of 31 May 2024.

[9] Published in the Official Journal no. 191 of 21 February 2022.

554/2004 of the contentious administrative.[10] As a result of the selection made, RetuRO was appointed in the capacity of DRS administrator, which has a dedicated DRS website in Romania, namely: returosgr.ro.[11] According to art. 3 of Government Resolution no. 1074/2021 there is established the obligation for producers placing packaged products (i.e. non-reusable primary packaging) on the national market to register with the database managed by the system administrator by 28 February 2023. Therefore, we take into consideration the registration with RetuRO.

It is important to note that the 2021 legislation requires producers to meet minimum annual targets for the return of DRS packaging through the administrator, covering 2024–2026 period, as follows:

a) 65% bottle, 65% plastic, 64% metal for 2024;
b) 75% bottle, 75% plastic, 80% metal for 2025;
c) 85% bottle, 90% plastic, 90% metal for 2026.

3 Case-Study on the Efficiency of DRS Implementation in Romania

According to Directive (EU) 2018/850 of the European Parliament and of the Council of 30 May 2018 amending Directive 199/31/EC on the landfill of waste (text with EEA relevance)[12] art. 1 item 4 the following paragraph is added in art. 5 para. (5) of Directive 199/31/EC: "Member States shall take the necessary measures to ensure that by 2035 the amount of municipal waste landfilled is reduced to 10% or less of the total amount of municipal waste generated (by weight)". As the doctrine has shown, at European level, legislative acts with a direct impact on the Member States are adopted, including the European Climate Law.[13] This Regulation sets out a binding objective of climate neutrality in the Union by 2050 (art. 1).[14]

In order to find out whether the DRS is effective one year after the date of its entry into operation, statistical research was carried out, documenting several reports of the system administrator. To this end, the legal interpretation[15] of the

[10] Published in the Official Journal no. 1154 of 7 December 2004, as further amended and supplemented.

[11] https://returosgr.ro/.

[12] Published in OJEU L 150, 14.06.2018.

[13] Regulation (EU) 2021/1119 of the European Parliament and of the Council of 30 June 2021 establishing the framework for achieving climate neutrality and amending Regulation (EC) no. 401/2009 and (EC) no. 2018/1999, published in Official Journal of the European Union L343/1 of 9.07.2021, pp.1–17, online https://eur-lex.europa.eu/legal-content/RO/TXT/?uri=CELEX:32021R1119; Ştefan (2004), p. 73.

[14] Regulation (EU) 2021/1119.

[15] Comprehensive information on legal interpretation in the work of Boghirnea (2018), pp. 50–57.

collected information was performed. Therefore, by consulting public reports of RetuRO on the amount of packaging placed on the market in 2024, no later than 01.10.2024, by categories: plastic, metal and glass, the following public information is available:

- in what concerns plastic packaging: 2,633,968,199 pieces (88,490,376 kg);
- in what concerns metal packaging: 1,183,650,678 pieces (16,451.498 kg);
- in what concerns bottle packaging: 948,557,595 pieces (245,400,798 kg[16]).

At the same time, we were interested to know the amount of DRS packaging returned in 2024 by 01.10.2024. This resulted in the following quantities of plastic, metal and glass packaging returned:

- plastic: 1,305,049,183 pieces (44,122,141 kg);
- metal: 572,578,619 (8,093,920 kg);
- bottle: 445,531,917 (110,365,034 kg).[17]

We also take into account the rate of return of plastic, metal and glass packaging, until 01.10.2024, as follows:

- Plastic: 50%
- Metal: 48%
- Bottle: 47%[18]

Moreover, the rate of return of plastic, metal and glass packaging for the month of September 2024 was also checked to find out whether citizens participate in the collection of packaging and its return to the machines specially set up to collect packaging. Therefore, the return rate for plastic was of 79%, for metal 82% and for bottle 82%. Furthermore, the administrator of the system publishes several categories of reports, by county and by locality. At the same time, it seems that homeless people are actively participating in the DRS, as it results from media reports.[19]

Specialized literature has also identified the problems faced by business environment in relation to DRS, as follows:

- "issues concerning the setting up as a point of return. For example, in Teleorman, the Environmental Guard has sanctioned all the traders controlled, with areas under 200 square meters, because they did not set themselves up as a point of return;
- monthly reports (...);

[16] https://returosgr.ro/sites/default/files/2024-10/Raportare%20RetuRO%20-%2025%20oct%20 2024.pdf.

[17] Idem.

[18] Idem.

[19] For example, https://www.replicaonline.ro/cauta-prin-gunoaie-ca-sa-supravietuiasca-pet-urile-returnabile-sgr-o-gura-de-oxigen-pentru-oamenii-strazii-video-594760.

- inconsistencies between what traders submit to the system administrator and what ends up in the system, etc."[20]

From another perspective, at first sight it may seem onerous the way DRS works, strictly from the consumer's perspective who is obliged to pay both the price of the desired product and a deposit of 0.5 lei for all types of DRS packaging, as shown in the documented RetuRo Reports. Nevertheless, the new nationwide system is starting to look attractive, as the figures reported by the system's administrator show. Moreover, according to the legal provisions, the value of the deposit will be recovered later, when the packaging is returned.

4 Conclusions

This paper has analyzed the way in which the collection of non-reusable primary packaging works, by means of the DRS, one year after its implementation in Romania. A few brief conclusions can be drawn.

First of all, our country has undertaken under the law to achieve minimum annual targets for the return of DRS packaging, in line with European legislation in force. The paper presented the applicable regulatory framework, mainly composed of Government Resolution no. 1.074/2021 on the establishment of the deposit-return system for non-reusable primary packaging and of other administrative acts. Our perception on the implementation of such a large-scale mechanism that covers the entire country is that the state has widely opened its doors by inviting individuals, economic operators and authorities to participate in these public services for the benefit of all. As already pointed out "public services are unquestionably a pillar of society."[21]

Second of all, in order to see what the state of achievement of the clear targets is that Romania has undertaken to meet, for 2024–2026 period, a statistical data collection research was carried out, analyzing the public reports of the administrator of the DRS system, RetuRO for 2024. In this respect, the results show that the monthly recycling targets for non-reusable primary packaging are not only achieved, but also exceeded. However, the large, annual targets cannot be said to have been reached, although the October–December 2024 contributions remain to be added. Even if the repaid deposit for each non-reusable primary packaging returned may seem small, in the amount of only 0.5 lei per DRS packaging, in the short term, the system implemented can help at least the disadvantaged categories to ensure their minimum subsistence from these guarantees. Therefore, we believe that in our country the use

[20] Voiculescu S, Implementarea SGR vine cu dificultăți mari pentru operatorii economici și cu amenzi colosale. Câteva dintre problemele comercianților și producătorilor, https://www.avocatnet.ro/articol_67723/Implementarea-SGR-vine-cu-dificult%C4%83%C8%9Bi-mari-pentru-operatorii-economici-%C8%99i-cu-amenzi-colosale-Cateva-dintre-problemele-comercian%C8%9Bilor-%C8%99i-produc%C4%83torilor.html.

[21] Cliza (2023).

of DRS will continue at the population level, this will ensure the elimination of packaging abandoned on the streets and unclaimed by anyone.

The final conclusion of the paper is that, in our opinion, the DRS is an attractive legal way for the population to participate in reducing pollution by collecting and returning packaging to the centers specially set up for this purpose, although its functioning is not perfect, but of course, leaves room for improvement.

References

Books and Articles

Bogasiu G (2015) Legea contenciosului administrativ comentată şi adnotată, 3rd edition, revised and supplemented. Universul Juridic, Bucharest

Boghirnea I (2018) The interpretation—obligation for the judge imposed by the application of the law. Legal and Admin Stud XVII(2)

Calabrese A, Costa R, Ghiron NL, Menichini T, Miscoli V, Tiburzi L (2021) Operating modes and cost burdens for the European deposit - refund systems: a systematic approach for their analysis and design. J Clean Prod 288. https://doi.org/10.1016/j.jclepro.2020.125600

Cliza MC (2023) Public services at the service of citizens - case study: cleaning services. Int J Legal Soc Order 3(1):49. https://doi.org/10.55516/ijlso.v3i1.130

Lazăr RA (2004) Legalitatea actului administrativ. Drept românesc şi drept comparat. All Beck, Bucharest

Martinho G, Santos P, Alves A, Ramos M (2024) Indicators and characteristics of PET packaging collected in the deposit and refund system pilot project. Helion 10(3). https://doi.org/10.1016/j.hcliyon.2024.e25182

Ştefan EE (2004) Implementation of the deposit-return-system, an absolute first for Romania. In: Popa Tache CE, Treneska Deskoska R, Boyd N (eds) Adapting to change business law insights from today's international legal landscape. ADJURIS—International Academic Publisher, Bucharest

Ştefan EE (2024) The deposit-return system in the current European background. Athens J Law 10(3). https://doi.org/10.30958/ajl.10-3-5

Voiculescu S, Implementarea SGR vine cu dificultăţi mari pentru operatorii economici şi cu amenzi colosale. Câteva dintre problemele comercianţilor şi producătorilor, https://www.avocatnet.ro/articol_67723/Implementarea-SGR-vine-cu-dificult%C4%83%C8%9Bi-mari-pentru-operatorii-economici-%C8%99i-cu-amenzi-colosale-Cateva-dintre-problemele-comercian%C8%9Bilor-%C8%99i-produc%C4%83torilor.html

Regulations

Directive (EU) 2018/850 of the European Parliament and of the Council of 30 May 2018 amending Directive 199/31/EC on the landfill of waste (text with EEA relevance), published in OJEU L 150, 14.06.2018

Government Resolution no. 1.074/2021 on the establishment of the deposit-return system for non-reusable primary packaging, published in the Official Journal no. 1120 of 21 November 2021, with latest amendment by Government Resolution no. 580/2024, published in the Official Journal no. 510 of 31 May 2024

Law no. 249/2015 on the management of packaging and packaging waste, published in the Official Journal no. 809 of 30 October 2015, as further amended and supplemented
Law no. 5542004 of the contentious administrative, published in the Official Journal no. 1154 of 7 December 2004, as further amended and supplemented
Order no. 459/2022 of the Minister of the Environment, Water and Forests on the approval of the Procedure for the selection of the administrator of the deposit-return system, published in the Official Journal no. 191 of 21 February 2022
Regulation (EU) 2021/1119 of the European Parliament and of the Council of 30 June 2021 establishing the framework for achieving climate neutrality and amending Regulation (EC) no. 401/2009 and (EC) no. 2018/1999, published in Official Journal of the European Union L343/1 of 9.07.2021, pp. 1–17, https://eur-lex.europa.eu/legal-content/RO/TXT/?uri=CELEX:32021R1119

The Principle of Solidarity in European Union Law. Solidarity and Energy Security

Gabriel Liviu Ispas

Abstract Among the fundamental principles of European Union law is the principle of solidarity, even if its approach has been marginal. The economic, social and political realities of the last decade have, however, highlighted the importance of this principle for the Union as a whole, but also for the Member States. The principle of solidarity has been highlighted since the migrant crisis, the health crisis caused by the COVID pandemic and the energy crisis, and the Court of Justice has ruled on this principle. The present study will highlight the importance of the CJEU ruling in the OPAL case, but also how energy policy can be aborted in the broader context of economic competitiveness, taking into account the Letta and Draghi reports. The study highlights the Union's energy strategy as well as regulatory developments in national law, both in terms of energy solidarity and in particular in the broad area of energy security. The study also shows how Romania has positioned itself in the various cases before the Court of Justice concerning energy security or the application of the principle of energy solidarity.

1 Introductory Aspects

The establishment of the Communities and later the European Union was based on the concept of solidarity in a divided Europe, where human and economic losses were high and the political rift between democratic and communist countries was effective. Robert Schuman, in preparing the first Community, stated that: "Europe will not be built all at once or as the result of a single plan, but through concrete achievements which will first and foremost generate a de facto solidarity...The solidarity of production thus established will demonstrate that any war between France and Germany becomes not only unimaginable but also materially impossible. The establishment of this powerful productive unit, open to all countries willing to

G. L. Ispas (✉)
Faculty of Business and Administration, University of Bucharest, Bucharest, Romania
e-mail: gabriel.ispas@faa.unibuc.ro

C.-S. Săraru, C. E. Popa Tache (eds.), *AI, Sustainability and Solidarity in Advancing European Values in a Globalized Age*, European Union and its Neighbours in a Globalized World 28, https://doi.org/10.1007/978-3-032-06508-7_6

collaborate, will lay the real foundations of economic unification, by undertaking to supply all member countries with the main elements of industrial production on equal terms".[1] Without detailing limits or a limited scope of application, solidarity appears consistently in the legal concerns and motivations behind the emergence of the founding treaties, then in the oil crisis of the 1970s. Subsequently, both the Maastricht Treaty and the Treaty on the Functioning of the European Union set out solidarity as a fundamental principle of the European Union, but its effective application was realized in the three major crises that have affected the Union over the last decade: the migrant crisis, the health crisis and the energy crisis caused by Russia's invasion of Ukraine.

The paper addresses the application of the principle of solidarity, especially in the recent energy crisis, highlighting the provisions of the Treaties, the regulatory acts realized at EU level, the case law of the Court of Justice of the European Union, but also the national developments in Romania regarding energy security and solidarity.

2 Solidarity, a Fundamental Principle of the European Union

The Treaties of the European Union do not define, in a comprehensive manner, the notion of solidarity, its content or purpose, leaving space for numerous scientific or jurisprudential approaches. Thus, there have been interpretations that position solidarity as a fundamental principle, as a basic idea of Community construction, as a constitutional value of the Union, or as a unifying political concept.[2] Mention of solidarity is made in the Treaties, as early as in the common provisions, as one of the values on which the Union is founded, shared by the Member States in a society characterized by pluralism, non-discrimination, tolerance, justice, solidarity and equality between women and men.[3] It goes on to state that the Union shall promote economic, social and territorial cohesion and solidarity among Member States.[4] Subsequently, solidarity appears as a concept relating to the Union's external action, based on the principles that define its role in international society, based on the values it wishes to affirm and promote, as a major player in international law.[5] An analysis of the three references to the concept of solidarity shows that it has a threefold representation: on the one hand, among the fundamental values of the Union,

[1] https://european-union.europa.eu/principles-countries-history/history-eu/1945-59/schuman-declaration-may-1950_en.

[2] Huhta and Reins (2023).

[3] Article 2 of the Treaty on European Union, consolidated version, OJ C 202, 7.6.2016, p. 17.

[4] Art. 3 para. 3, para. 3 of the Treaty on European Union, consolidated version, OJ C 202, 7.6.2016, p. 17.

[5] Ibid, Art. 21 para. 1.

by reference to the rights of citizens in a Europe of values, as an internal vision of the Union, as a fundamental concept in relations between states, which go beyond their national interests and visions and become effective support for other Member States that may have or are experiencing difficulties, without there being a limitative enumeration of causes in which states must take an active conduct, or the situations in which States are relieved of such an obligation, in a manner that also involves the exercise of State sovereignty and, lastly, in a global perspective, in which the Union does not limit itself to its own values in relation to its Member States and citizens, but extends its sphere of interest in the international relations it develops.

The Treaty on the Functioning of the European Union mentions solidarity both in the chapter on economic policy and in the chapter on the environment. By regulating the Union institutions' interventions in economic matters, the Treaty allows measures appropriate to the economic situation to be adopted in a spirit of solidarity between Member States, in particular in the event of serious difficulties in the supply of certain products, especially in the field of energy.[6] Thereafter, solidarity is referred to by reference to the functioning of the internal market. In the spirit of solidarity between States, in order to improve the quality of environmental programs, the Union may adopt energy measures aimed at the functioning of the energy market, its supply, the promotion of energy diversity and the promotion of interconnection.[7] The two provisions create the legal framework within which the Union institutions can legislate on energy policies, even if, according to the principle of conferral of powers, the field is shared between the Member States and the Union.

The lack of definition and the slightly ambiguous use of the concept of solidarity[8] can also be interpreted in a positive way, in which states, when negotiating and signing the treaties, agreed to allow a margin of appreciation for situations that they could not have anticipated at the time. Given that the Union Treaties, as the primary source of law, enjoy an absolute presumption of legality, it must be borne in mind that the mechanism for adapting and revising the Treaty is difficult and lengthy, and a rapid amendment would be difficult to achieve.[9] In this manner, which is typical of national constitutional law,[10] the Member States have ensured that the enunciation of the principle is sufficient, clear and predictable and enables the Union institutions (an important role of which is played by the ministers of the Member States meeting in the Council in various working configurations) to intervene when necessary, within the limits of the provisions of the Treaties, to achieve the objectives laid down in the Treaty, even if sometimes the instruments are not provided for. This approach does not exclude the possibility that complainants, respecting the procedural qualities, may bring actions before the Court of Justice for annulment of acts

[6] Treaty on the Functioning of the European Union, Article 122, consolidated version, OJ C 202, 7.6.2016, p. 97.

[7] Ibid.

[8] Quandt and Lomazzi (2023).

[9] Ispas and Panc (2021a).

[10] Muraru and Tănăsescu (2023).

issued by the institutions.[11] This avoids unilateral action by Member States which, at certain historical moments, may behave in a way which violates the common fundamental values and principles established for the Union as a legal order distinct from that of the Member States. The reasoning given by the Court of Justice in an early but fundamental case for the supremacy of Union law is thus decisive, stating that 'unlike the ordinary international treaties, the EEC Treaty established a legal order of its own, integrated into the legal system of the Member States at the time when the Treaty entered into force and binding on the national courts'.[12]

3 Solidarity and Migration

Over the last decade, the European Union has been affected by an unprecedented wave of migration, which has created the need for an adequate, efficient and effective response from institutions and states. Regardless of the reasons behind this veritable exodus, or miscommunication on the part of officials in some destination countries, the reality is that more than three million citizens, most of them from the Middle East, have embarked on a journey that has turned into illegal migration. The immediate consequence has been increased pressure on Italy and Greece, the frontline states, which have had to call on the EU institutions and other countries for help. The rapid response was given by the Commission, but it did not slow down the flow of immigration and did not relieve the pressure on border states.[13] The reactionș of the states varied, depending on a number of objective or subjective factors,[14] and it was necessary to activate solidarity in order to relocate migrants and provide financial support to the states severely affected by the migration phenomenon.

In 2015 two Decisions[15] were issued for the *establishment of interim measures in the field of international protection for the benefit of Italy and Greece, with a view to assisting these countries to better cope with an emergency situation characterized by a sudden influx of third-country nationals into their respective Member States.* Several Member States, the Czech Republic, Hungary, the Slovak Republic, Romania and the Czech Republic, were against the adoption of Decision 2015/1601 in the Council, arguing that it violated national sovereignty.[16] Subsequently, in the face of the opposition expressed by Hungary and Slovakia to Decisions 2015/1601 and 2016/1754[17] the Commission opened infringement pro-

[11] Ispas and Panc (2021b).

[12] C.J.C.E., Case 26/62, NV Algemene Transport-en Expeditie Onderneming van Gend&Loos v. Netherlands Inland Revenue Administration, judgment of February 5, 1963.

[13] https://ec.europa.eu/commission/presscorner/detail/en/IP_15_4813.

[14] Ispas (2021).

[15] Decision 2015/1523 and Decision 2015/1601.

[16] https://oda.oslomet.no/bitstream/handle/10642/7231/Migration-Solidarity+Crisis+MTakle.pdf?sequence=1&isAllowed=ysaw.

[17] Council Decision (EU) 2016/1754 of September 29, 2016 (OJ 2016, L 268, p. 82).

ceedings against them as Member States, and the Slovak Government[18] and the Hungarian Government[19] brought actions for annulment before the Court of Justice, invoking the lack of proportionality of the measures adopted in the Decisions.[20] Before the Court of Justice, the Republic of Poland intervened in favor of the applicants, and the Kingdom of Belgium, the Federal Republic of Germany, the Hellenic Republic, the Hellenic Republic, the French Republic, the Italian Republic, the Grand Duchy of Luxembourg, the Kingdom of Sweden and the Commission intervened in favor of the Council.

In its decision, the Court holds that where one or more Member States are in an—emergency situation within the meaning of Article 78(3) TFEU, the obligations entailed by provisional measures adopted on the basis of the contested—provision in favor of one or more Member States must, in principle, be shared between all the other Member States in accordance with the principle of solidarity and fair sharing of responsibility between Member States, since, according to Article 80 TFEU, that principle governs the Union's asylum policy.[21] On the basis of the principle of solidarity, the Union institutions were obliged to allocate migrants to Hungary, even if Hungary had relinquished its first line state status as a result of administrative measures at the external border with Serbia, which reduced the flow of migrants to its territory.

The Court also examines the fact that the Republic of Poland, in its intervention, developed a more general argument in order to criticize the alleged disproportionate effects of these allocations on some receiving Member States which, in order to -meet their -transfer obligations, would have to make efforts and bear burdens which are clearly greater than those of other receiving Member States. Thus, the Member States concerned are 'almost ethnically homogenous Member States such as Poland' whose population is culturally and linguistically different from the migrants to be transferred to their territory. The Court finds, on the one hand, that the arguments put forward are inadmissible because they go beyond the procedural framework applicable to applications to intervene,[22] but it also considers the substantive arguments, pointing out that if the transfer were to be made strictly conditional on the existence of cultural and linguistic ties between each applicant for international protection and the Member State of transfer, it would be impossible to allocate those applicants among all the Member States in compliance with the principle of solidarity laid down in Article 80 TFEU and, therefore, to adopt a compulsory transfer mechanism. The ethnic origins of applicants for international protection cannot be taken into account as this would clearly be contrary to EU law and in particular to Article 21 of the Charter of Fundamental Rights of the European Union.

---

[18] Case C-643/15 Slovak Republic v. Council of the European Union, ECLI:EU:C:2017:631.

[19] Case C-647/15 Hungary v. Council of the European Union.

[20] http://curia.europa.eu/juris/document/document.jsf?docid=197500&mode=req&pageIndex=1&dir=&occ=first&part=1&text=&doclang=RO&cid=18451325.

[21] Recital 291, https://curia.europa.eu/juris/document/document.jsf?text=&docid=194081&pageIndex=0&doclang=RO&mode=lst&dir=&occ=first&part=1&cid=6214798.

[22] See Ispas and Panc (2021b), pp. 80–89.

The doctrine has taken nuanced positions which emphasize the principle of solidarity. Thus, "the Court of Justice could have opted for a direct approach, similar to that of its Advocate General, to deliver one of the praetorian phrases of which it alone has the secret, consisting in conspicuously recognizing all its legal strength to the principle formulated in article 80 TFEU. Yet, it took a biased approach, relying on a manifest error of assessment to arrive at the same conclusion. When considering the motivations expressed by the Council, the Court noted that the Council "considered it essential to demonstrate the following Solidarity." Relying on the incentives behind the measure, the Court found that the Council had been conveniently bound by Article 80 TFEU and required to "give effect to the principle of solidarity and fair sharing of responsibility" (para 252). Obviously, complying with a legal obligation by adopting a relocation decision in view of the specific urgency of the situation cannot constitute a manifest error of assessment. What is more, the Council decided on this binding mechanism on the basis of Article 78 TFEU, read in the light of the principle of solidarity enshrined in Article 80 TFEU. The binding nature of the principle of solidarity within the EU's migration policy is therefore clearly laid down, which is a key point in the Courts judgement, putting an end to the controversy.[23]

Institutional steps continued and in 2024 the Pact on Migration and Asylum was adopted and entered into force in June 2024, applicable from June 2026. The Pact is based on the principle of solidarity and regulates, in a comprehensive manner, border control issues, asylum and immigration procedures, the return of third-country nationals, the strengthening of databases, including fingerprinting and facial recognition of those in the process of migration.

4 Applying the Solidarity Principle in Energy Policies

Prior to the invasion of Ukraine by the Russian Federation, the principle of solidarity did not have a major exposure in the European Union's public or legislative policies. Of course, there have been cases before the Court of Justice highlighting the application of this principle at European level. However, the energy crisis was a direct and immediate consequence of the measures taken at EU and Member State level to sanction the aggressor state, including by limiting and subsequently stopping oil and energy imports in their various forms.

Member States, especially those dependent on Russian gas and oil, saw their economic situation jeopardized and the competitiveness of their products uncertain. At the same time, energy prices have risen dramatically, affecting Member States' economies and domestic users, creating risks to energy security. The EU institutions reacted by adopting a series of legislative acts[24] aimed at protecting the economy

[23] Labayle (2017).

[24] Council Regulation (EU) 2022/1369 of 5 August 2022 concerning coordinated measures to reduce gas demand, OJ L 206, 8.8.2022, p. 1-10, Council Regulation (EU) 2022/1854 of 6 October 2022 concerning emergency action to tackle the problem of high energy prices, OJ L 261I,

and citizens through a series of measures to increase energy production capacity, diversify the types of renewable energy, including by stimulating the development of new production capacity and identifying new partnerships with energy-producing countries. At the same time, a number of measures proposed to reduce household consumption have aroused rumors and recalled the unfortunate times of the communist regime, which involved rationalizing energy distribution in order to reduce consumption at peak times.

Energy policies cannot be separated from international geopolitical developments and the evolution of international markets, in particular beyond 2020. The major international competitors, in particular the US, the European Union and China, have set their sights on global economic leadership and domestic market development, in parallel with export development and expansion into new markets, especially in emerging economics. While the monolithic positioning of the USA had the privilege of energy supply, especially gas and oil, as well as technological advancement and advanced research, China's positioning was based on a highly centralized economy, with the supply of raw materials from domestic production, cheap labour The European Union has enjoyed a well-regulated internal market with clear competitive rules, but has been hampered by its dependence on imported energy, mostly from Russia, and by poor investment in new technologies and advanced research.[25] Faced with a real realignment of energy policies, the EU has decided to focus on green energy, but also on climate neutrality policies and the identification of new energy sources. At the same time, states' recovery and resilience plans have included possible investments in economic development and reengineering to achieve environmental goals of making the economy more competitive, greener and more sustainable, and RePowerEu has prompted institutional and state positioning. The policies of interconnection, but also of securing the energy needs of other neighboring countries, including the Republic of Moldova and Ukraine, have affected the supply and distorted the price of energy. This has led to Romania, Bulgaria and Greece buying the most expensive energy, even though Romania is a net producer and, in terms of gas production, is one of the top producers in the European Union. Without suggesting operations of speculative market manipulation, we cannot fail to note that, in the absence of clear regulations on interconnection between national networks and the lack of effective measures to counterbalance the artificial price increases, the economies of these states, as well as the standard of living of the residents of these states, have been seriously affected, while the Union has failed to take compensatory measures.

7.10.2022, p. 1-21, Council Regulation (EU) 2022/2576 of December 19, 2022 on reinforcing solidarity through better coordination of gas purchases, reliable price reference indices and cross-border exchanges in gas, OJ L 335, 29.12.2022, p. 1-35, Council Regulation (EU) 2022/2577 of 22 December 2022 establishing a framework for accelerating the deployment of energy from renewable sources, OJ L 335, 29.12.2022, p. 36-44, Council Regulation (EU) 2022/2578 of 22 December 2022 establishing a market correction mechanism to protect Union citizens and the economy against excessive prices, OJ L 335, 29.12.2022, p. 45–60.

[25] Jerzyniak (2024).

In this way, we can extend the concept of solidarity to a genuine energy security, where the analysis is multidimensional, under a wide variety of threats to geopolitical and economic organization. The current energy crisis is nothing new for European society, as the 1970s brought a deep crisis in energy supply (oil and gas) for the member states of the Communities, in an emblematic period of the Cold War. In the view of some researchers on the subject, "the justification by Germany (and to some extent by the EU) to promote energy interdependence with Russia because of the availability, accessibility, affordability and acceptability of gas supplies has come to an end. Rooting these motives in the security paradigm of the 1970s and the era of external energy interdependence for the EU and its Member States now seems to be over as Europe moves to a new energy security order. Energy sovereignty and solidarity are not independent variables of energy security, but rather create energy security. In the EU, they either help or hinder market participation. The internal energy market requires Member States to transfer some of their energy sovereignty to the EU. When energy is used as a weapon to undermine energy sovereignty, the price goes up. A high price indicates an inability to ensure adequate supply and an undermining of energy sovereignty as well as a failure of energy solidarity".[26]

5 OPAL and the New Dimensions of Energy Solidarity[27]

The origins of the dispute go back to OPAL's connection to the Gazprom pipeline, through which Russia was connected to the entire northern market of the European Union. As early as 2009, the Commission asked Germany to change the rules exempting the capacity of the pipeline's cross-border connection. In 2016, Germany notified the Commission of its intention to amend the connection rules, and the approval prompted Poland, Latvia and Lithuania to oppose the Commission, including by bringing the action in the present case.

In its appeal against the judgment of the General Court, Germany asked the Court of Justice to set aside the judgment and refer the case back to the Court of Justice for a fresh judgment, while Poland, supported by the interveners Lithuania and Latvia, sought, in essence, to dismiss the appeal as unfounded. The pleas in law focused on the manner in which the principle of solidarity should be applied, in particular in relation to the energy component, and the limits of the discretion of that principle.

[26] Carnegie LaBelle (2024).

[27] Judgment of the Court (Grand Chamber) of July 15, 2021, Federal Republic of Germany v European Commission, Appeal - Article 194(1) TFEU - Principle of energy solidarity - Directive 2009/73/EC - Internal market in natural gas - Article 36(1) - European Commission decision on the re-examination of the conditions for the derogation of the OPAL pipeline from the rules on third party access and tariff regulation following a request by the German regulator - Action for annulment, Case C-848/19 P, ECLI: ECLI:EU:C:2021:598.

Regarding the erroneous assessment in law of the principle of solidarity, the Grand Chamber of the Court effectively positions solidarity as a principle of European Union constitutional law. It points out, in recitals 37 to 53 of the judgment, that under Article 194 para. (1) TFEU, the spirit of solidarity between Member States referred to in that provision constitutes a specific expression, in the field of energy, of the principle of solidarity, which is itself one of the fundamental principles of Union law. The principle of solidarity underpins the entire legal system of the Union and is closely linked to the principle of loyal cooperation enshrined in Article 4(3) TEU, under which the Union and the Member States respect and assist each other in the performance of the tasks arising out of the Treaties. In that regard, the Court has held in particular that that principle not only obliges the Member States to take all appropriate measures to ensure the application and effectiveness of Union law, but also imposes on its institution's reciprocal obligations of loyal cooperation with the Member States. The principle underlies the objectives of public policies on energy, and the interpretation of subsequent legislative acts of the Union must be carried out in accordance with it and is binding on the States and on the Union's legislative and executive institutions alike. In recital 49, the Court states that the principle of solidarity entails rights and obligations for both the Union and the Member States, the Union having an obligation of solidarity towards the Member States and the Member States having an obligation of solidarity towards each other and towards the common interest of the Union and the policies pursued by it.

In recitals 69 to 79, the Court points out that there are no limitations in the Treaty as to how energy solidarity may be applied, all the more so as limitations to the provisions of Article 222 TFEU would be capable of calling into question the very validity of the express Treaty provision. The spirit of solidarity should, in the Court's view, guide the actions of all the State or institutional actors involved. In conclusion, as the Court states in recital 69, the principle of energy solidarity, laid down in Article 194 TFEU, must be taken into account by the Union institutions and the Member States when establishing or operating the internal market, and in particular the internal market in natural gas, ensuring security of energy supply in the Union, which means not only dealing with emergencies when they occur but also taking measures to prevent crisis situations. To that end, it is necessary to assess the existence of risks to the energy interests of the Member States and the Union and in particular to the security of energy supply in order to carry out benchmarking.

The Opal case brings a new approach to the principle of solidarity in the case-law and doctrine of EU law, not only vertically—through relations between States—but also horizontally, by imposing the principle on the institutions. Solidarity is thus approached in relation to the development of the Union's internal market, through possible development objectives, but also through energy security, which must ensure the functioning of national economies and the comfort of citizens. Another approach to solidarity envisages risk-sharing between Member States through intervention and support when one of the Member States is seriously affected or there is an imminent action that may jeopardize its energy security. Risk-sharing is directly linked to the concept of the internal market, in which Member States' economies operate. In a third approach, energy solidarity is the instrument through which disadvantaged citizens or communities can be protected. This approach allows the Commission to support Member States in providing incentives to ensure that the price of energy for household users is not above their purchasing power and that the financial burden is not impossible or severely affects their standard of living.

6 National Developments in Romania

Without being a significant voice at European level, although it is the largest gas producer in the Union, Romania has embraced the fundamental values and principles of Union law. Romania's failure to bring its policies into line with the legislative regulations issued by the EU institutions has led to a failure to refer Romania to the Court of Justice over its application of the principle of solidarity.

However, with reference to the fundamental elements of analysis of the principle of solidarity, taking into account social rights, it can be seen that Romania's population is in a state of real vulnerability, especially in terms of ensuring energy needs, in relation to the population's income. In 2023, 13.6% of the population had difficulties in paying their energy bills and 12.5% were unable to heat their homes adequately in winter.[28]

In order to connect the principle of solidarity and energy security with the need to ensure competitiveness and respect for the social rights of citizens, especially those from vulnerable areas, Romania's Just Transition Plan focuses on phasing out coal by 2032 and supporting the transition of regions with carbon-intensive industries. The plan, financed with €2.1 billion from the Just Transition Fund, aims to develop renewable energy sources, modernize industries and retrain the workforce.[29] In this context, taking into account the fact that Ukraine, which was a net exporter in the past, is in a situation where it needs massive energy imports, Romania, together with Bulgaria and Greece, raised the issue of interconnectivity and solidarity at the Council meeting in the Energy configuration, at its October 2024 session,[30] the proposals being summarized in 3 actions[31]: Strict monitoring by the European Commission of the capacity of cross-border flows in transit countries (where lines exist but are only used to a small extent) and coordination of maintenance works to prevent blocking of interconnections that would lead to a price increase; acceleration of investments in new interconnections and assumption of a clear timetable by all Member States. Romania indicated that, for its part, it is already interconnected

[28] https://www.caleaeuropeana.ro/wp-content/uploads/2024/09/Raportul-de-tara-privind-starea-uniunii-energetice-din-2024.pdf.

[29] https://energy.ec.europa.eu/document/download/e1691f7a-c47e-4a3d-8b3c-238d2f10b335_en?filename=23_RO_SoEUr%20Fiche_2024.pdf.

[30] https://www.consilium.europa.eu/ro/meetings/tte/2024/10/15/.

[31] https://www.caleaeuropeana.ro/romania-cere-raspicat-o-singura-europa-cu-aceleasi-drepturi-pentru-toti-pe-piata-de-energie-transmite-sebastian-burduja-in-intalnirea-cu-omologii-din-ue-e-o-ch estiune-de-competitivitate-pe-termen-l/.

with its neighbors through 9 functional lines, and work is underway on 9 more lines. As of October 2024, Romania had 3500 MW of capacity, representing 20% of total capacity and 38% of maximum daily production, well above the minimum limit of 15% required by the Union. Romania has shown that there is a lack of concern at the level of all Member States to ensure interconnectivity, which directly affects the price of energy, exceptional short-term measures to protect European citizens and Member States' economies, to ensure fairness for economies and citizens.

At the national level, Romania's Energy Strategy 2025–2035, with a 2050 perspective, was adopted by government decision.[32]

Given the imperative of energy security, in the context of significant challenges stemming from market fluctuations and regional vulnerabilities caused by the war provoked by the Russian Federation's invasion of Ukraine and, implicitly, by Romania's geostrategic position on the eastern border of the European Union, it is necessary to build a resilient energy sector, capable of reacting promptly and efficiently in the context of any type of crisis, in order to guarantee a continuous and secure energy supply.[33]

The Strategy sets out the following principles, developed horizontally[34]: prioritization of security of supply and crisis response capacity, development of the energy sector on the principle of efficiency and economic rationality, economic and social equity for regions and people, achieving climate neutrality by 2050, creating a free, competitive and entrepreneurial energy market; technological neutrality and exploitation of all energy resources that can contribute to reducing emissions and strengthening the production chain; development of the electricity and thermal energy storage sector, strengthening the supply chain dedicated to the energy industry, development of the circular economy (for example by using energy from industrial processes in efficient centralized heating and cooling systems).

The objectives of the Energy Strategy were regulated as follows: energy security, low carbon energy, energy efficiency, physical access to energy for all consumers and energy affordability and economic competitiveness, efficient energy markets, digitalization, smart grid development and cyber security.

Even if the strategy covers regulatory developments at European level, in particular those concerning the Strategy for an Energy Union of the European Union, there are no references to energy solidarity and the OPAL case, or to the doctrinal or jurisprudential developments that have developed since this judgment. There is also no reference to the security risks of transmission networks, even if these are publicly known.

Romania has committed to an 89% reduction of GHG emissions in the energy sector by 2035, and a 99% reduction by 2050 compared to 1990 GHG emissions. To achieve the objectives and targets set, the process of phasing out solid fossil fuels

---

[32] Decision 1491/2024 for the approval of Romania's Energy Strategy 2025-2035, with the perspective of 2050, published in the Official Monitor, part I, no. 1226 of 05.12.2024.

[33] https://energie.gov.ro/wp-content/uploads/2024/08/Strategia-Energetica-a-Romaniei-2025-2035-cu-perspectiva-anului-2050_23.08.2024.pdf, p. 4.

[34] https://sgg.gov.ro/1/wp-content/uploads/2024/11/ANEXA-34.pdf, p. 9.

from the energy mix is a necessary action, thus Romania has set 2032 as the deadline for decommissioning its coal and lignite-based energy production capacities.[35] In view of the targets set, there is a general consensus for achieving the objective of climate neutrality, and the investments envisaged from funds coming from the EU budget, the resilience and recovery plan and national funds are aimed at innovation and research, as well as the development of green energy production capacities.

7 Conceptual Developments at EU Level: The Letta and Draghi Reports

The report by former Italian Prime Minister Enrico Letta, entitled More than a Market, was published in April 2024 and is an in-depth analysis of the European Union's internal market. Noting that in the areas of research, education and innovation the Union has no coordinated policy and no significant investment compared to the situation in the United States and Asia, the author proposes a fifth freedom in the internal market, covering research, data use, education, skills, innovation and knowledge. All of these areas could be secondary to technological freedom in order to increase the Union's competitiveness and positioning on the global economic market.[36]

The report presents the internal energy market as an important policy which can be a useful tool in the international positioning of the Union's economic market. The energy crisis has affected trust between states, particularly in the setting of the final price of energy, and the population and entire sectors have been affected. However, the prospect of a cross-border electricity market remains a possibility and an opportunity which would be designed to avoid sudden and unjustified price increases. Investment in energy generation, storage and transmission infrastructure remains a priority and increasing the resilience of the energy market is vital to ensure minimum costs for industry and citizens. Administrative measures to establish a single agency to coordinate investment and the energy market are proposed, and increased diplomacy is proposed to build sustainable partnerships with energy producers, to secure the needs for the operation of savings and to secure the needs for household consumption.[37]

An important document underpinning the European Commission's strategic program for 2024–2029 is the report by former European Central Bank President Mario Draghi, EU Competitiveness: Looking ahead.[38]

---

[35] https://energie.gov.ro/wp-content/uploads/2024/08/Strategia-Energetica-a-Romaniei-2025-2035-cu-perspectiva-anului-2050_23.08.2024.pdf.

[36] Letta (2024).

[37] Ibid, pp. 60–69, viewed on 12.11.2024.

[38] https://commission.europa.eu/topics/strengthening-european-competitiveness/eu-competitiveness-looking-ahead_en#paragraph_47059.

The author notes that "Europe has suddenly lost its most important energy supplier, Russia. All the while, geopolitical stability is weakening, and our dependencies have proven to be vulnerabilities. Technological change is accelerating rapidly. Europe has largely missed the internet-fueled digital revolution and the productivity gains it has brought; in fact, the productivity gap between the European Union and the United States is largely explained by different advances in technology. The EU is underperforming in new technologies that boost future economic growth."[39]

In order to strengthen the Union's position on the global market, Draghi identifies three areas of intervention: investment in innovation to reduce the gap with the US and Asian countries, decarbonization and the development of the circular economy, and increasing security and decreasing dependence on energy and raw materials. Fully in line with the Letta report, the Draghi report emphasizes investment in renewable energy,[40] diversification of sources and increased productivity, as well as the identification of new international partnerships.

However, these developments must be linked to political, geostrategic and war developments in Ukraine. The ambiguous stance of some states, doubts about the violation of sanctions imposed on Russia, including through companies resident in the territory of Member States, and the possible takeover of gas distribution under non-transparent conditions may all represent obstacles to development and ensuring economic competitiveness.

8 Conclusions

The principle of solidarity is a common value of the European Union and a guarantee that no one is left behind, no one is abandoned. However, from the provisions of the Treaties and the case law of the Court of Justice to actual practice in institutional or national policies, there is a visible gap which must be reduced through joint action.

While in other areas, such as public health and asylum, the trend has been in favor of supporting states in difficulty, there is an appearance that the immediate interest of the state is more important than the principle of solidarity in energy solidarity. The economic crisis has publicly exposed a reality of the economy—many of the Member States' economies were sustaining their competitiveness through direct negotiations with Russia, while agreements remained bilateral. The risk of reduced competition through the use of power mechanisms or non-transparent access to public decision-making creates distrust between Member States and between economic operators in production.

[39] https://commission.europa.eu/document/download/97e481fd-2dc3-412d-be4c-f152a8232961_en.

[40] https://commission.europa.eu/document/download/ec1409c1-d4b4-4882-8bdd-3519f86bbb92_en?filename=The%20future%20of%20European%20competitiveness_%20In-depth%20analysis%20and%20recommendations_0.pdf.

The energy crisis period has shown that the unilateral policies on which both France and Germany have relied cannot counterbalance a systemic supply crisis, and the consequence is rising energy prices, up to four times higher than in the United States. Large differences in energy prices between countries and between household consumers reduce competitiveness, weaken the Union's position on the global market, lower citizens' standard of living and strengthen nationalist and sovereigntist movements in Member States.

Agreeing with Mario Draghi, we conclude that in the absence of firm, uniform policies at Member State level, if productivity does not increase, the Union will have to choose between being a developer of new technologies to multiply on emerging markets, being a significant player in environmental, climate change and climate neutrality policies, or a promoter of the European social model. We add that, if solidarity policies are predominantly directed towards the economy and state interests, to the detriment of citizens' interests, the Union will be led by those who predict its demise. The interest of policies must continue to be the social welfare, security and stability of the citizen, and other policies could be conceived as modern and efficient instruments to achieve this goal.

References

Carnegie LaBelle M (2024) Breaking the era of energy interdependence in Europe: a multidimensional reframing of energy security, sovereignty, and solidarity. Energ Strat Rev 52:101314. https://doi.org/10.1016/j.esr.2024.101314

Huhta K, Reins L (2023) Solidarity in European Union law and its application in the energy sector. Int Comp Law Q 72:771–791. https://doi.org/10.1017/S002058932300026X

Ispas GL (2021) Impact of the COVID-19 on the migration in the European Union. Juridical Tribune-Tribuna Juridica 11(1):30–41

Ispas GL, Panc D (2021a) Drept instituţional al Uniunii Europene, 2nd edn. Hamangiu, Bucharest

Ispas GL, Panc D (2021b) Organizarea justiţiei în Uniunea Europeană. Hamangiu, Bucharest

Jerzyniak T (2024) The EU De-risking of energy dependencies: towards a new clean energy geopolitical order? Politics Governance 12. https://doi.org/10.17645/pag.8285

Labayle H (2017) Solidarity is not a value: Provisional relocation of asylum-seekers confirmed by the Court of Justice (September 6, 2017, Joined Cases C-643/15 and C-647/15 *Slovakia and Hungary v Council*), https://eumigrationlawblog.eu/solidarity-is-not-a-value-provisional-relocation-of-asylum-seekers-confirmed-by-the-court-of-justice-6-september-2017-joined-cases-c-64315-and-c-64715-slovakia-and-hungary-v-council/?print=print

Letta E (2024) Much more than a market, https://www.consilium.europa.eu/media/ny3j24sm/much-more-than-a-market-report-by-enrico-letta.pdf

Muraru I, Tănăsescu S (2023) Drept constituţional şi instituţii politice, vol 1, 16th edn. CH Beck, Bucharest

Quandt M, Lomazzi V (2023) Solidarity: a European value? In: Polak R, Rohs P (eds) Values—politics—religion: the European values study, Philosophy and politics - critical explorations, vol 26. Springer, Cham, pp 249–280. https://doi.org/10.1007/978-3-031-31364-6_7

Treaty on European Union, consolidated version, OJ C 202, 7.6.2016

Treaty on the Functioning of the European Union, consolidated version, OJ C 202, 7.6.2016

European Sustainability Reporting Standards in the Slovak Accounting Legislation

Darina Saxunova, Daniela Novackova, and Rita Szalai

Abstract The European Green Agreement currently has an impact, apart from other things, on the business environment and the system of reporting information on the business sustainability. To achieve the proper functioning of the common market, the institutions of the European Union adopt secondary acts that strengthen the competitiveness of the economy in the EU member states, strengthen the social market economy and the sustainable economic activities of companies. Secondary EU acts are an important tool for promoting common EU policies and activities. The objective of the scientific study is to clarify the process of introducing EU regulation related to sustainability with a focus on accounting aiming at improving reporting quality to augment comparability and reliability of information provided by businesses in Slovakia. The contribution of the scientific study is to open the discourse on European Sustainability Reporting Standards and to identify problem matters.

1 Introduction

The current world of financial markets and investments is constantly changing and developing. Investors face an ever-increasing amount of information that affects their investment decisions. Apart from traditional financial indicators, investment decisions are increasingly influenced by non-financial factors comprising environmental, social, and governance (ESG) aspects. "The most valuable information document compiled by a company and published for the external and internal environment is the annual report." The annual report is a complex document whose purpose is to provide public information regularly about the company's

D. Saxunova (✉) · D. Novackova · R. Szalai
Faculty of Management, Comenius University, Bratislava, Slovakia
e-mail: darina.saxunova@fm.uniba.sk; daniela.novackova@fm.uniba.sk; rita.szalai@fm.uniba.sk

C.-S. Săraru, C. E. Popa Tache (eds.), *AI, Sustainability and Solidarity in Advancing European Values in a Globalized Age*, European Union and its Neighbours in a Globalized World 28, https://doi.org/10.1007/978-3-032-06508-7_7

performance, financial position and risk, timing and amount of cash flows from operating, investing and financial activities for the latest financial year. It is created in accordance with legal norms and, on the other hand, is also based on the recommendations of the national code for corporate governance. For many companies, it becomes a strategic need to present successful business results and social activities in various areas through an annual report. This document is aimed at shareholders, owners, investors, creditors, analysts, and employees, as well as other stakeholders, including the government, business partners, suppliers, media and communities. European companies are obliged to fully disclose the proportion of their revenues, capital, and operating expenses linked to environmentally sustainable economic activities. For instance, financial organizations such as large banks, asset managers, investment firms, and insurance and reinsurance companies will have to disclose the proportion of environmentally sustainable economic activities in the total assets they finance or invest in.[1] Companies shall report on ESG activities via a special sustainability report which can be a part of the annual report or the economic efficiency report.

2 Literature Review

Back to twentieth century, the Brundtland Report IN 1987 was the landmark in the pathway to sustainability where the problems of protecting and enhancing environment were highlighted and considered as one of the important goals of the agenda for action to be taken in the long run. In 1992 the Earth Summit, held in Rio de Janeiro, so-called Agenda 21 anchored sustainability concept and identified basic sustainability principles.[2]

For many years economic priorities were more urgent than sustainability matters, on the other hand the scarce capital must have been available and invested to support social dimension. Sustainable development enabled to widespread concerns about the condition and viability of environmental, economic, and social components of the present and future worlds. It gained particular attention from international institutions, political factors, business sectors, civil society, and the academic and scientific community, seeing that prosperity is possible only with the aid of sustained, inclusive and sustainable economic growth of all countries and regions.[3]

The concept of sustainable development can be conveyed as wise utilization, sound planning and budgeting or responsible evolution/progress. Responsible business conduct is based on the premises that all businesses should always make a

[1] Moneva et al. (2022).

[2] Wefersová et al. (2016).

[3] Fleacă et al. (2023).

positive contribution to the economic, environmental and social progress of the countries where the businesses function.[4]

Social sustainability is defined by the United Nations Global Compact as all business impacts, whether positive or negative, on people (employees, workers in the value chain, customers, and local communities), and it represents a key dimension of sustainability reporting. However, social dimension lacks appropriate focus and depth, it has been found to be underdeveloped in the context of sustainability; companies pay more attention to the environmental dimension.[5,6] The extent to which companies are committed to integrating corporate sustainability is often related to the potential benefits perceived in terms of cost reductions, efficiency gains, and improvements in market position, image, and company reputation.[7]

Until now, companies that were required to report information on corporate sustainability had the option to choose the standards and scope of reporting. Their obligation was to disclose information that included environmental, social, and governance factors, the way employees were treated, respect for human rights, the fight against corruption and bribery, as well as the diversity of corporate boards (concerning age, gender, education, and professional qualifications). For the investors or non-governmental organizations, the information disclosed for similar businesses was often not comparable.

ESG Reporting has become a crucial component in corporate reputation and success, and therefore the years of the second decade of the twenty-first century really have brought „a recent breakthroughs in the sustainability reporting standard-setting process with relatively new institutions in the field, such as examples—Global Reporting Initiative (GRI), the International Integrated Reporting Council (IIRC), the Sustainability Accounting Standards Board (SASB), the World Resources Institute and the World Business Council for Sustainable Development“[8] which, with a great deal, have contributed to understanding the dynamic and rapidly growing field of environmental, social and governance (ESG) sustainability reporting. Certain experts raised the questions into the debate suggesting that some kind of public intervention in sustainability information is needed to improve the quality of such disclosure.[9] Thus, public institutions or private ones with strong public support could be expected to be at the forefront of regulating sustainability reporting.

The European Union (EU) is a crucial player having been active and supporting this change by adopting legislation that governs disclosure of (i) companies' sustainability aspects (Corporate Sustainability Reporting Directive), (ii) the

[4] Wils et al. (1998).

[5] An et al. (2020).

[6] Vila and Moya (2023).

[7] Sukitsch et al. (2015).

[8] Giner and Luque-Vílchez (2022).

[9] Deegan (2002).

Table 1 Examples of relevant legislation norms leading to ESRS development

Framework/Standard	Scope	Characteristics
GRI (Global Reporting Initiative)	Global	International standards to report non-financial information, including impacts related to climate change, the environment, human rights and governance.
SASB (Sustainability Accounting Standards Board)	Global	Provides specific standards for industries to report relevant financial sustainable information to investors
TCFD (Task Force on Climate-related Financial Disclosures)	Global	Framework to develop financial information related to the climate, focusing on risks and opportunities.
CDP (Carbon Disclosure Project)	Global	Platform that permits companies, cities, states and regions to report information on their environmental impact.
ISO 26000	Global	Guide informing on social responsibility, providing recommendations on sustainability principles and practices
European Taxonomy	Europe	EU legal framework that classifies economically sustainable activities, helping companies to align their operations with EU sustainability objectives
CSRD (Corporate Sustainability Reporting Directive)	Europe	EU directive that increases sustainability reporting requirements to a higher number of companies and reinforces reporting norms
ESRS (European Sustainability Reporting Standards)	Europe	Obligatory standards proposed for sustainability reporting within the EU, based on GRI structuring

Source: Own elaboration on (PwC, 2022)

sustainability of economic activities (Taxonomy Regulation), (iii) the sustainability of financial products (Sustainable Finance Disclosure Regulation), and (iv) the environmental, social and governance risks of credit institutions (Pillar 3 disclosures).[10]

It was pointed out that more standards could impede transparent reporting for organizations, which in turn hinders stakeholders in making fair judgments about the sustainability of organizations.[11] Therefore the effort was directed to the establishment of future reporting of non-financial information elaborating and approving sustainability reporting directive. Table 1 demonstrates relevant legislation norms linked to sustainability reporting of financial and non-financial information being in effect in the Global and in the European level.

[10] Hummel and Jobst (2024).

[11] Oorschot et al. (2024).

3 Corporate Sustainability Reporting Directive Development

CSRD's concept is to stimulate changes in corporate behavior and eventually align sustainability reporting with financial reporting by mandating extensive disclosure of information on environmental, social, and governance topics. It aims to bring clarity and certainty about what sustainability information is to be reported when mandatory EU standards will come into effect. While it may seem like it's "just" about compliance, it's also an opportunity for forward-thinking businesses to share their sustainability stories with investors and other stakeholders.

But the strong voice and rich expertise of institutions as the European Commission cooperating with the European Financial Reporting Advisory Group (EFRAG) and IFRS Foundation marked a big initiative in the area of sustainability reporting and their increased activity was triggered with an initiative taken by SEC in the USA via the Investor Advisory Committee's recommendation of incorporating environmental, social and governance (ESG) factors into reporting requirements for Financial statements issuers. "As far as encouraging a shift in entity's behavior towards achieving sustainable development is concerned, EC and EFRAG have taken a proactive attitude. However, the IFRS Foundation has been adopting a more reactive attitude since the IFRS Foundation was invited to participate in the process. In addition, unlike the EC/EFRAG's aim, the Foundation has not aimed at changing entity' behavior with IFRS but to constitute standards that portray economic reality rather than shaping it."[12] In November 2022, the European Financial Reporting Advisory Group (EFRAG) submitted the first set of draft standards to the European Commission for consideration. Within the framework of the EU standards, EFRAG merged the existing requirements for non-financial reporting with the requirements of the European Green Deal and the EU taxonomy. Following an extensive consultation process and an additional public feedback period on the revised draft standards it issued on 9 June 2023, the European Commission adopted the final standards on 31 July 2023. The 2-month review period by the European Parliament and the Council of the European Union ended on October 21, 2023 and the European Sustainability Reporting Standards are now adopted as declared acts.

The Sustainability Reporting Standards cover all aspects of sustainability reporting—environmental, social, and governance topics. Their aim is to provide an overview of the risks and opportunities in the field of corporate sustainability, including its sustainability strategy, goals and progress, products and services, business relationships, incentive programs, or the value chain.[13] The new CSRD directive combines measures to achieve the goals of the European of the Green Deal, such as efforts to mitigate and adapt to climate change, with the initiatives of the Action Plan for Sustainable Finance. These amendments aim to strengthen transparency and uniformity in reporting, which will enable investors to better understand the

[12] Giner and Luque-Vílchez (2022), p. 1285.

[13] Worldwide impact of CSRD - are you ready? PwC – In the loop, https://viewpoint.pwc.com/dt/us/en/pwc/in_the_loop/assets/worldwideimpactcsrd12oct23.pdf.

risks and opportunities associated with the sustainability of their investments, as well as to assess the impact of these investments on the company and the environment.

The CSRD directive builds on the already established requirements of the NFRD directive, expanding them, as can be seen in figure no. 5. It also tightens the rules regarding the reporting of non-financial information on sustainability. The number of companies obliged to report on sustainability will increase to approximately 50,000, while in Slovakia it should be approximately from 650 to 700 companies.

The current free choice of standards through which companies fulfill their ESG reporting requirements will be replaced by the mandatory European Sustainability Reporting Standards (ESRS). This will harmonize the sustainability reporting format, allowing for better comparability of information among businesses with a similar focus. The Directive introduces a mandatory audit for the sustainability reporting and the digitization of information. It is expected that the CSRD directive will bring a restriction on the so-called greenwashing. The first businesses will follow the new rules in the financial year 2024, with reports drawn up according to the European Sustainability Reporting Standards (ESRS), which will be published in 2025.

Demand for external assurance of this reporting is also escalating as indicated by the CSRD requiring companies to obtain at least limited assurance of their sustainability reports and the SEC including a requirement that large, accelerated filers ultimately get reasonable assurance of their GHG disclosures.[14]

4 Objectives and Methodology

The research object of this scientific study is to analyze the CSRD's environment in the background, which resulted in incorporating this new sustainability reporting directive into new legislation linked to accounting in all EU member states. The main objectives of the scientific study is to examine the latest information and carry out legal analysis of the new legislation related to accounting in connection with the Directive on Corporate Sustainability Reporting (CSRD) approved in 2022. Moreover, the scientific study also highlights (a) the specific changes constituted in the Accounting Act in Slovakia, (b) strives to clarify specific obligations business entities will have to fulfill, and (c) clarifies the process of introducing EU regulation in the field of accounting related to improving the reporting quality focusing on the comparability and reliability of information provided by businesses in Slovakia and d) focuses on the fundamental relevance of introducing the European Sustainability Reporting Standards in the EU member states. As part of the investigation, we focused on the following research questions applying methods of comparison and critical analysis.

[14] Christensen et al. (2024).

RQ1: What is the goal of the corporate sustainability reporting directive since 2022?
RQ2: What are the specific changes established in the Accounting Act?
RQ3: What specific obligations do business entities have?

5 Non-financial Reporting Directive vs Corporate Sustainability Reporting Directive

Looking at the sustainability concept from the perspective of the semantic meaning, we can conclude that the meaning of words "sustainability" (noun) and "sustain" (transitive verb) can be interpreted as ability to continue over a long period of time. Having in mind socially responsible business and and at the same time sustainable business, changing the business strategy and system towards sustainability requires adopting the principles of prosperity and carrying out economic activity without negative impact on the environment. The profit itself shall not be a key priority considered for an economic entity, but also entity's contribution and impact on the society and the environment within its economic activity.

5.1 Sustainability in EU Secondary Legislation

Currently, the term sustainability includes the following criteria, namely: "Environmental, Social, Governance "(ESG)". The enterprise must be prepared and equipped with the know-how and specific knowledge, how to monitor, measure and report findings under all of the following criteria. When the environmental dimension/aspect is controlled, the entity focuses on measuring:

- air, water and soil pollution, water consumption, amount of recycled water,
- description of used resources, waste and its recycling and reuse.
- When the social dimension/aspect is controlled, the entity focuses on measuring/monitoring:
- working hours, collective bargaining, employee councils,
- adequate food and accommodation, water and hygiene, access to information, working conditions for employees.
- When the governance dimension/aspect is controlled, the entity focuses on measuring/mentoring:
- anti-corruption mechanisms,
- training, political involvement and lobbying.

In the interest of correct interpretation and correct application in practice, Regulation (EU) 2019/2088 defines the term "aspects of sustainability" as aspects of sustainability: taking into consideration environmental, social or employment relations, respect for human rights and the fight against corruption and bribery. The

Table 2 Internal and external factors affecting the sustainability of the enterprise

Internal factors	External factors
Digitization Cyber security Innovations Artificial intelligence	Geopolitical situation Energy supply Plenty of raw materials International standards

Source: Own elaboration

inseparable part of the sustainability concept according to the EU law, in addition to ESG aspects, is already mentioned fight against corruption and bribery, which we consider logical, because within the framework of economic activities, companies must conduct the activity with the aim not to violate legal regulations, moreover, consistent with responsible/inclusive management (Tomas and Jan Antonin Bata, twentieth century/Linda Rothschild, twentieth to twenty-first century) or ethical code, only to emphasize that this ESG aspects did not appear only by accepting CSRD, but ESRS is the consequence of many boiling hot issues addressed in CSR by general public, corporations, politicians. There is a variety of other internal and external factors which have an influence on the sustainability of the company, sumarized in Table 2.

In this context, it is also necessary to refer to Regulation (EU) 2020/852 of the European Parliament and of the Council of 18 June 2020 on the establishment of a framework to facilitate sustainable investment[15] constituting the classification system of environmentally sustainable economic activities. In other words, which companies, from their strategy perspective, carry out sustainable economic activity regarding the environmental protection. The regulation precisely constitutes the six environmental objectives which conclude the following: climate change mitigation; climate change adaptation; the sustainable use and protection of water and marine resources; the transition to a circular economy; pollution prevention and control; and the protection and restoration of biodiversity and ecosystems.[16]

5.2 *General Characteristics of the Corporate Sustainability Reporting Directive*

Directive (EU) 2022/2464 of the European Parliament and of the Council of 14 December 2022 amending Regulation (EU) No 537/2014, Directive 2004/109/EC, Directive 2006/43/EC, and Directive 2013/34/EU, as regards corporate

[15] Official Journal of the European Union L 198/2020. EUR-Lex, https://eur-lex.europa.eu/legal-content/EN/TXT/?uri=OJ%3AL%3A2020%3A198%3ATOC

[16] Art. 9 of Regulation (EU) 2020/852 of the European Parliament and of the Council of 18 June 2020 on the establishment of a framework to facilitate sustainable investment, and amending Regulation (EU) 2019/2088 (OJ L 198, 22.6.2020, p. 13–43).

sustainability reporting[17] was adopted by the institutions of the European Union with the aim of:

a) ensuring compliance with international instruments such as the UN 'Guiding Principles on Business and Human Rights: Implementing the United Nations 'Protect, Respect and Remedy' Framework' ('UN Guiding Principles on Business and Human Rights'), the OECD Guidelines for Multinational Enterprises and the OECD Due Diligence Guidance for Responsible Business Conduct (Para 31 Directive (EU) 2022/2464);
b) higher quality reporting of sustainability information, which would enable individual citizens and savers, including trade unions and employee representatives to be adequately informed and, thus, to be able of being more engaged in a social dialogue, that would be ultimately beneficial for all mentioned parties involved (Para 9 Directive (EU) 2022/2464);
c) reporting information related to aspects of sustainability, which can help businesses identify and manage their opportunities and their own risks related to aspects of sustainability. It can provide a basis for enhanced dialogue and communication among businesses and their stakeholders and thereby contribute to augmented businesses' reputation (Para 12 Directive (EU) 2022/2464);
d) providing information on sustainability of the third countries'companies that carry out economic activity on the territory of the EU member states, in order to provide information on sustainability, in particular on their impact on social and environmental issues, enabling all companies operating in the internal market to function under the equal conditions (Para 20 Directive (EU) 2022/2464);
e) establishing terms for Public Interest Entities on consolidated sustainability reporting.
f) setting standards for the sustainability reporting that businesses must disclose on social factors, including working conditions, social partners involvement, collective negotiation, equality, non-discrimination, diversity and inclusion, and human rights (Para 49 Directive (EU) 2022/2464);

The introduced directive is one of the instruments that contribute to the social fair transition of economic entities to a sustainable economic system with regard to sustainable investments. In this context, the directive strengthens the transparency and long-term outlook of financial and economic activity. Regulation (EU) 2021/1119 of the European Parliament and of the Council of 30 June 2021 establishing the framework for achieving climate neutrality and amending Regulations (EC) No 401/2009 and (EU) 2018/1999.[18]

Its predecessor was mainly Non-financial Reporting Directive (NFRD) and the following table compares, critically analyses arguments and the results are presented in the Table 3 and it is an evidence that voluntary disclosure converts into

[17] Directive (EU) 2022/2464 of the European Parliament and of the Council, EUR-Lex, https://eur-lex.europa.eu/legal-content/EN/TXT/?uri=CELEX%3A32022L2464

[18] Official Journal of the European Union L 243/2021. EUR-Lex, https://eur-lex.europa.eu/legal-content/EN/TXT/?uri=OJ%3AL%3A2021%3A243%3ATOC

Table 3 Comparing the scopes of NFRD a CSRD Directives

	NFRD guideline	CSRD guideline
Subjects	– Large enterprises that are Public Interest Entities (PIE) with more than 500 employees during the accounting period	– Large enterprises – SMEs that are Public Interest Entities (PIE) – Captive insurance companies and captive reinsurance companies – Companies with Outside-EU-headquarters
Submission format	– Part of the management report (in Slovakia part of the annual report submitted in pdf.), or – Separately in a document, published on the company's website, to which a link is provided in the management report (annual report)	– Only a part of the management report in the unified electronic reporting format .xhtml
Disclosed Information in the Report	– Mandatory disclosure of information containing environmental issues and treatment of employees, respect for human rights, fight against corruption and bribery, diversity in company boards (in terms of age, gender, education, and professional background) – No binding standards are prescribed for the reporting of non-financial information – Existing standards e.g. GRI (Global Reporting Initiative), IFRS (International Financial Reporting Standards)	– ESRS (European Sustainability Reporting Standards) mandatory sustainability reporting standards for information to be adopted in delegated acts – ESRS specify the information to be disclosed by companies on environmental, social, and human rights factors and governance factors
Auditor's Verification	– Optional	– Mandatory (so-called assurance in the field of sustainability reporting
Efficiency	– Since 2017 the individual effectiveness of the CSRD application	– From 2024, individual effectiveness of the CSRD directive by category

Source: Own elaboration based on NFRD a CSRD directives

mandatory reporting with an identified content, reporting format and the obligation to have Sustainability report audited by the competent auditor.

The CSRD defines and imposes precisely which ESG criteria must be included into the Sustainability report. CSRD came into effect in 5th January 2023 and by the end of the year 2023 there were first twelve European Sustainability Reporting Standards ESRSs approved and available for implementation. The Table 4 summarizes the names and areas (substance of the individual ESRSs) addressed by the particular standards.

Within individual ESRSs the following matters must be addressed, precise data identified, assessed and disclosed by economic entities in:

Table 4 Sustainability reporting standards

	Standard	Substance
CROSS-CUTTING STANDARDS:	ESRS 1 General requirements	Materiality assessment is a key tool for identifying impacts, risks and opportunities.
	ESRS 2 General disclosures	It constitutes the general characteristics and information for sustainability reporting.
STANDARDS ON ENVIRON-MENTAL MATTERS	ESRS E1 Climate change	It provides a framework for climate change disclosures
	ESRS E2 Pollution	It structures the publication of information on pollution.
	ESRS E3 Water and marine resources	It improves understanding of the impact of businesses on water and marine resources.
	ESRS E4 Biodiversity and ecosystems	It provides insight into the impact of a business on biodiversity and ecosystems.
	ESRS E5 Resource use and circular economy	It focuses on resource use and the circular economy.
STANDARDS ON SOCIAL MATTERS	ESRS S1 Own workforce	It deals with the impact of an organization on employees.
	ESRS S2 Workers in the value chain	It focuses on workers in the organization's value chain.
	ESRS S3 Affected communities	It deals with the organization's impact on affected communities.
	ESRS S4 Consumer and end-users	It focuses on the organization's impact on consumers and end users.
STANDARDS ON GOVERNANCE MATTERS	ESRS G1 Business conduct	It ensures transparency about the ethical behavior and performance of the business.

Source: Elaborated by authors

A. Environmental matters—climate change mitigation, including as regards scope greenhouse gas emissions; climate change adaptation; water and marine resources; resource use and the circular economy; pollution; biodiversity and ecosystems.
B. Social and human rights matters—treatment and opportunities for all, including gender equality and equal pay for work of equal value, training and skills development; working conditions, consultation and participation rights of workers, work-life balance, and health and safety; respect for the human rights, fundamental freedoms, democratic principles and standards established in the Documents in International Organisations (UN, ILO).
C. Governance matters—the role of the undertaking's administrative, management and supervisory bodies regarding sustainability matters; the main features of the undertaking's internal control and risk management systems; business ethics

and corporate culture, including anti-corruption and anti-bribery; activities and commitments of the undertaking related to exerting its political influence, including its lobbying activities—the management and quality of relationships with customers (Chapter 6a: Sustainability reporting standards. Directive (EU) 2022/2464).

6 Corporate Sustainability Reporting Directive Transposition into the Slovak Legislation and Other Secondary European Acts

The membership of the Slovak Republic in the European Union is determined by several international commitments. These commitments also include the approximation of law (Art.114 TFEU) and the correct transposition of secondary European Acts into the Slovak legal order. This fact is the consequence of the primary legislation, namely the Article 4(2) of the Treaty on European Union.[19]

Regulations and directives are appropriate instruments for the proper functioning of the internal market. These secondary acts are also legal instruments for deepening European economic integration and instruments for fulfilling the goals established in the strategic documents of the European Union. According to Article 288 TFEU2: a) a regulation shall have general application. It shall be binding in its entirety and directly applicable in all Member States; b) a directive shall be binding, as to the result to be achieved, upon each Member State to which it is addressed, but shall leave the choice of form and methods to the national authorities.

Control over the correct transposition and implementation of secondary acts is ensured by the European Commission and the Court of Justice of the European Union. The Court of Justice EU is the highest judicial authority in matters of Union law. To monitor Union law application, regarding the conduct of the EU institutions when implementing treaty provisions, as well as regarding the fulfilment of obligations under Union law by the Member States and individuals.[20] In order to achieve the goals established in the European Green Deal, the institutions of the European Union adopted several secondary acts related to sustainability and sustainable business within the European Economic Area. Such acts also include Directive (EU) 2022/2464 of the European Parliament and of the Council of 14 December 2022 amending Regulation (EU) No 537/2014, Directive 2004/109/EC, Directive 2006/43/EC and Directive 2013 /34/EU, as regards corporate sustainability reporting.[21] The given directive must be transposed into the national legislation by

[19] Official Journal of the European Union C 326/2012. EUR-Lex, https://eur-lex.europa.eu/legal-content/EN/ALL/?uri=OJ%3AC%3A2012%3A326%3ATOC

[20] Borchardt (2017).

[21] Official Journal of the European Union L 322/2022, pp. 15–80. https://eur-lex.europa.eu/legal-content/EN/TXT/?uri=OJ%3AL%3A2022%3A322%3ATOC

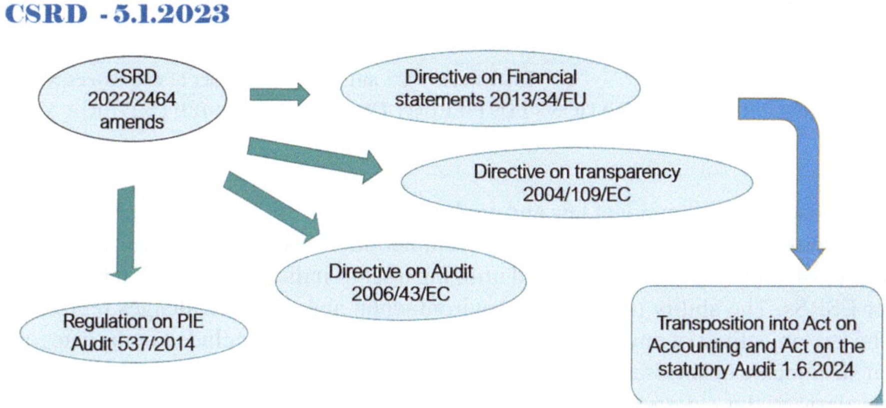

Fig. 1 Transposition of the CSRD into Slovak Acts. *Source*: own elaboration based on the EU directives

member states. The Slovak Republic incorporated the directive into the Accounting Act and other laws (see Fig. 1).

Also Act no. 513/1991, the Commercial Code establishes precisely prohibited unfair practices in business. Economic entities currently must take measures to monitor information and collect data as part of sustainability reporting in accordance with Directive (EU) 2022/2464:

6.1 Requirements and Obligations for ESG Criteria

The information to be presented in a sustainability report of selected accounting entities is focused now on the information linked to the ESG criteria. Key priorities are the quality improvement, augmentation of comparability and reliability of this targeted information. Sustainability report is the part of the annual report, data on sustainability includes information on governance and management, strategy, risk management, and company indicators and goals.

Larger business entities compliant with the recent legislation are committed to prepare sustainability reporting. Public Interest Entities meeting two of three size criteria (see below) prepare the report already in 2025 for 2024 and larger businesses will assess their size criteria A, B, C, whether they have (a) the number of employees, precisely more than 500 employees, (b) the value of total assets—minimum of total assets required, the value of 25 million EUR and (c) the turnover value controlled is over 50 mil. EUR. The obligation to submit the first report in 2026 will be for the fiscal year 2025 for large companies that meet two of the three mentioned criteria.

PIE and larger companies will follow ESRSs standards and will prepare Sustainability reports addressing all areas in ESG dimensions defined by CSRD

Table 5 PIE and larger companies

A:		B:		C:
Turnover > 50 mil. €	or	Total assets > 25 mil. €	or	Number of employees > 500
PIE AND LARGE CORPORATIONS FULFILLING TWO OF THREE SIZE CRITERIA A, B, OR C				

transposed into the national law and applying also ESRSs. There are many attempts to propose the proper methodology of sustainability measurement, variety of methods exist, and they are implemented utilizing a set of indicators defined in the CSRD or ESRSs. The ability to transform environmental and social challenges represents the key objectives of any business that is interested in being included in the category of sustainable businesses. To accomplish the level of sustainability, it is necessary to implement the elements of sustainable development thoroughly in the corporate strategy as well (see Table 5).

6.2 *New Legislation in the Field of Accounting in Slovakia*

Amendment of Act no. 431/2002 Coll. on Accounting represents the fulfillment of the Slovak Republic's obligations resulting from its membership in the European Union and it reflects Directive (EU) 2022/2464 which was transposed into Act 431/2002 on Accounting and Act on statutory Auditing. Both acts were approved in the Slovak Parliament and came into effect on June 1st, 2024. Slovak Sustainability Reporting will comprise:

a) sustainability reporting complying to §20c of the Accounting Act (individual sustainability reporting), or
b) in accordance with §20g of the Accounting Act (consolidated sustainability reporting),
c) while complying with the requirements for the selection of information specified in §20c par. 1 or § 0g par. 1 proposal (principle of double materiality must be respected consisting of Impact Materiality: Inside-Out (it demonstrates impact of a company performance and its activities on Sustainability measurements and Financial Materiality: Outside-In, i.e. Sustainability measurements, that are focused on when implemented CSRD and ESRS how they influence business development, its performance, financial positions and cash flow),
d) and presenting the information in accordance with European standards for sustainability reporting, while the annual report containing sustainability reporting must be prepared in an electronic format.
e) amended Act also defines new size criteria for micro, small, middle and large businesses, because to prepare the sustainability report is organized gradually starting the first report in 2025 until 2028 taking the size of the business into account.

Other obligations imposed by the Slovak Accounting Act are:

a) the amended Act on accounting also requires description of the data, how they were collected, brief description of the business model and business strategy of the economic entity including evaluation of the health and state of the business, entity's opportunities and risks that are related to sustainability, plans of the entity including all measurements and conducted activities linked to the financial and investing plans to ensure that business model and business strategy will be compatible with transition to circular economy.
b) obligation of setting goals compliant to ESG criteria imposed by ESRSs,
c) obligation of having sustainability report audited by the auditor or European auditor (§20 h, or the auditor who fulfill competency criteria (experience, education, training)
d) obligation of storing the sustainability report (§20d6) into the Register of Financial statements of entities, maximum within 12 months, after the period for which the sustainability report was prepared together with the auditor's assuring report.
e) the auditor or auditing company must be insured. The size of insurance is also defined by the Act, as well as penalties if the economic entity will not fulfill its obligation. The Act specifies also the reward for the audit.
f) the following Table 7 specifies precisely schedule of the first Sustainability reports prepared by companies based on their size and fulfilling the criteria specified in the Act (see Table 6).
g) the act also identifies which entities are exempted from this obligation to prepare sustainability report (not fulfilling the size criteria plus certain exceptions).

Regarding the RQ3 research question, considering the data provided in the Explanatory Report of the Act on Accounting, we have compiled a transparent and systematic table that contains a list of the obligations of economic entities that shall provide sustainability report in some EU member states as a part of the Annual report.

Table 6 Economic entities size criteria

Size criterion	Micro accounting unit §2 par. 6 letters a), b) Accounting Act	Small accounting unit §2 par. 7 letters a), b) Accounting Act	Large accounting unit §2 par. 8 letters a), b) Accounting Act
Total assets TA	TA ≤ 450,000 €	450,000 € < TA ≤ 5,000,000 €	TA > 5,000,000 €
Net turnover NT	NT ≤ 900,000 €	900,000 € < NT ≤ 10,000,000 €	NT > 10,000,000 €
Average number of employees-NoE	NoE ≤ 10	10 < NoE ≤ 50	NoE > 50

Source: Own elaboration based on Act on Accounting 431/2002 ammended

Table 7 Identification of obligations for economic entities (for Public Interest Entities)

Entity's obligations	Business entities	Number of subjects
– Individual sustainability reporting in the annual report for the accounting period since 1 January 2024, – report preparation and submission to the Register of the Financial Statements (tax authority in Slovakia, or e.g. IRS in the USA, report due in 2025	Public Interest Entity (SVZ)—number of employees >500, or asset value >25mil*. €; or turnover >50 mil.** €. *, ** means: the value in two preceding years before the year when the report on sustainability will be prepared. Obligatory reporting compliant with CSRD for companies following NFRD	about 6
– Consolidated sustainability reporting in the annual report for the accounting period since 1 January 2024, – report preparation and submission to the Register of the Financial Statements report due in 2025	Public Interest Entity (SVZ)—number of employees >500, or asset value >25 mil.* €; or turnover >50 mil.** €. Obligatory reporting compliant with CSRD for companies following NFRD	about 17
– Individual sustainability reporting in the annual report for the accounting period since 1 January 2025, – report preparation and submission to the Register of the Financial Statements report due in 2026	Large entities fulfilling 2 out 3 terms Number of employees >250, asset value >25* (20 mil.*) €; or turnover >50** (40 mil.**). Obligatory reporting compliant with CSRD for companies not following NFRD	about 560
– Individual sustainability reporting in the annual report for the accounting period since 1 January 2026, – report preparation and submission to the Register of the Financial Statements report due in 2027	Entities with number of employees from the interval: (50, 250), or asset value >25 mil. (20 mil*) €; or turnover >50 mil. (40mil**) €. SME issuing Securities on the EU stock exchange in Europe	about 270
Entities from the third countries krajín, their obligation to prepare sustainability report covering the year 2027, Report due in 2028.	Turnover >150 mil € outside of the EU Turnover >50 mil in Slovakia	
Sustainability report for the accounting period since 1.1.2028, prepared and archived as the part of the Annual report report due in 2029	Entities with number of employees from the interval: (10, 50), or asset value X falling into the interval: X is from (450,000, 5mil. €) Turnover T is from (900,000 to €10 million.)	230

Source: Amended Slovak Accounting Act 105/2024 ("105/2024 Z.z." Slov-Lex, https://www.slov-lex.sk/ezbierky/pravne-predpisy/SK/ZZ/2024/105/20240601)
Legend: The values achieved in: *the first preceding year and then **second preceding year

7 Conclusion

Sustainability reporting shall augment the position of responsible companies. It is a tool to educate customers as well, they will better understand the effort of the company which is compliant to new regulations and directives supporting the sustainability, protection of the planet, people and prosperity of the businesses as well. The law is needed to ignite desirable behaviour of the companies. We may summarize internal and external advantages for the companies preparing sustainability report.

Internal advantages are as follows:

- Better understanding of risk and opportunities, enabling comparison of divisions,
- Emphasizing the interconnection of financial and non-financial perfpormance,
- The processes will be more efficient, it will help to prepare long-term business plans, strategy with the aim lowering costs, increasing economic efficiency,
- Preventing from environmental, social and and governance crises,
- Tool for comparisom within the company or among companies in the industry.
- External advantages:
- Tool for removing and eliminating negative ESG impacts,
- Improvement of the reputation, and positive impact on the loyalty of the customers,
- Outsiders can better understand the economic entity, enabling comparison of companies
- Demonstration how the economic entity is influenced by expectations or has impact on expectation in the area of sustainability development.

Finally, we stress the start of this sustainable development goals accepted in 2015 by United Nations. This was duly addressed by the 2030 Agenda with its 17 Sustainable Development Goals (SDGs), indivisible and interconnected that defined an ambitious framework to foster peaceful, just and inclusive societies all over the world. As a result, the governments transformed them into national action plans, programs, and initiatives that reflected the various realities and capabilities that their respective countries have. Also, a significant number of policy documents and provisions, legislations and regulatory instruments have been elaborated to promote sustainability practices in businesses that can contribute conjunctively to the progress of countries toward SDGs and transition towards a more sustainable economy.[22] We believe that Sustainability report will be the positive obligation which will force companies to start behaving responsibly and brings the desired fruit.

[22] Fleacă et al. (2023), pp. 275 et seq.

Appendix: Time Schedule of CSRD Development

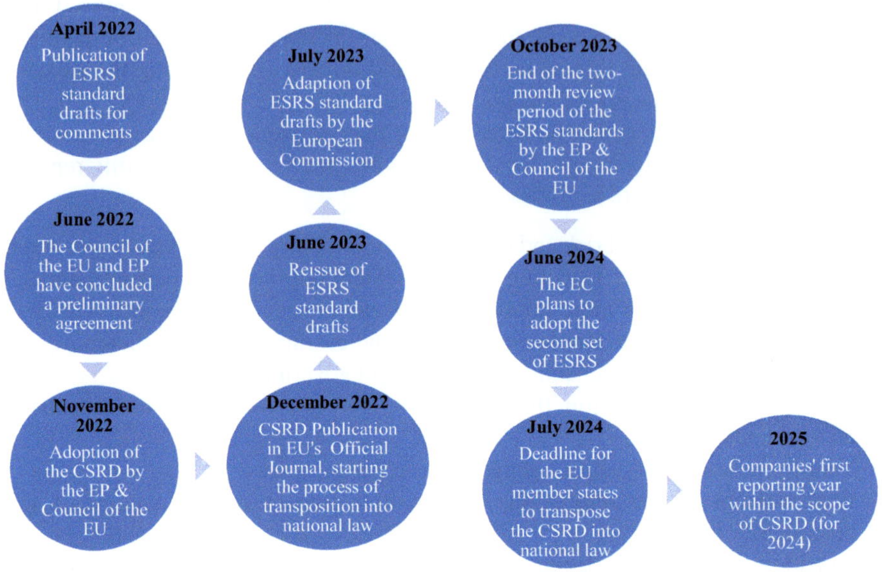

Source: Own elaboration based on (Pwc, 2024)

References

An Y, Davey H, Harun H, Jin Z, Qiao X, Yu Q (2020) Online sustainability reporting at universities: the case of Hong Kong. Sustain Account Manag Policy J 11(5):887–901. https://doi.org/10.1108/sampj-06-2018-0161

Borchardt K-D (2017) The ABC of the EU law. Publications Office of the European Union, Luxembourg. https://op.europa.eu/en/publication-detail/-/publication/5d4f8cde-de25-11e7-a506-01aa75ed71a1

Christensen H, Hales J, O'Dwyer B, Peecher ME (2024) Accounting for sustainability and climate change: special section overview. Acc Organ Soc 113:101568. https://doi.org/10.1016/j.aos.2024.101568

Deegan C (2002) Introduction: the legitimizing effect of social and environmental disclosures – a theoretical foundation. Account Audit Account J 15(3):282–311. https://doi.org/10.1108/09513570210435852

Directive (EU) 2022/2464 of the European Parliament and of the Council of 14 December 2022 amending Regulation (EU) No 537/2014, Directive 2004/109/EC, Directive 2006/43/EC and Directive 2013/34/EU, as regards corporate sustainability reporting (OJ L 322, 16.12.2022, pp. 15–80)

Fleacă B, Fleacă E, Corocăescu M (2023) Sustainability information – analysis of current trends in sustainability monitoring & reporting. Entrep Sustain 10(3):274–287. https://doi.org/10.9770/jesi.2023.10.3(18)

Giner B, Luque-Vílchez M (2022) A commentary on the ‘new’ institutional actors in sustainability reporting standard-setting: a European perspective. Sustain Account Manag Policy J 13(6):1284–1309. https://doi.org/10.1108/sampj-06-2021-0222

Hummel K, Jobst D (2024) An overview of corporate sustainability reporting legislation in the European Union. Account Eur 21(3):320–355. https://doi.org/10.1080/17449480.2024.2312145

Moneva JM, Scarpellini S, Aranda-Usón A, Etxeberria IA (2022) Sustainability reporting in view of the European sustainable finance taxonomy: is the financial sector ready to disclose circular economy? Corp Soc Responsib Environ Manag 30(3):XXX. https://doi.org/10.1002/csr.2423

Oorschot KE, Johansen VA, Thorup NL, Aspen DM (2024) Standardization cycles in sustainability reporting within the global reporting initiative. Eur Manag J 42(4):492. https://doi.org/10.1016/j.emj.2024.04.001

Regulation (EU) 2020/852 of the European Parliament and of the Council of 18 June 2020 on the establishment of a framework to facilitate sustainable investment, and amending Regulation (EU) 2019/2088 (OJ L 198, 22.6.2020, pp. 13–43)

Sukitsch M, Engert S, Baumgartner RJ (2015) The implementation of corporate sustainability in the european automotive industry: an analysis of sustainability reports. Sustainability 7(9):11504–11531. https://doi.org/10.3390/su70911504

Vila M, Moya S (2023) Social sustainability reporting in European business schools. Sustain Account Manag Policy J 14(1):242–264. https://doi.org/10.1108/SAMPJ-02-2022-0100

Wefersová J, Wefers H, Saxunová D, Szarková R (2016) Austrian strategy (institutional support) for tourism development inspiration for tourism oriented countries. Vilakshan 13(2):41–66

Wils A, Kamiya M, Choucri N (1998) Treats to sustainability: simulating conflict within and between nations. Syst Dyn Rev 14(2–3):129–162. https://doi.org/10.1002/(SICI)1099-1727(199822/23)14:2/3<129::AID-SDR146>3.0.CO;2-6

Worldwide impact of CSRD - are you ready?. PwC – In the loop, https://viewpoint.pwc.com/dt/us/en/pwc/in_the_loop/assets/worldwideimpactcsrd12oct23.pdf

Shaping the Future of Shipping: Legal and Policy Impacts of EU Emissions Trading and Fuel EU Maritime Regulations

Leonidas Sotiropoulos

Abstract The shipping sector accounts for about 8% of total greenhouse gas emissions in the European Union (EU). To address this, the EU will include shipping in its Emissions Trading System (ETS) starting in 2024, aiming for climate neutrality by 2050. This article explores the legislative frameworks and strategies necessary for achieving this goal, focusing on the European Commission's "Fit for 55" package, the ETS, and the FuelEU Maritime Regulation. The central research question is: How can the shipping sector transition to climate neutrality while complying with emerging regulations? Using qualitative methodology, the article examines existing legislative measures, compliance obligations, and technological advancements in the maritime industry. Through qualitative dogmatic analysis, it evaluates the implications of recent regulations on emissions reduction. Part I discusses strategies for achieving climate neutrality, detailing the FuelEU Maritime regulations and the EU ETS, thus providing a comprehensive understanding of the regulatory landscape. Part II will further explore the role of the EU Taxonomy and IMO sustainability standards. The findings highlight industry challenges and opportunities, offering recommendations for policymakers and stakeholders to promote a sustainable maritime sector aligned with EU climate objectives.

1 Introduction

Gas emissions, particularly greenhouse gases (GHGs), are at the forefront of global environmental governance, significantly influencing climate change dynamics. The evolution of the international legal framework, marked by pivotal agreements such

L. Sotiropoulos (✉)
European University of Cyprus, Nicosia, Cyprus

C.-S. Săraru, C. E. Popa Tache (eds.), *AI, Sustainability and Solidarity in Advancing European Values in a Globalized Age*, European Union and its Neighbours in a Globalized World 28, https://doi.org/10.1007/978-3-032-06508-7_8

as the Kyoto Protocol[1] and the Paris Agreement,[2] reflects a concerted effort to establish binding commitments and regulatory mechanisms aimed at emissions reduction. Within this context, the European Union's Emissions Trading System (EU ETS) stands out as a pioneering initiative, employing a cap-and-trade approach to incentivize emissions reductions across various sectors, including power generation and aviation. However, the maritime industry, which facilitates approximately 90% of global trade by volume, presents unique challenges due to its substantial GHG emissions and growing demand for shipping services. The urgency to address these emissions has led to the development of targeted regulatory measures, such as the International Maritime Organization's (IMO) strategies and the EU's FuelEU Maritime initiative, which seeks to promote sustainable fuels and set rigorous emission reduction targets for the sector.

The pursuit of climate neutrality in the shipping sector is a critical component of the European Union's broader energy and climate goals, which aim for comprehensive decarbonization by 2050. The shipping industry is a significant contributor to global greenhouse gas emissions,[3] accounting for approximately 8% of the total emissions in the EU. In light of increasing climate change concerns, the European Union (EU) has decided to include shipping in its Emissions Trading System (ETS) starting in 2024. This decision is a crucial step towards integrating maritime transport into broader climate policies.[4]

This article investigates the strategies and legislative frameworks necessary to achieve this ambitious objective, focusing on the European Commission's "Fit for 55" package,[5] which includes pivotal regulations such as the FuelEU Maritime Regulation. The central research question guiding this inquiry is: How can the shipping sector effectively transition towards climate neutrality while ensuring compliance with emerging regulatory frameworks? To address this question, the article employs a qualitative dogmatic methodology that examines existing legislative measures, compliance obligations, and technological advancements within the maritime industry. It analyzes recent regulations, including the Emissions Trading System (ETS) and the EU Taxonomy, to identify key strategies for reducing greenhouse gas emissions and promoting sustainable practices in shipping. The significance of this article lies in its potential to inform policymakers, industry stakeholders, and researchers about the pathways to achieving a sustainable maritime sector, thereby contributing to the global fight against climate change.

---

[1] United Nations Framework Convention on Climate Change. (n.d.). *Kyoto Protocol.* https://unfccc.int/resource/docs/convkp/kpeng.html.

[2] Council of the European Union. (n.d.). *Paris Agreement.* https://www.consilium.europa.eu/en/policies/climate-change/paris-agreement.

[3] See analytically, The impact of GHG emissions in shipping: an overview, available at https://sinay.ai/en/the-impact-of-ghg-emissions-in-shipping-an-overview/.

[4] See Dong et al. (2022).

[5] European Commission (2021) Regulation of the European parliament and of the council on the use of renewable and low-carbon fuels in maritime transport and amending directive. Available at: https://eur-lex.europa.eu/legal-content/EN/TXT/?uri=CELEX:52021AE36302009

More specifically, Part I examines the strategies for achieving climate neutrality in the maritime sector, beginning with an overview of sustainable practices in shipping, which highlights the urgent need for collaboration across all economic sectors. It then discusses the FuelEU Maritime Regulation, a landmark initiative aimed at promoting the use of renewable and low-carbon fuels in shipping, detailing its obligations and compliance requirements. Additionally, this section explores the legislative measures related to the EU Emissions Trading System (ETS), which serves as a critical tool for reducing emissions, and outlines the monitoring and reporting commitments imposed on shipping companies. Through these discussions, the text aims to provide a comprehensive understanding of the regulatory landscape governing the transition to sustainable shipping practices, setting the stage for further exploration of the role of the EU Taxonomy and IMO sustainability standards in Part II. The insights gained will inform stakeholders about the challenges and opportunities that lie ahead in the pursuit of a greener maritime future. The article ends with the appropriate conclusion and critical remarks and recommendations. The article aims to provide a comprehensive understanding of the frameworks and strategies necessary for achieving climate neutrality in the shipping sector, ultimately contributing to the EU's climate objectives.

2 Strategies for a Green Maritime Sector

2.1 Introduction to Sustainable Practices in Shipping

The shipping industry, vital for global trade, faces significant scrutiny due to its environmental impact, particularly in terms of greenhouse gas emissions. In light of the EU's Fit for 55 initiatives, which aims for a 55% reduction in net emissions by 2030, sustainable practices in shipping have become crucial. These practices include adopting alternative fuels, utilizing energy-efficient technologies, and optimizing logistics to minimize emissions. Regulatory frameworks like the EU's FuelEU Maritime initiative support these efforts by promoting cleaner fuels and setting ambitious emission reduction targets. By embracing sustainability, shipping companies can comply with regulations while fostering innovation and enhancing their competitiveness in a rapidly evolving market.

The implementation of the European Union's energy and climate goals, with the ultimate ambition of achieving climate neutrality by 2050,[6] requires the simultaneous collaboration of all sectors of the economy, with shipping now at the forefront. On July 14, 2021, the European Commission adopted a package of legislative proposals known as "Fit for 55," primarily aimed at ensuring the implementation of the

[6] See analytically Psaraftis (2019), p. 18.

European Green Deal.[7] The relevant legislative proposals are now largely being finalized and gaining legal force. In this context, the decarbonization of the shipping[8] sector is central to this package, with key points of interest being the reduction of carbon dioxide emissions and the use of more sustainable fuels on ships. At the same time, at the international level, the same objectives have been adopted by the International Maritime Organization, establishing corresponding compliance obligations.

2.2 *FuelEU Maritime, Regulation and Initiatives*

The FuelEU[9] Maritime Regulation, enacted on July 13, 2023, represents one of the most significant legislative initiatives within the Fit for 55 packages aimed at decarbonizing the shipping sector.[10] The main goal is to increase the demand and consistent use of renewable and low-carbon fuels, which contribute to reducing greenhouse gas emissions from ships, without jeopardizing the smooth flow of maritime traffic. Its provisions will be binding starting from January 1, 2025. One of the two main obligations imposed on companies—understood as shipowners, managers, or charterers—is to reduce the carbon intensity of the fuels used for ship propulsion by 2% by 2025 and gradually up to 80% by 2050.[11]

To comply with this obligation, companies are expected to primarily turn to the use of renewable fuels of non-biological origin, which show great potential for decarbonization,[12] unlike fossil fuels, which will be excluded from the certification process outlined by the Regulation.[13]

[7] See Goyal and Llop (2024). Also, European Green Deal: Agreement reached on cutting maritime transport emissions by promoting sustainable fuels for shipping, https://ec.europa.eu/commission/presscorner/detail/en/ip_23_1813.

[8] Gilbert and Bows (2012).

[9] FuelEU Maritime accompanied from the characteristic legislation: A. Regulation (EU) 2021/1238: Establishes the FuelEU Maritime initiative to promote the use of renewable and low-carbon fuels in the maritime sector. B. Directive (EU) 2018/2001: Sets sustainability criteria for biofuels, bioliquids, and biomass fuels, relevant to the fuels used in maritime transport. C. Regulation (EU) 2021/1796: Addresses specific requirements for the use of renewable and low-carbon fuels in the maritime sector under the FuelEU initiative.

[10] Cullinane and Yang (2022).

[11] Ibid.

[12] However, due to the significantly higher costs associated with acquiring and using these fuels compared to traditional fuels, a "multiplier" has been suggested to be used until the end of 2033. This would allow the energy derived from these fuels to count as double for the purpose of meeting carbon intensity reduction targets.

[13] This process, outlined in Article 10 of the Regulation, requires that the fuels utilized by ships must also comply with the requirements set forth in Article 29 of Directive (EU) 2018/2001, which pertains to the sustainability criteria and greenhouse gas emissions reductions for biofuels, bioliquids, and biomass fuels.

The second main requirement set by the Regulation relates to the Onshore Power Supply system. Specifically, ships,[14] both passenger and container ships, are now required to use onshore power supply for all their electricity needs when they are anchored in European ports for at least 2 h. This obligation will start in 2030 for ships anchoring in European ports covered by Article 9 of the Regulation,[15] and in 2035 for ships anchoring in European ports outside the scope of this article. Overall, shipowners are required to monitor and report, with the timeline developed as follows: (a) by August 31, 2024, companies must submit a monitoring report for each ship, detailing the quantity, type, and emission factor of the fuel used while the ship is anchored or at sea, and (b) starting from January 1, 2025, based on the aforementioned monitoring report, companies must expand their monitoring scope to include issues such as the quantity of each type of fuel consumed by the ship while anchored or at sea, the use of onshore power supply, the amount of electricity provided to the ship, the type of engine, and any presence of wind propulsion technology on the ship.[16] Ensuring successful compliance with this obligation requires the documentation of all reporting elements and their inclusion in a monitoring plan.

2.3 *Legislative Measures and Emissions Trading System*

The Emissions Trading System (ETS) is the primary tool for mitigating greenhouse gas emissions in the European Union,[17] covering approximately 40% of such emissions.[18] According to relevant national legislation,[19] obligated operators of facilities

---

[14] Prior to the Regulation's adoption, the responsibility for installing onshore power supply systems fell on the ports themselves.

[15] Key maritime ports within the Trans-European Network, as well as integrated maritime ports in the same network, are defined as those where the average number of port calls by sea-going container vessels over 5000 gross tons exceeds one hundred annually over the past 3 years.

[16] If companies adhere to the regulations, they will receive a compliance certificate, which they must retain as evidence of meeting the carbon intensity limits of the energy used on board and the obligation to utilize onshore power supply.

[17] The EU ETS is a cornerstone of the EU's climate policy and its key tool to reduce greenhouse gas emissions cost-effectively. It is the world's first carbon market and remains among the largest ones globally. See analytically, EU Emissions Trading System (EU ETS), available at: https://climate.ec.europa.eu/eu-action/eu-emissions-trading-system-eu-ets_en.

[18] The EU-ETS legislation consists from: A. **Directive 2003/87/EC**: Establishes the EU ETS and sets the framework for greenhouse gas emission allowance trading. B. **Directive 2018/410/EU**: Amends Directive 2003/87/EC to enhance cost-effective emission reductions and promote low-carbon investments. C. **Regulation (EU) 2019/943**: Addresses the functioning of the internal electricity market and includes provisions relevant to the ETS. D. **Regulation (EU) 2021/1119**: Establishes the European Climate Law, which aims to set a framework for achieving climate neutrality by 2050. E. **Regulation (EU) 2023/959**: Implements the inclusion of maritime transport in the EU ETS.

[19] For instance see the Greek legislation. This is in accordance with Joint Ministerial Decision 181478/965 (published in Government Gazette B′ 3763/26.10.2017), as amended by Joint

must submit the required Emissions Report for the previous year to the Market Mechanisms and Emissions Registry Department of the Directorate of Climate Change and Air Quality at the Ministry of Environment and Energy by the end of March each year (along with the report from the accredited verifier). Specifically, by the end of April, they must return to their accounts in the EU Greenhouse Gas Emissions Registry emissions allowances corresponding to the verified tons of pollutants emitted in the previous year. For this purpose, they can procure any necessary emissions allowances either through organized markets or bilaterally, and a relevant registration in the EU Registry is required for the formal completion of each transaction.

As part of the legislative measures of the Fit for 55 packages, and to align emission reduction targets with the goals of the European Green Deal, a proposal for the revision of the ETS was accepted in April 2023, which is reflected in the new Directive (EU) 2023/959. This Directive includes, among other things,[20] a gradual extension of the ETS to the shipping sector during the period 2024–2026. Specifically, starting in 2024, ships with a total capacity of over 5000 tons that carry goods or passengers for commercial purposes[21] will be required to acquire and surrender carbon dioxide emissions allowances.[22] The responsible party for surrendering allowances is considered to be any individual or legal entity responsible for the operation of the ship (shipowner, manager, or charterer). The Directive establishes a principle of surrendering allowances for 100% of emissions occurring during voyages and dockings in ports within the Union, while the obligation is reduced to 50% for emissions occurring during voyages where either the destination or departure port is outside the Union.[23] The surrender obligations will escalate over the years, starting with a requirement to surrender 40% of verified emissions for which the shipping company submitted a report for the year 2024, 70% of verified emissions for the year 2025, and 100% of emissions from 2026 onward.[24] Finally, no free allowances are provided to shipping.

Ministerial Decision 105040/2297/2019 (published in Government Gazette B′ 4315/29.11.2019), which remains in effect.

[20] Significant amendments include the gradual elimination of free allowances for the aviation sector by 2026, alongside the implementation of the Carbon Offsetting and Reduction Scheme for International Aviation (CORSIA) for flights outside Europe from 2022 to 2027. Additionally, a separate Emissions Trading System (ETS) for buildings and road transport will be established, starting in 2027.

[21] The obligations for offshore activity vessels will commence in 2027 as well.

[22] Certain exceptions and reduced obligations apply to ice-class ships, vessels serving remote islands, and ships providing public services.

[23] Cargo ships docking at transshipment ports outside the Union but within 300 nautical miles of its borders must surrender fifty percent (50%) of the emissions incurred on their route to those ports.

[24] Companies that fail to surrender enough allowances by April 30 each year to cover their previous year's emissions will incur a fine of €100 per ton of carbon dioxide equivalent emissions for which they did not provide allowances. According to Regulation 2023/959, if a shipping company is non-compliant for two consecutive years, the Union may ultimately prohibit the entry of its ships into European ports.

2.4 The Commitment of Monitoring and Reporting

Related to the recently imposed obligation on ships is the requirement for monitoring and reporting their emissions, which has already been introduced with Regulation (EU) 2015/757. This commitment currently applies to ships with a total capacity of over 5000 tons that carry goods or passengers and have a port of call within the jurisdiction of a Member State. With the amendment of the above Regulation by the most recent Regulation 2023/957, starting from January 1, 2025, the obligation will also apply to general cargo ships and offshore activity vessels. Further obligations established by the new Regulation include, starting from January 1, 2024, the obligation to review the monitoring plan that shipping companies must have developed for each of their ships.

Additionally, starting in 2025 and by March 31 of each subsequent year, shipping companies is required to submit an emissions report for each ship under their jurisdiction for the entire reference period of the previous year.[25] The main goal of the Regulation is that, by the year 2030, no ship should emit greenhouse gas emissions while in port or at anchor. This ambitious target aims to significantly reduce the environmental impact of maritime operations and contribute to the overall goals of the European Green Deal.

To ensure compliance with these obligations, shipping companies must implement robust monitoring systems to accurately track and report emissions. The monitoring plan must detail the methodologies used for calculating emissions, including the types of fuels consumed and the operational patterns of the vessels.[26] Companies are also required to maintain comprehensive records that can be verified by accredited third parties.

The new regulations emphasize transparency and accountability, mandating that all emissions data be submitted in a timely manner to the relevant authorities. This data will not only help in assessing compliance with the ETS but will also play a crucial role in shaping future environmental policies within the EU.

In addition to emissions reporting, the regulations encourage the adoption of cleaner technologies and practices within the shipping industry. Companies are incentivized to invest in renewable energy sources and innovative solutions to minimize their carbon footprint. This includes exploring alternative fuels such as hydrogen, biofuels, and other low-emission options.[27] Furthermore, the EU is expected to provide support mechanisms, including funding and technical assistance, to facilitate the transition toward greener shipping practices. By fostering collaboration between governments, industry stakeholders, and research institutions, the EU aims to create a sustainable maritime sector that aligns with its climate objectives.

---

[25] Starting January 1, 2024, the obligations will also include methane and nitrous oxide emissions, in addition to the currently covered carbon dioxide emissions.

[26] Flodén et al. (2024), p. 971.

[27] Ibid, p. 973.

Through these comprehensive measures, the EU seeks to lead by example in the global effort to combat climate change, ensuring that the shipping industry plays its part in achieving a sustainable and environmentally friendly future.

3 Advancing Green Shipping: The Role of EU Taxonomy and IMO Sustainability Standards

3.1 EU Taxonomy and Green Shipping

The particular importance of achieving the green transition in the shipping sector is further evidenced by the inclusion of this sector among the activities that, according to the European Union Taxonomy (Regulation EU 2020/852), are classified as environmentally sustainable,[28] provided they meet the specified criteria.[29] This classification makes investments in these activities more attractive.[30]

Specifically, the mention of the shipping sector in the Taxonomy was already present in the first delegated Climate Act of the Regulation (Regulation EU 2021/2139) and pertains to specific maritime activities (the activities of inland waterway transport of passengers and/or cargo, the upgrading of ships used for these activities, maritime and coastal transport of goods and passengers, vessels for port operations and auxiliary activities, as well as the upgrading of related vessels).[31] Technical criteria for assessing the sustainability of these activities were established; however, these criteria required zero carbon dioxide emissions from the respective ship as a fundamental component of sustainability. At the same time, it was provided that, based on proven economic and technical reasons, compliance could be partial, but only for a temporary period until the end of 2025. With the amendment of the aforementioned act, new, more lenient technical criteria were introduced, with an application period starting from January 1, 2026. Specifically, it is no longer required that a ship emits zero carbon dioxide emissions for its operation to be considered sustainable. Instead, if the goal of zero emissions is technologically and economically unfeasible for the shipowner, the ship only needs to comply with higher (though gradually decreasing) emission limits, which extend until 2050 when emissions must be zero.

The regulatory scope of the Taxonomy covers all companies subject to Directive EE 2014/95 (NFRD), and its application began on January 1, 2023. Specifically, from January 1, 2024, the application of Directive EU 2022/2464 (CSRD) will commence, which expands the scope of the NFRD regarding the subject matter of

---

[28] See EU taxonomy for sustainable activities, available at: https://finance.ec.europa.eu/sustainable-finance/tools-and-standards/eu-taxonomy-sustainable-activities_en.

[29] Fernandez and Willman (2023).

[30] Schinas (2023).

[31] Pettingale et al. (2022).

reporting and the companies covered.[32] In particular, the above will form part of the reporting obligations imposed—until now—on large and listed companies.[33] The obligation extends to the submission of an annual management report from their Board of Directors, in a separate section titled Non-Financial Statement or Consolidated Non-Financial Statement, through which they disclose the percentage of their turnover from products or services related to economic activities characterized as environmentally sustainable, as well as the percentage of their capital expenditures and the ratio of their operating expenses related to assets or processes connected to economic activities classified as environmentally sustainable.

3.2 *International Maritime Organization (IMO) and Sustainable Development*

Finally, increased obligations for achieving sustainability and energy efficiency are established for the member states of the International Maritime Organization, aiming to reduce the carbon intensity of the shipping sector by 40% by 2030 and by 70% by 2050 compared to 2008 levels.[34] Specifically, as of January 1, 2023, all existing ships[35] must calculate (a) their energy efficiency and (b) the annual operational carbon intensity they emit, with the goal of reducing greenhouse gas emissions.[36]

Regarding energy efficiency, the relevant compliance measure is indicated by the Energy Efficiency Existing Ship Index (EEXI). This index focuses on the technical characteristics of the ship and reflects the extent to which the fuels used for the ship's propulsion are energy-efficient. The obligation applies to ships with a gross tonnage of over 400 tons and requires obtaining EEXI approval once during the ship's lifetime. The main function of this measure is to certify existing ships as being twenty percent (20%) more energy-efficient compared to 2012 levels. The

[32] The directive applies to small and medium-sized enterprises (SMEs) with at least 250 employees whose securities are traded on a regulated market within the Union, as well as large enterprises whose securities are not traded in such markets.

[33] This includes companies with over 500 employees or those whose balance sheet totals at least 20 million euros or whose net turnover is at least 40 million euros.

[34] See Jones (2023). Also see IMO (2020a) IMO Action to reduce greenhouse gas emissions from international shipping. Available at: https://wwwcdn.imo.org/localresources/en/MediaCentre/HotTopics/Documents/IMO%20ACTION%20TO%20REDUCE%20GHG%20EMISSIONS%20FROM%20INTERNATIONAL%20SHIPPING.pdf.

[35] These obligations pertain to entities established prior to the introduction of the Energy Efficiency Design Index (EEDI) in 2013.

[36] The relevant requirements are reflected in the recent decision by the Marine Environment Protection Committee 328(76).

same obligation already exists for new ships (built after 2013) and is measured through the Energy Efficiency Design Index (EEDI).[37]

As for carbon emissions, the Carbon Intensity Indicator (CII) serves as the primary measure of operational compliance and requires each ship to progressively and annually reduce its carbon emissions. The reduction levels are related to (a) the number of nautical miles the ship has traveled and (b) its deadweight tonnage, while the obligation applies to ships with a gross tonnage of over 5000 tons. These requirements must be reflected in the Ship Energy Efficiency Management Plan (SEEMP), which is mandatory for every shipowner and for each individual vessel they operate.

4 Conclusion, Critical Remarks and Recommendations

The journey toward climate neutrality in the shipping sector is both imperative and complex, necessitating a multifaceted approach that combines regulatory frameworks, technological innovation, and industry collaboration. The European Union's ambitious goals, as outlined in the "Fit for 55" package and the FuelEU Maritime Regulation, represent significant strides towards reducing greenhouse gas emissions in maritime operations. However, several critical challenges and considerations must be addressed to ensure the successful implementation of these initiatives. While the regulatory frameworks provide a solid foundation for decarbonization, the practical challenges of compliance remain substantial. Many shipping companies, especially smaller operators, may struggle with the financial and logistical implications of transitioning to renewable fuels and implementing onshore power supply systems.

Of course, the reliance on renewable fuels of non-biological origin poses questions about availability, scalability, and cost-effectiveness. The current technology may not be sufficient to meet the ambitious carbon intensity reduction targets, particularly in the short term. Also, the extensive monitoring and reporting obligations can impose significant administrative burdens on shipping companies. Ensuring accurate and timely data collection will require robust systems and may divert resources from operational priorities.

Undeniably, the international nature of shipping means that unilateral EU regulations may create competitive disadvantages for European operators compared to those in regions with less stringent environmental standards. This could lead to carbon leakage, undermining global efforts to reduce emissions. The EU should consider implementing financial incentives, such as grants or low-interest loans, to support shipping companies in their transition to greener technologies. Targeted

---

[37] Essentially, the Index measures the same parameters as the Energy Efficiency Design Index (EEDI) established in 2013, which, along with the Ship Energy Efficiency Management Plan (SEEMP), has become mandatory for ships (62nd decision of the Marine Environment Protection Committee (MEPC)).

funding for research and development in alternative fuels and energy-efficient technologies is essential.

Furthemore simplifying the monitoring and reporting requirements could alleviate the administrative burden on shipping companies. Developing standardized reporting frameworks and leveraging digital technologies for data collection can enhance efficiency. In addition, encouraging collaboration between industry stakeholders, research institutions, and regulatory bodies can foster innovation and facilitate the exchange of best practices. Establishing platforms for sharing knowledge on successful decarbonization strategies can benefit the entire sector.

The EU should engage in dialogue with international organizations, such as the International Maritime Organization (IMO), to promote the adoption of similar environmental standards globally. Coordinated action can mitigate the risks of competitive disadvantage and carbon leakage. Undoubtedly, the regulatory landscape should remain flexible and adaptive to technological advancements and emerging challenges. Regular reviews of the effectiveness of the regulations and the progress towards targets will ensure that the shipping sector remains on track to achieve climate neutrality.

In conclusion, while the path to climate neutrality in shipping is fraught with challenges, it also presents significant opportunities for innovation and leadership. The inclusion of shipping in the EU ETS represents a critical step towards reducing GHG emissions in the maritime sector. However, the challenges identified in the study must be addressed to ensure the effectiveness of this initiative. Recommendations include fostering collaboration among stakeholders, enhancing customer education about the EU ETS, and implementing supportive policies that facilitate the transition to greener shipping practices. By addressing these critical issues and implementing the recommended strategies, the EU can pave the way for a sustainable maritime future that aligns with its climate objectives and sets a precedent for global efforts in combating climate change.

References

Books and Articles

Cullinane K, Yang J (2022) Evaluating the costs of decarbonizing the shipping industry: A review of the literature. J Mar Sci Eng 10(7):946. https://doi.org/10.3390/jmse10070946

Dong J, Zeng J, Yang Y, Wang H (2022) A review of law and policy on decarbonization of shipping. Front Mar Sci 9:1076352. https://doi.org/10.3389/fmars.2022.1076352

Fernandez V, Willman T (2023) EU taxonomy: explaining new requirements due January 2024. https://clarity.ai/research-and-insights/regulatory-compliance/eu-taxonomy-explaining-new-requirements-due-january-2024/

Flodén J, Zetterberg L, Christodoulou A, Parsmo R, Fridell E, Hansson J, Rootzén J, Woxenius J (2024) Shipping in the EU emissions trading system: implications for mitigation, costs and modal split. Clim Pol 24(7):969–987. https://doi.org/10.1080/14693062.2024.2309167

Gilbert P, Bows A (2012) Exploring the scope for complementary sub-global policy to mitigate CO2 from shipping. Energy Policy 50:613–622. https://doi.org/10.1016/j.enpol.2012.08.002

Goyal S, Llop M (2024) The shipping industry under the EU Green Deal: an input-output impact analysis. Transp Res A Policy Pract 182:104035. https://doi.org/10.1016/j.tra.2024.104035

Jones F (2023) EU signs off on new legislation for maritime emissions. Available at https://www.offshore-technology.com/news/eu-signs-off-maritime-emissions-regulation/?cf-view

Pettingale H, de Maupeou S, Reilly P (2022) EU Taxonomy and future of reporting. https://corpgov.law.harvard.edu/2022/04/04/eu-taxonomy-and-the-future-of-reporting/

Psaraftis H (2019) Sustainable shipping: a cross-disciplinary view. Springer

Schinas O (2023) Sustainable maritime transport: European policy perspective and potential impact. In: Leal Filho W, Dinis MAP, Moggi S, Price E, Hope A (eds) SDGs in the European region: implementing the UN Sustainable Development Goals – regional perspectives. Springer, Cham, pp 1078–1079. https://doi.org/10.1007/978-3-031-17461-2_70

Regulations and Directives for EU Emissions Trading System (EU ETS)

Directive 2003/87/EC. Establishes the EU ETS and sets the framework for greenhouse gas emission allowance trading

Directive 2018/410/EU. Amends Directive 2003/87/EC to enhance cost-effective emission reductions and promote low-carbon investments

Regulation (EU) 2019/943. Addresses the functioning of the internal electricity market and includes provisions relevant to the ETS

Regulation (EU) 2021/1119. Establishes the European Climate Law, which aims to set a framework for achieving climate neutrality by 2050

Regulation (EU) 2023/959. Implements the inclusion of maritime transport in the EU ETS

Regulations and Directives for FuelEU Maritime

Directive (EU) 2018/2001. Sets sustainability criteria for biofuels, bioliquids, and biomass fuels, relevant to the fuels used in maritime transport

Regulation (EU) 2021/1238. Establishes the FuelEU Maritime initiative to promote the use of renewable and low-carbon fuels in the maritime sector

Regulation (EU) 2021/1796. Addresses specific requirements for the use of renewable and low-carbon fuels in the maritime sector under the FuelEU initiative

Public Property and Governance in the Cyber Age

Public Property Rights. Origins and Developments in the Cyber Age

Cătălin-Silviu Săraru

Abstract Public property rights, so important for the stewardship of common pool resources, have evolved throughout history under the influence of political, economic and technological factors. In the cyber age, this concept faces new challenges, such as digitisation and the management of digital resources as public goods. The article delves into the origins and evolution of public property law, highlighting the impact of new technologies on the legal regime applicable to it. Analysed from an interdisciplinary and comparative perspective, it proposes the possibility of codifying the law of cyber public property, the legal regime applicable to essential digital resources. The article also identifies the link between physical and cyber public property, suggesting a legal framework to ensure the responsible and sustainable use of digital resources for the benefit of the entire global community.

1 Introduction

Public ownership, as a fundamental concept, forms the basis for the management of common resources by the state or other public entities. Over time, its evolution has been influenced by political, economic and technological factors. In the cyber age, this concept is caught up in new confrontations such as digitisation, global access to information and the stewardship of digital resources as part of public goods.

In order to develop a well-grounded analysis, I will begin with the origins of public property law, its significant developments, and how the cyber age is transforming its perception and administration. Through an interdisciplinary, comparative approach, the article analyses the impact of new technologies on the legal regime applicable to public property and proposes solutions to respond to these changes.

C.-S. Săraru (✉)
Faculty of Law, Bucharest University of Economic Studies, Bucharest, Bucuresti, Romania
e-mail: catalin.sararu@drept.ase.ro

C.-S. Săraru, C. E. Popa Tache (eds.), *AI, Sustainability and Solidarity in Advancing European Values in a Globalized Age*, European Union and its Neighbours in a Globalized World 28, https://doi.org/10.1007/978-3-032-06508-7_9

Public property is an ancient concept, found in various forms in ancient civilisations. In Ancient Rome, 'res publica' included roads, aqueducts, harbours and other goods for collective use. Later, in the Middle Ages, the Church and monarchies had primary control over public resources, but the principles of public administration were influenced by canon law.

The modern concept of public property developed with the emergence of nation-states and the idea of sovereignty. The French Revolution introduced the principle of the separation of public and private property, which was later reinforced in the Napoleonic Civil Code. International law, through treaties, codified rules for the administration of international public resources, such as the seas and airspace. From here to a possible codification of the cyber public domain, it is only a step. As for cyber public property law, it is not yet an established concept in doctrine or international law, but it can be analysed from an emerging perspective, based on the characteristics of cyberspace, the rules of international law and the characteristics of its governance. However, this article will limit itself to the premises of the possibility of codifying some rules on this right from the perspective of administrative law.

At a definitional level, cyber public property rights could be the legal regime applicable to essential digital resources and infrastructure under the administration of States or international organisations, which are fundamental to the functioning of cyberspace as a global common. Theoretical discussions concern a set of rights, obligations and restrictions designed to ensure equal access, security, sustainability and responsible use of these resources for the benefit of the entire global community.

Analogous to the concept of physical public property (e.g. roads, parks), cyber resources could be governed by legal regimes that promote shared use but impose restrictions to prevent excessive or inappropriate use. Therefore, in the following, the article will start from the evolution of public property law to identify pathways towards cybernetic public property and, further, towards a space-time cybernetic public domain.

2 Discussion and Results

2.1 Nature of the State's Right Over Public Domain Goods: Theory of General Use and Denial of Ownership

In the past, the right of ownership of the State and administrative-territorial units over public property was contested on the grounds that they had only a right of custody and supervision (*droit de garde et surintendance*) over the property in question and not the three attributes of ownership: possession, use and disposition. This theory of general use and denial of ownership was enshrined in French private law[1] and public law[2] at the end of the 19th and beginning of the twentieth century, with nuances from one author to another. Essentially, this theory had as its starting point Art. 538 (repealed on July 1, 2006) of the French Civil Code of 1804, which stated that 'roads, communication routes and streets in charge of the State, navigable or floating rivers, sea shores, additions to the shore and places from which the sea water has receded, natural or artificial ports, and, in general, any portion of French territory *not susceptible of private ownership* (s.n. n. C.S.S.) is considered as public domain'.[3] For a long time, it was considered, judged solely from the point of view of civil law, that the assets forming the public domain could not be the subject of a property right as conceived in the Civil Code. In other words, it was considered that there was only the right of private property and that the goods which made up the public domain of the State were not susceptible of being the subject of private property.

The theory of general use and the denial of property rights have also been advocated in Romanian private law[4] and public law.[5]

---

[1]Aubry and Rau (1897), pp. 48 ff. These authors maintain that as long as property is assigned to general use, it becomes public property and cannot be the subject of 'true private property'; Colin and Capitant (1930), p. 711.

[2]Proudhon (1843), pp. 242, 243 (this author argues that the state does not own the goods that make up the public domain, given that in the case of property rights, only the owner has the right to use it and to profit from its exploitation, whereas the state exercises only protective possession over the goods in the public domain in order to ensure free use of the goods by all, the public domain being unproductive); Ducrocq (1900), p. 85 (this author points out that public domain goods are by their very nature not subject to ownership, the State having only the custody and supervision of these goods, with the task of preserving them for future generations); Berthélémy (1933), pp. 470 et seq. (the author, starting with the fact that the public domain is inalienable, considers that the administration has no *jus utendi*, *jus fruendi* or *jus abutendi* over it, and is therefore not the owner of the public domain. It is pointed out that no one has *jus abutendi* over the public domain, *jus fruendi* are conceivable only exceptional, and *jus utendi* belongs to everyone, even foreigners).

[3]Article 538 (abrogated on July 1, 2006) Civil Code created by Law 1804-01-25 promulgated on February 4, 1804: Les chemins, routes et rues à la charge de l'Etat, les fleuves et rivières navigables ou flottables, les rivages, lais et relais de la mer, les ports, les havres, les rades, et généralement toutes les portions du territoire français qui ne sont pas susceptibles d'une propriété privée, sont considérés comme des dépendances du domaine public—www.legifrance.gouv.fr. This article was taken over in large part by Article 476 of the Romanian Civil Code of 1864, which reads as follows: 'The large roads, small roads and ulițele which are the responsibility of the State, the navigable or floating rivers and streams, the shores, the additions to the shore and the places from which the sea water has receded, the natural or artificial harbours, the shores where ships draw, and generally all parts of the Romanian land, which are not private property, are considered as dependencies of the public domain.' We note that the Romanian legislator has discarded the presumptive French wording 'which is not susceptible of private ownership' by using the concrete phrase 'which is not private property'.

[4]Hamangiu et al. (1928), pp. 918 et seq.; Luțescu (1947), pp. 166–167.

[5]Vermeulen (1927), pp. 282 ff.

2.2 Public Property Theory

The theory of general use and the denial of property rights received the objection that the exercise of all the attributes of property rights is also found in the case of public property, albeit in a specific form. In France, it was Maurice Hauriou who, as early as 1892, advocated the theory of the property rights of administrative authorities in the public domain. This author considers that administrative persons exercise an administrative property right over public property, on the basis of the following justifications:[6]

1. there is no dependency in the public domain which, once decommissioned, cannot be alienated by the administration and, consequently, be considered an object of property. It being difficult to admit that decommissioning had the power to create the quality of the asset as an object of administrative property; therefore this quality pre-exists the decommissioning;
2. the administration has the right to use the action in revendication to recover the outbuildings in the public domain of which it has lost possession, but the action in revendication belongs only to the owner and, moreover, it is imprescriptible like the public domain;
3. in French case law, numerous decisions have recognised that the public domain is subject to ownership. Thus the judgment of the Council of State of January 17, 1923, *Piccioli*, held that the land on which seaports are located belongs to the State.

Similarly, Marcel Waline has shown that administrative persons have more than a simple right of security over the public domain, given that goods in the public domain can be acquired by the administration through the usual ways of acquiring property and especially by prescription; administrative persons can exercise possessory actions, but also actions for revendication; also administrative persons have the obligation to maintain the domain property and to bear the costs of maintenance.[7] Reviewing these particularities, the author concludes that the State has a property right in the public domain.

Also in France, Louis Rolland states that, 'in principle, we must consider that legal persons governed by public law have a property right over the dependencies of their domain'.[8] French authors on public law[9] and private law[10] in the interwar period expressed similar views.

---

[6] Hauriou (1925), pp. 296, 297.

[7] Waline (1939), p. 555.

[8] Rolland (1932), pp. 345, 346.

[9] Bonnard (1926), p. 295. Similar to Hauriou's justifications, this author, starting from the fact that public domain goods can be disused and thus alienated, concludes that the rule of inalienability is not an absolute rule.

[10] See Planiol (1926), pp. 119 et seq.; Josserand (1932), pp. 798 et seq.

In German doctrine Otto Mayer has argued that the public domain 'is civil property transposed into the sphere of public law and modified accordingly. This property, whose management and administration are governed by public law, is called public property'.[11]

In Romania, this theory has been embraced since the interwar period,[12] and today it is unanimously accepted, given that it is also provided for in Article 136 of the revised Constitution. We note that Romanian case law from the interwar period recognised that the state has a property right over the public domain.[13]

Applying the theory of property rights in the public domain to the concept of 'cyberspace-time public property', we can consider that the state or public authorities could exercise a property right in such a domain in a similar way as the classical public domain theory is applied. However, in this cyber context, there are some particularities that need to be taken into account.

As Hauriou argues for the traditional public domain, it can be argued that public authorities (the state or other public law entities) exercise a right of 'administrative property' over cyberspace time. In fact, it is based on the management and regulation of the use of cyberinfrastructure, networks and data that constitute this digital 'space'. Similar to the physical assets of the public domain, this 'cyberspace time' could be protected by regulations prohibiting its privatised alienation, even if the forms of use and management are different from physical assets. As for the pre-existence of property rights in cyber-assets, analogous to the physical public domain, it could be argued that 'cyberspace time' has a pre-existing quality of 'administrative property' that does not depend on its active use or specific management technologies. For example, authorities could have the right to regulate the use of and access to this cyberspace, even if the technology constituting it changes or evolves (e.g. cloud computing technologies, blockchain, internet of things, etc.).

The right to claim and protect the integrity of cyberspace-time needs to be regulated unequivocally from this administrative perspective. In a similar way to the right to reclaim public domain property, public authorities could have (and, in reality, almost never use) the right to protect and reclaim control over portions of 'cyberspace time' that have been 'lost' or are being illegally accessed. Specific actions can be established to protect data, to prevent cyber-attacks, and to keep the cyber-infrastructure under state control, preventing misuse by private entities or other states.

Just as administrative entities can acquire public domain assets in various forms, public authorities could have the ability to 'acquire' and manage cyber infrastructure (e.g. public data centres, state telecommunication networks, digital education

[11] Mayer (1905), pp. 87 ff.

[12] See Ionaşcu (1941), pp. 219 et seq.; Tarangul (1944), p. 357. For a critique of the theory of the non-existence of the property rights of the state and administrative-territorial units over goods in the public domain in current Romanian doctrine see Chelaru (2008), pp. 43, 44; Bîrsan (2008), pp. 85–87.

[13] Civil Judgment no. 51/1935 pronounced by Section IV of the Prahova County Court *apud* Tarangul ED, *op. cit.*, p. 358.

or e-government platforms). Moreover, they could be obliged to maintain and protect this 'cyber space-time' to ensure the proper functioning of public services and the protection of users. This maintenance obligation must be taken on and well regulated.

Another feature is the imprescriptibility and protection of public property in cyberspace. Similar to the classical public domain, authorities could exercise imprescriptible rights over 'cyberspace time'. The means by which this is achieved are the very legal regulations that protect public information networks, electronic communications and digital infrastructure, based on clear provisions that they cannot be privatised or taken over by private entities without strict regulation. Like public land that cannot be sold without a rigorous legal procedure, essential cyber resources could remain under state control. Similar to the French Council of State rulings on the public domain, judicial and administrative authorities in various countries could recognise that ownership of critical cyber infrastructure (public internet networks, government databases, public service platforms) belongs to the State, even if this does not imply a physical property right, but one based on infrastructural control and access regulation.

Therefore, applying the theory of property rights in the public domain to 'cyberspace time' implies a similar vision to the one applied to physical goods in the public domain, but with the adaptation to the specificities of digital infrastructure.

3 The Capacity in Which the State Exercises Public Property Rights

Today, the State exercises public ownership over public domain assets of national interest as a legal person of public law and on the basis of the prerogatives of public power.[14] These assets are placed under the general administration of the Government.

There have been various theories in the doctrine over the years as to the capacity in which the state exercises the right of public ownership (independently of whether it is a legal person under the right of sovereignty or as a legal person):

3.1 *The State:* Sui Generis *Legal Person*

Some authors have taken the view that the State is a legal person only in private law relations, whereas in public law relations it acts as the holder of sovereignty (of the prerogatives of public power) and not as a legal person. The theory originated in

[14] Săraru (2015).

France and among the first authors who supported it was H. Berthélemy[15] who pointed out that the state exercises the right of public power (the right to command, the right to impose taxes, the right to coerce its inhabitants) as an authority, without needing to have a legal personality to do so. In Romanian doctrine this theory has been supported, especially by private law authors.[16] The theory starts from the idea that the legal person can act only in the sphere of legal relations that do not involve the exercise of state authority. It has thus been shown that only 'in certain categories of legal relations—which do not directly concern the exercise of their competence, but are in one way or another connected with it—can state bodies also appear as legal persons'.[17]

An author of the interwar period pointed out that 'the administrative person has a dual character: public power and private person. In the first capacity, the administrative person is subject to a special legal regime: its acts have certain particularities, which distinguish them from those committed by private individuals and which escape the censure of the ordinary courts. As a private person, the acts of a public authority are subject to the legal regime applicable to those performed by private persons'.[18]

This theory has been opposed on the grounds that any organisation can be the subject of patrimonial legal relations only if it has legal personality. In other words, only if an entity is recognised by the legal system as a person can it participate as such in legal property relationships.[19] If by legal person is meant any organisation, which is a distinct subject of legal relations, regardless of their nature, it is irrelevant whether the State appears in these relations in a position of legal equality or as the holder of sovereignty; it is, in both cases, a distinct subject of the legal relation, endowed, for it is the only way it can be a subject, with legal personality.[20] The elimination of the State from the category of legal persons, which some authors based on the impossibility of applying general rules, is not justified, both in the light of the legal provisions, which distinguish only two broad categories of legal subjects, namely natural persons and legal persons, and in the light of the fact that the State unambiguously meets the constituent elements of legal personality.[21]

[15] Berthélemy H, *op. cit.*, pp. 470 et seq.

[16] See Calmuschi (1981), p. 51; Stătescu (1970), p. 471; Popa (2002), p. 268; Costin and Costin (2007), p. 921 («stat»). In administrative law, for the support of this theory in the interwar period, see Costi (1945), pp. 7 and 17.

[17] Popa (2002), p. 270.

[18] Costi (1945), p. 7.

[19] See Dănişor et al. (2008), p. 324.

[20] Idem, p. 90.

[21] Eminescu (1981), p. 52.

3.2 Dual Personality Theory of the State

The State, as a legal person, exercises two categories of powers: some of public law and others of private law. Hence some authors have supported *the theory of the dual personality of the State:* with regard to the management of private property, the State would have a private law personality, and with regard to the management of public property and the realisation of acts of authority, a public law personality.[22] In this respect, one author points out that 'a categorical distinction should be made between the status of the State or administrative-territorial units as legal persons under private law, owners of the private domain, and their status as legal persons under public law, owners of the public domain. For the "administration" of private property, the State enters into ordinary civil relations, by virtue of its civil law capacity, whereas for the "administration" of public property, it enters into relations of power, by virtue of its administrative law capacity…'.[23]

We consider that this theory can no longer be accepted under Romanian positive law for the following reasons. In the first place, it presupposes that the State has two legal personalities, as if they were two distinct legal persons, each with its own organisation, its own patrimony and its own purpose, which is affected by social interests. If this were the case, it would be impossible to explain how the satisfaction of state creditors for claims resulting from the operation and maintenance of public property (which is part of the state patrimony as a legal person under public law) can be achieved through the enforcement of private property (which would be part, according to this theory, of the state patrimony as a legal person under private law) under the conditions provided for by the Government Ordinance No. 22/2002 *on the enforcement of payment obligations of public institutions, established by enforceable titles*[24] and the Civil Code. Therefore, it is more than obvious that the State can only have a single legal personality that also incorporates the prerogatives of public power, namely the legal personality of public law.

3.3 Theory of the Uniqueness of the Personality of the State: Some Considerations on State Liability

The theory of the uniqueness of the personality of the state, which promotes the idea of the existence of only the legal personality of public law, is very important in the doctrine. This theory was advocated in France by Esmein, Michoud, Ripert, and in

[22] Jacquelin (1899), p. 19; Hauriou (1925), p. 150; Vecchio (1995), p. 217. In Romanian law for discussions related to this theory see Stancu-Ţipişcă (2006), pp. 73 et seq.

[23] Iorgovan (2005), p. 171.

[24] Published in the Official Journal no. 81 of February 1, 2002, and approved with amendments by Law no. 288/2002 (published in the Official Journal no. 344 of May 23, 2002), with subsequent amendments.

France by Paul Negulescu and Anibal Teodorescu, who stated that from the beginning the state has been a subject of law, exercising all rights, whether patrimonial or of public authority.[25] It has been considered that only by adopting the thesis that the State has a single legal personality one can explain, 'The Continuity of the State, the debts of one government being binding on another government, since the government that fell did not commit itself, but the State, a legal person'.[26] The same opinion is held in current Romanian doctrine. Thus, it is considered that it is inconceivable that the same entity should have two legal personalities, one under public law and the other under private law, determined by the different powers it exercises and the legal acts it concludes. The State also has the same single legal personality when it adopts or issues an act of public law and when it concludes an act of private law, because—in both cases—if it fails to comply with its obligations, it will be liable and will pay damages for the harm caused either by acts of public law or by acts of private law.[27]

Taking into account the doctrinal guidelines and current legal regulations, we consider that the state is a *legal person of public law*,[28] in which capacity it is the holder of both the public property right over public goods of national interest and the private property right over private goods of national interest.

The uniqueness of state personality theory emphasises that the state has a single legal personality, irrespective of the nature of its activities (public or private law). Applied in the context of the cyber public domain, this theory suggests that the State should exercise unitary control over cyber infrastructure, considering it as an asset of national interest under the jurisdiction of public authorities.

Even though the state could have private law acts (such as contracts for the provision of digital services), the single legal personality does not distinguish between these acts and public law acts, and in both cases the state would be responsible for protecting digital infrastructure and ensuring fair access to it.

3.4 State Liability in the Cyber Public Domain

According to the theory of the uniqueness of the personality of the State, the State is always liable for its obligations, whether acting as a public authority or as an entity entering into private law. In the context of the public cyber domain, state liability could be applied in cases where public cyber infrastructure is misused, cyber-attacked or where authorities fail to comply with data protection regulations. Thus, the state should be liable for damages caused by mismanagement of this domain or breach of existing legal rules on cybersecurity.

---

[25] Iorgovan (2005), p. 50, note 1. For details see also Stancu-Țipișcă (2006), pp. 76 et seq.

[26] Văraru (1928), p. 69.

[27] Prisăcaru (1996), p. 44.

[28] See also Dănișor et al. (2008), p. 324.

With regard to the protection of the cyber public domain, given the continuity of the state, explained by the theory of uniqueness of personality, it is considered that the responsibility for protecting the cyber public domain should remain with the state, even in the face of technological changes or digital infrastructure developments. This means that the state, as a single legal person, should protect this 'cyber space-time' for all successive governments and authorities, regardless of the nature of technological change, in order to prevent privatisation or undermining its control of over-critical infrastructure.

Here, too, we must take into account the obligation to maintain and regulate the cyber public domain. In the same logic, the state has the obligation to maintain and protect the public cyber infrastructure, including through regulations to prevent the misuse of cyber resources by private or foreign entities. Applying the theory of uniqueness of personality, the state not only ensures the effective management of public law assets (such as public internet networks), but is also liable for damages that may arise as a result of misuse or negligence in their protection.

Finally, just as in the classical public domain, where the state is responsible for protecting assets and infrastructure of national interest, in the cyber public domain, state liability will apply when there are losses related to cyber attacks or security breaches. State liability is not only limited to damage caused by direct actions, but also includes the obligation to protect the infrastructure and ensure the continuity of essential public services.

In conclusion, the application of the theory of the uniqueness of the personality of the state to the cyber public domain suggests that the state, as a single legal person, is responsible for managing, protecting and regulating this public law 'cyber space-time'. It should be accountable both to citizens and to other entities for damage caused by mismanagement of cyberinfrastructure, thus being a guarantor of the protection of this vital domain in the digital age.

4 Public Property Rights in Cyberspace

The article's main argument is that there is an interest in creating a regime to ensure fair use and protection of essential digital resources. Its development could represent a milestone in global internet governance and international cyber law. States today seek to protect the cybersecurity of networks and information systems, particularly those in areas related to essential services as well as those critical to national security. In these initiatives, state actors have begun to cooperate on strategic lines even within international organisations. Cyber, space and emerging technologies have profoundly changed the strategic environment, and NATO, for example, needs to integrate them into its future strategic concept to enhance the Alliance's resilience and effectiveness.[29]

Cyberspace today can be seen as the virtual environment generated by computer networks and systems, including the information content processed, stored or transmitted, as well as the actions performed by users within it. Physical infrastructure (e.g. submarine cables, servers), spectrum, domain names or even certain collective data could be considered as part of the public cyber heritage.[30]

Each state's cyber public domain is already a complex ecosystem of public information systems, is part of a country's digital infrastructure, and refers to all digital elements and information systems controlled or regulated by a state. Why is there still no clear regime? The main reasons, considered individually or collectively, are the lack of international consensus, the dominant role of the private sector, and the fact that legal regulation is often outpaced by new technologies.

All these aspects have, as we can deduce, public and private characteristics.[31] Critical infrastructure is the backbone of the functioning of public and private services, consisting of the information systems and networks essential for energy supply, transportation management, healthcare and communications. Energy grids (electricity, gas), air, rail and road traffic infrastructure, hospital information systems and telecommunications networks are an integral part of this critical infrastructure, along with the financial systems that support payments and banking transactions. Why is the cyber space-time vision important? The answer can be extracted from the following example that few studies have focused on the fragmentation of human activities due to limited access to relevant data, such as using massive data from call detail records (CDRs) and URLs of mobile phone users to analyse the fragmentation of activities in both cyber and physical spaces. The results show that physical (PHAF) and cyber (CHAF) activity fragmentation are inversely correlated, and cyber activities are less influenced by the built environment, being less restricted in time and space compared to physical activities.[32] Thus, space and time here become the guiding elements of legal protection and liability.

Another fundamental pillar is government networks, i.e. all the digital systems used by state institutions to carry out their work. These include the government intranet, digital platforms for interministerial communication and collaboration, as well as e-government services that facilitate interaction between citizens and public administration.

In terms of cybersecurity systems, vital for protecting digital infrastructure from cyber-attacks, security measures are built around intrusion detection and monitoring

[29] In this context, the Alliance has sought to take three main directions: building a preemptive consensus for nonviolent action and defining cyber and space actions that trigger Article 5, promoting deterrence through communicating capabilities and resolve, and working with industry partners to maintain a technological lead. See Gottemoeller et al. (2022).

[30] For more on the lines of evolution of this field see in general Popa Tache (2023), pp. 70 et seq.

[31] Ishikawa and Kryvoi (2023), pp. 1–11.

[32] Liao et al. (2024).

systems, advanced encryption and authentication solutions, as well as cybersecurity operations centres (SOCs) and specialised agencies such as national CERTs.

Digital public data and resources are another important aspect of the cyber public domain. This includes national registers such as the population register, cadastral databases and open data made available to citizens and businesses to stimulate innovation and transparency. They are joined by e-government platforms that allow citizens to access various public services online. Such platforms make it easier to pay taxes, request official documents and access information on education, health and other social services.

To support connectivity and communication between public institutions, communications systems and network infrastructure are at the core. The national internet backbone, national data centres and secure networks used by intelligence agencies and the military ensure the optimal functioning of the state. Another central element is the government cloud infrastructure, which allows data to be stored and processed in secure, state-managed environments. These cloud services are essential for public institutions, providing advanced data and digital asset management capabilities. Finally, cyber incident warning and response systems complement this ecosystem by detecting, managing and recovering from security incidents. CSIRTs, national response plans and national cybersecurity coordination centres are indispensable tools in this respect.

A few distinctions need to be made here.

The most important of these, as a starting point, is the distinction between cyberspace and the public domain cyberspace. The difference really lies in the scope and accessibility of each concept as defined. In both cases. There must be an international perspective.[33]

Cyberspace is a general term for the virtual space created by the interconnection of computer networks and the internet, created by/from all networks, digital platforms, connected devices and electronically transmitted information. As a global environment, cyberspace encompasses both private elements, such as protected servers or databases, and public elements, such as web pages accessible to anyone. The governance of cyberspace is a complex endeavour, based on rules related to state sovereignty, user rights, cybersecurity and data protection.[34]

On the other hand, the public domain of cyberspace is the part of cyberspace that is freely accessible, unprotected by intellectual property rights or other legal restrictions. In this context, users have the right to access, use and distribute content without infringing copyright or other property rights. The concept is inspired by the traditional public domain, as we described it as an evolution in Chap. 2. This also includes cultural works or inventions that are no longer protected by copyright or patent, but are expanding into cyberspace. Other examples of resources in the public domain of cyberspace could be open educational materials (OER), open-source software or publicly available government information.

[33] Siroli (2018).

[34] See more in Harnisch and Zettl-Schabath (2022).

Table 1 Key differences

Feature	Cyberspace	The public domain of cyberspace
Definition	Global virtual environment	Subset of freely accessible cyberspace
Accessibility	Partially restricted (e.g. private data)	Fully open to the public
Own	Includes public and private components	No exclusive property rights
Governance	Supervised by states and organisations	Promotes global accessibility

So, while cyberspace is a general digital environment, we have a public domain of cyberspace that is a subset defined by accessibility and freedom of use (see Table 1).

At first glance, the public domain of cyberspace is a specific component of cyberspace, which focuses on accessibility and free use without legal or financial constraints. If this is the reality, then what is the competence of administrative law? The regulation of the public domain of cyberspace by states, and thus the regulation of public property through administrative law, raises multiple issues today, given the global and decentralised nature of cyberspace.[35] After all, the aim is efficient management in line with public interests.

To achieve this, ideally, states should rely on administrative regulations that define the limits and rules for the use and protection of this space. These include the definition of the digital public domain, which entails identifying digital content (inventorying it) and infrastructure belonging to the public domain, such as publicly accessible government documents or open data. At the same time, rules can be developed for the re-use of public resources, setting clear conditions that promote transparency and innovation in the use of this data.

Monitoring and protection of public domain resources becomes imperative. To oversee activities in this space, states can set up dedicated institutions or administrative departments to manage public digital resources to protect them from misuse through cybersecurity measures and prevent tampering. These efforts are leading to the establishment of public data governance agencies to provide guidelines for the ethical and secure re-use of these resources.[36] How many countries worldwide have this institutional framework?

Given the transnational character of cyberspace, based on the principle of cooperation, states have the possibility of entering into public-private partnerships, through agreements with digital platforms such as Google or Wikipedia, to ensure open access to certain resources. This achieves that level of normality, which is followed by the exemption of citizens from having to pay individually from their own resources for this access. International cooperation with organisations such as UNESCO or ITU to establish global standards in the management of public data is also along the same lines. Regulating access and use can also be done through administrative law, as states can impose strict rules to promote the responsible use of public resources, such as preventing breaches of privacy rules, hate speech or

[35] Nakayama (2022) and Couzigou (2018).

[36] Some useful considerations can be found in Tao et al. (2024).

fraudulent use of resources. Administrative law has the potential to support digital inclusion by making it within the competence of public administrations to guarantee access to digital infrastructure and resources for all citizens.

Another aspect worth considering is **that** states may adopt administrative regulations requiring the use of open licenses for resources created by the public sector. Relevant examples include Creative Commons (CC BY) licenses, which allow public data to be accessed, shared and modified under certain conditions. Administrative law provides states with tools to prevent infringements by penalising entities that misuse public domain resources in cyberspace. In the same way, States can impose interoperability rules to facilitate the use of public resources across different platforms and jurisdictions. All this is necessary because the well-known transnationality of cyberspace means that states do not have complete control over networks and resources that are not exclusively under their jurisdiction. They need to strike a balance between open access and security, protecting the public domain without restricting innovation or open access, especially as there is a risk of conflict between public and private interests. In this context, the state has a responsibility to manage public resources without harming commercial interests.

The following distinction takes the analysis further into its complexity by attempting to delineate a public domain cyberspace from a public domain cybertime. The expression or concept of a 'public domain of cybertime', at least at a theoretical level, suggests that 'cybertime' is a distinct concept belonging to the public domain, i.e. a space open to all, without restrictions of access or ownership. The idea of a virtual space in which time, defined in cybernetic terms, is available to all, possibly in a context of networks or technologies that transcend traditional temporal boundaries, emerges. Interpreting this hypothesis, cyber time could be defined as the continuous flow of digital interactions, accessible and democratised.

On the other hand, the cyber public domain of time shifts the focus to a 'cyber public domain' (a shared digital space) in relation to time. It refers more to time as an integrated dimension in this cyber public space. Imagine, for example, a global digital space (such as a blockchain or metaverse) in which time is a shared resource, either through precise measurements or cybernetic synchronisations.

From a theoretical point of view, which variant is 'more correct'? The answer can only be that both are valid, but, while 'public cyber domain of time' seems more specific to explore time as a dimension, 'public cyber domain of time' suggests, rather, the integration of time into a broader public cyber space. From an administrative law point of view, both variants deserve attention.

The administrative legal protection of cybersecurity is a top priority for any modern state in the context of the increasing frequency and sophistication of cyber attacks. To face these threats, strong public-private partnerships, academic involvement and citizen participation are indispensable. Collaboration between all these parties facilitates the development of innovative solutions and the provision of a secure and functioning digital environment.

5 Conclusions

Over the last 200 years, we have witnessed a marked evolution in the public domain, from the denial of the State's right of ownership over it, to the establishment of the State as a legal person under public law exercising the right of public ownership, and recently the extension of this right into a new domain: cyberspace.

Public property law cannot remain immobile in traditional patterns, but must evolve to respond to new cyber realities. The fragmentation and flexibility of cyberspace call for appropriate regulation that understands that public property is no longer just a static concept linked to physical assets, but a dynamic, adaptable notion. In this context, cyber public property law is at the intersection between administrative law and emerging technologies, and the need for a legal framework to regulate digital resources is becoming increasingly evident. If in the past public ownership was shaped by well-defined political and economic structures, today it is time for the same principles to be applied to the protection and management of a global 'commons'—cyberspace.

New regulations must encourage fair and responsible access to digital resources while promoting their security and sustainability for future generations. In this light, cyber public property rights may be the key to a delicate balance between innovation and the protection of collective interests, between technological development and social responsibility. Addressing such ownership therefore requires a different overall vision, where digital governance ensures not only the protection of state or private interests, but also the fundamental rights of citizens in a shared cyberspace. Therefore, in the face of new realities, defining and strengthening cyber public property rights is no longer just an option, but a necessity for a future where technology and law coexist harmoniously.

References

Aubry C, Rau C (1897) Cours de droit civil français. tome II, Paris
Berthélémy H (1933) Traité élémentaire de droit administratif. Rousseau, Paris
Bîrsan C (2008) Drept civil. Drepturile reali principale, 3rd edn. Hamangiu, Bucharest
Bonnard R (1926) Précis élémentaire de droit administratif. Recueil Sirey, Paris
Calmuschi O (1981) Subiectele colective de drept în România. Academiei, Bucharest
Chelaru E (2008) Administrarea domeniului public şi a domeniului privat, 2nd edn. C. H. Beck, Bucharest
Colin A, Capitant H (1930) Cours de droit civil français, Paris, vol I
Costi G (1945) Noţiunea contractului administrativ. Imprimeria Centrala, Bucharest
Costin MN, Costin CM (2007) Dicţionar de drept civil de la A la Z, 2nd edn. Hamangiu, Bucharest
Couzigou I (2018) Securing cyber space: the obligation of states to prevent harmful international cyber operations. Int Rev Law Comput Technol 32(1):37–57. https://doi.org/10.1080/13600869.2018.1417763
Dănişor DC, Dogaru I, Dănişor G (2008) Teoria generală a dreptului, 2nd edn. C. H. Beck, Bucharest
Ducrocq T (1900) Cours de droit administrative, vol. IV, Paris

Eminescu Y (1981) Collective subjects of law in Romania. Academiei, Bucharest
Gottemoeller R, Hedgecock K, Magula J, Poast P (2022) Engaging with emerged and emerging domains: cyber, space, and technology in the 2022 NATO strategic concept. Def Stud 22(3):516–524. https://doi.org/10.1080/14702436.2022.2022.2082955
Hamangiu C, Rosetti Bălănescu I, Băicoianu A (1928) Tratat de drept civil român, vol I. «Națională» S. Ciornei, Bucharest
Harnisch S, Zettl-Schabath K (2022) Secrecy and norm emergence in cyber-space. The US, China and Russia interaction and the governance of cyber-espionage. Democr Secur 19(1):82–110. https://doi.org/10.1080/17419166.2022.2097074
Hauriou M (1925) Précis élémentaire de droit administratif. Société anonyme du Recueil Sirey, Paris
Ionașcu A (1941) Curs de drept civil român. tom I, Sibiu
Iorgovan A (2005) Tratat de drept administrativ, vol II. All Beck, Bucharest
Ishikawa T, Kryvoi Y (2023) Introduction. In: Ishikawa T, Kryvoi Y (eds) Public and private governance of cybersecurity: challenges and potential. Cambridge University Press, Cambridge, pp 1–11
Jacquelin R (1899) Une conception d'ensemble du droit administratif, Paris
Josserand L (1932) Cours de droit civil positif français, vol. I, Paris
Liao M, Kwan M-P, Liu X (2024) Exploration of human activity fragmentation in cyber and physical spaces using massive mobile phone data. Ann GIS 30(4):417–434. https://doi.org/10.1080/19475683.2024.2024.2341704
Luțescu GN (1947) Teoria generală a drepturilor reale. Teoria patrimoniului. Clasificarea bunurilor. Drepturile reale principale, Bucharest
Mayer O (1905) Le droit administratif allemand, Special Part, vol. I
Nakayama BJ (2022) Information vs the cyberspace domain. J Cyber Policy 7(2):213–229. https://doi.org/10.1080/23738871.2022.2022.2083976
Planiol M (1926) Traité pratique de droit civil français, vol. III, Paris
Popa N (2002) Teoria generală a dreptului. All Beck, Bucharest
Popa Tache CE (2023) Le dynamisme du droit international public contemporain et la transdisciplinarité, Préface de Florent Pasquier. L'Harmattan, Paris. collection «Le droit aujourd' hui»
Prisăcaru V (1996) Tratat de drept administrativ român. General part., 2nd edn. revised and added. All Publishing House, Bucharest
Proudhon V (1843) Traité du domaine public, tom I, 2nd edn
Rolland L (1932) Précis de droit administratif, 4th edn. Dalloz, Paris
Săraru CS (2015) Owners of public property in Romania. Jurid Trib Trib Jurid 5(1):17–23
Siroli GP (2018) Considerations on the cyber domain as the new worldwide battlefield. Int Spect 53(2):111–123. https://doi.org/10.1080/03932729.2018.1453583
Stancu-Țipișcă M (2006) Persoanele juridice de drept public. C. H. Beck, Bucharest
Stătescu C (1970) Civil Law. Persoana fizică. Persoana juridică. Drepturile reale. Didactică și Pedagogică, Bucharest
Tao L, Wan J, Wen B (2024) The effects of artificial intelligence and victims' deservingness information on citizens' blame attribution towards administrative errors. Public Manag Rev:1–21. https://doi.org/10.1080/14719037.2024.2024.2411632
Tarangul ED (1944) Tratat de drept administrativ român. Tipografiei Glasul Bucovinei, Cernăuți
Văraru M (1928) Tratat de drept administrativ român. Librăriei Socec & Co., Bucharest
Vecchio G (1995) Lecții de filozofie giuridica. Europa Nova. translated by JC Drăgan
Vermeulen J (1927) Noțiunea de domeniu public. Revista de drept public
Waline M (1939) Manuel élémentaire du droit administratif, Paris

Towards a Public Domain of Cybernetic Space-Time as a Challenge for International Law. About the Cybercommons

Cristina Elena Popa Tache

Abstract The universality of cyberspace as an international network has introduced new dimensions and even mutations for international law, demanding a reconceptualisation of territorial, jurisdictional, and temporal boundaries. This paper examines the viability and implications of establishing a special 'public domain' in cyberspace, where legal norms could operate universally to support transparency, inclusivity, and equitable access, as a kind of metamorphosis of the Commons. Such a framework would allow cyberspace to function as a collective resource, filling gaps in current international regulations and aligning with the principles underpinning other public domains, such as outer space and the high seas. The study discusses theoretical models of the public domain, from Hardin's 'tragedy of the commons' to Ostrom's 'governance of common-pool resources', applied to cyberspace to identify legal mechanisms that could facilitate shared governance without infringing upon state sovereignty or individual rights. The temporal dimension of cyberspace-characterised by immediacy and perpetual access-present challenges for traditional legal systems and requires adaptable legal interpretations to address the continuous digital presence and threats. A potential solution that emerges is that the delineation of an internationally recognised 'public domain' in cyberspace could contribute to equitable access, security, and sovereignty in the digital age, advocating for international cooperation that reflects the unique characteristics of digital environments, functioning as an extension of the global commons doctrine.

C. E. Popa Tache (✉)
Faculty of Law and International Governance, Danubius International University, Galati, Romania

C.-S. Săraru, C. E. Popa Tache (eds.), *AI, Sustainability and Solidarity in Advancing European Values in a Globalized Age*, European Union and its Neighbours in a Globalized World 28, https://doi.org/10.1007/978-3-032-06508-7_10

1 Introduction

1.1 On the Context of Cyberspace Evolution and Its Impact on International Law

Over the last decade, the rapid bites of cyberspace have profoundly transformed the structures and functioning of contemporary societies. International law has become a 'must', through a constant and borderless connection between individuals, institutions and states given by the internet, which has also become a ubiquitous medium, influencing all aspects of economic, political and social life. This is not easy to achieve, especially for future generations, due to the specific expansion of new issues, including climate change, which have already led to new difficulties in the field of international law, which is built on the foundation of traditional, even conservatoires, principles and rules, which presuppose fixed territorial borders and a sequential time. The literature has not remained indifferent to these signals and one example is Humphreys and the reactions he provoked when he spoke of the generation of the future.[1] Whereas in the past, international regulations clearly applied to specific areas, the internet now challenges the same concepts, being a virtual domain where anything is possible and where jurisdictional authority and enforcement of rules are often difficult to establish. Added to this is the need for uniform international rules.

Although there are attempts at regulation, especially at the level of the European Union, international law continues to face a fundamental problem: how to regulate a 'space' that, by definition, does not respect the physical and temporal limits to which we have become accustomed? Will law succeed in redefining the notions of space and time?

On November 18, 2024, the Council of the European Union approved a declaration on a 'common understanding on the application of international law in cyberspace', signalling that international law remains relevant and applicable in this digital domain. The declaration emphasises that states must respect certain rules and obligations when conducting activities in cyberspace.[2] However, as I will detail in the main body of this article, this declaration also did not include cybertime as a concept which, in my opinion, cannot be treated totally separately from cyberspace nor can it be inferred as implicitly included.

The obvious complexity and dynamic nature of this environment requires, first of all, a reconceptualisation of the 'public domain' in which legal rules can be universally and effectively applied. Then comes the hardest task: (re)conceptualising the commons and its metamorphosis into cybercommons. In this sense, the idea of a

[1] Humphreys (2022). On reactions see Lawrence (2023); Wewerinke-Singh et al. (2023).

[2] Council of the European Union. Declaration on a Common Understanding of International Law in Cyberspace. 15,833/24, CYBER 334, COJUR 111, COPS 622. Brussels: General Secretariat of the Council, November 18, 2024. Text available here: https://data.consilium.europa.eu/doc/document/ST-15833-2024-INIT/en/pdf

'public domain' in cyberspace becomes a significant challenge, given the multiple political, economic and social interests involved, but also the need to guarantee equitable access and a security framework for all users. The concept itself has traditionally been linked to natural resources and areas that are of global interest, such as the international seas and outer space. In these areas, international law recognises the need for common regulation to ensure free and unfettered access while protecting these resources from abuse. So, the fundamental question is: can we apply the same principles to cyberspace? Could a public cyberspace domain and cybercommons ensure transparency, accessibility and fairness in the face of new technologies? Moreover, what implications would it have for the sovereignty and accountability of states and the protection of the fundamental rights of the individual?

The present analysis differs from other views in that it considers a specific unitary concept of cyberspace and time in relation to its unique characteristics. Legally, cybertime has not been analysed in detail, although technically (other disciplines) there is specialised literature.[3] Here will surface both the need for tailored international regulation, protecting specific rights and enabling appropriate protection. None of this can be achieved without promoting cooperation between states, so that cyberspace and time become a collective resource rather than a field of legal and economic conflict. All these arguments will ultimately lead to the conclusion that there is a need for an international law of cyberspace and time.

1.2 The Need to Redefine Areas of Law and Traditional Boundaries in the Digital Context

Whereas in the past, international rules were enforced through rules involving physical delimitations of territories and a fixed chronology, in cyberspace and time these delimitations dissolve. We need to rethink notions of jurisdiction, territory and even sovereignty in order to apply them effectively and fairly. Many of the fundamental rules and concepts of international law – such as the protection of national territories, state jurisdiction and the regulation of acts of aggression – have focused on territorial sovereignty and respect for effective boundaries.

If we were to identify at this point the international law of cyberspace time, I could say that it represents the totality of legal norms and principles regulating the activities of states, non-state actors (because such a subfield would considerably influence the group of subjects of international law) and individuals in the international digital environment, taking into account both the traditional territorial and temporal aspects of international law and the specificities of cyberspace. The discussions revolve around the regulation of access to digital resources, the protection

[3] Several engineering, communications and tourism papers have even explored cybertime. According to Andrade (2021), cybertime is: 'The rhythms that an internet user activates when s(he) explores the digital network's territories within cyberspace.' See also Zalot (2013).

of fundamental rights of the individual in cyberspace, state responsibility and the regulation of interactions between entities operating in this obviously and strongly interrelated space. International cyberspace-time law adapts to the unique characteristics of cyberspace, such as instantaneity, fluidity of borders and global interconnectivity, and aims to ensure order, security and fairness in the use of this transnational digital domain.

1.3 Objectives of the Study and Central Questions to Be Answered

Through this study, the central aim is to take another step towards identifying solutions for regulating digital resources and to propose a system of international governance that protects both state sovereignty and the fundamental rights of the individual.

The method is one of re-evaluating the applicability of international law to cyberspace time, developing a global governance framework, exploring the role of emerging technologies (artificial intelligence, blockchain) and identifying conflicts between traditional regulations and digital realities. Key questions are: how can this space be regulated? What are the relevant theoretical models for its governance? How can new technologies respect transparency and accountability? What are the implications of delineating a 'public domain' in cyberspace? What about cybercommons?

Before analysing these models, which start from educational models and converge towards applicative ones, some clarifications are in order regarding the notion of cybernetic space-time. It has been called cyberspacetime, cyberspace-time or cybernetic space and time. Whatever we call it or however we feel more comfortable, we need to go beyond the metaphorical aspect and identify the concrete legal relations. And for this we will exclude, from the outset, the superficiality of implicitly including the time component in the general notion of cyberspace.

As Mihalache said, an interpretation of Blake's works helps us to understand that cyberspace is not a purely spatial entity; it also involves time, but not in the sense of Einstein's special relativity theory. The cyberspace-time continuum is not a void waiting to be filled, but an aggregation of places (sites), which, like Blake's plates, are multimedia architectures resulting from the merging of space and time.[4] Even though space and time have been hastily lumped together in the notion of cyberspace, from a legal point of view a specific regime must be established for each dimension; otherwise the rigour of the law would no longer exist.

The CIRET-UNESCO Project: The Transdisciplinary Evolution of the University states in Article 6: 'The emergence of cyber-space-time represents, more than the fall of the Berlin Wall, a fabulous opportunity for democracy, for individual and

[4] Mihalache (2002).

social development and for the universal sharing of knowledge. Provided, of course, that this cyberspace time is not perverted into a huge financial pump. The medium of the creations broadcast in this cyber-spacetime has the texture of the depths of matter, being close to the quantum world. In other words, scientifically speaking, cyberspace is of a radically different nature from our ordinary space. If the earth can be divided into territories, whose borders separate the various nation-states and peoples of the world, such a division of cyberspace would simply be against nature? This is the scientific basis of the need for a radically new vision of the evolution of the public domain, in terms of its purposes, its extension and its quality. In cyberspace time, the public domain is planetary and not national in nature. If national and international organisations have the courage and intelligence to surface a new vision of the public domain, cyberspace could become a fabulous (…).'[5]

We deduce from all this that we can have cyber spacetime at both the national and international level. But what is this public domain and what does it comprise as elements of interest for international law? The public domain relevant for international law refers to those resources and spaces that could be normatively taken over by cybercommons, are accessible to all states, and are governed by international rules and principles, without being subject to exclusive national sovereignty. Mainly global resources and regions, which are considered to be in the interest of the entire international community and require common regulation and protection.

Some differences should be noted. Typically, while the commons and public domain have in common the idea of resources accessible and managed for the collective benefit, the term 'commons' has a broader and more global application, being used to designate natural or digital resources that are not under the exclusive control of a state or private entities. On the other hand, 'public domain' refers mainly to assets or resources that are owned and managed by the state at the national level. The commons also include essential global resources, such as natural ecosystems (water, air, animal species) or even digital goods (such as the internet or data commons), which are internationally regulated.

One example is outer space, including the regulation of the legal regime for satellites. Under international treaties, such as the 1967 Outer Space Treaty, outer space is an area of common use for all mankind, and activities in this area must be regulated for the benefit of all mankind. Seas and oceans from the second example. Under the United Nations Convention on the Law of the Sea (UNCLOS), the international seas, such as open water areas (exclusive economic zone, seabed and ocean floor), are considered as a kind of 'public domain'. Resources in these areas must be managed sustainably and equitably for all. More recently, although less directly regulated, the atmosphere is seen as an area of global concern, given the impact of

[5] CIRET-UNESCO Project: The Transdisciplinary Evolution of the University. Synthesis document, prepared by the International Center for Transdisciplinary Research and Studies (CIRET) in collaboration with UNESCO, 1997. Available at the international conference 'What kind of university for tomorrow? Towards a Transdisciplinary Evolution of the University,' Locarno, Switzerland, April 30–May 2, 1997, https://ciret-transdisciplinarity.org/bulletin/b12c8. php.

climate change, pollution and the need for collective management of atmospheric resources, regulated by international conventions such as the Paris Agreement.

Finally, there is also the category of multilateral treaties applicable to specific geographical areas or well-defined spaces that are beyond the sovereignty of the States parties to the treaty, such as, for example, the Antarctic Treaty of 1959, the Treaty on Principles Governing the Activities of States in the Exploration and Use of Outer Space, including the Moon and Other Celestial Bodies of 1967, etc. Antarctica is the ice-capped continent around the South Pole, not subject to the sovereignty of any state, whose regime is governed by the 1959 Washington Treaty on Antarctica (cooperation, peaceful use, denuclearisation and demilitarisation, and the prohibition of dumping radioactive waste).

From all these examples, we can extract a basis for customary regulation for the benefit of cyberspace time, including the disputes that have arisen over time.[6] From the UNESCO-CIRET project mentioned above, we extract that cyber space and time cannot be divided, but we can divide some rights and obligations.

In this area, the term ‘public domain’ can be extended to global digital networks and resources, which, similar to other public domains, should be regulated and managed in the interest of all humanity, ensuring fair access, data protection and respect for the rights, freedoms and even choices of individuals. From this point of view, it is ideal to regulate and protect digital infrastructure and data at the international level, in order to prevent misuse and promote transparent and accountable global governance, by including them in cybercommons.

2 Specificity of Delimiting a Public Domain in Cyberspace

An international cyber cyberspace time could be defined as a domain governed by international rules and principles, which govern both the digital (spatial) dimension and the temporal interactions and events within it. On the temporal dimension, some clarifications are needed. Cyberspace time not only embraces digital networks and

[6]An example of disputed sovereignty and associated maritime zones is the Australian Antarctic Territory (‘AAT’) and associated EEZ and continental shelf. Australia’s sovereignty in Antarctica is based on principles of customary international law, and Australia’s sovereign rights over waters within 200 nautical miles of the AAT and associated continental shelf are based on UNCLOS treaty law. The AAT was proclaimed by Australia in 1936 following a transfer of title from the United Kingdom and Australian pioneering work in the Antarctic area directly south and southwest of Australia. 13 The AAT is a sectoral claim over Antarctica, the continent and islands south of latitude 60° south (to the South Pole) and between longitudes 45° east to 136° east and 142° east to 160° east. Applying the normal principles of customary international law, while only four states (the United Kingdom of T.T., France, Norway and New Zealand) recognise Australia’s sovereignty over the AAT. See House of Representatives Standing Committee on Legal and Constitutional Affairs, Australian Law in Antarctica: The report of the second phase of an inquiry into the legal regimes of Australia’s external Territories and the Jervis Bay Territory (AGPS, Canberra, 1992), para. 2.8.

data flows, but is characterised by a specific dynamic in which time and data accessibility are indivisible and in continuous dynamics.

International cybertime is a concept that refers to the specific temporal dimension of cyberspace, where actions and events unfold in an almost instantaneous and continuous manner, having a direct impact on the information flows and behaviour of actors in this global space. Even if it is or can be considered a part of cyberspace, regulations must be explicit and not implicit. It is a term that is closely linked to rapid technological evolution and the way in which actions in this domain effect modify and interact in real time at a global level.

One indication of the existence of cyber time is the instantaneity of actions and reactions. In cyberspace, interactions happen in real time, regardless of the geographical location of the actors involved. Actions in one place can instantly affect users or infrastructure in another part of the world. A cyber-attack can be launched in one country but has immediate and global effects even in another corner of the world. Cyber time is therefore characterised by the absence of a delay in taking action, which implies the need for a regulatory body that is able to respond quickly and effectively to events as they occur.

Another important characteristic is the accelerating pace of technological change. Time in cyberspace is also defined by the rapid evolution of technologies and digital infrastructure, which we cannot ignore. New innovations such as artificial intelligence, blockchain or the internet of things (IoT) are developing at a much faster pace than in other areas. It means legal regulation needs to be constantly adapting to keep pace with technological progress. Cybertime must be *expressly mentioned* in the explanatory memoranda underpinning regulatory proposals because it is not only a factor governing interactions, but also a key parameter in determining the pace of adaptability of international rules.

L. Strate showed that three levels of cyberspace have been identified, the first being ontology, which includes the notions of cyberspace as paraspace or nonspace, as well as the concept of *cyberspacetime*. The second level is given by building blocks, such as conceptual and perceptual physical space or cyberspace. Finally, the third level is that of synthesis, composed of varieties of cyberspace, such as media space, aesthetic space, data space, and personal and social space.[7] The absence of a special legal treatment of cybertime, separate from cyberspace, may not result in adapted and adequate regulation and problems may arise.

In addition to all this, international cyber time also implies global, international synchronisation. Although each country or region has its own time zones, in cyberspace time becomes standardised through the use of a global time system (e.g. UTC – Universal Time Coordinated). This is a sine qua non for the proper functioning of networks, for global financial transactions, and for activities involving coordination between different parts of the world. The global interconnection of information systems creates the need for a time management system that allows actions and events to be carried out efficiently on a global scale.

---

[7] Strate (1999).

This is also where 24/7 accessibility and continuity, i.e. the perpetual nature of digital activities, come into play. Cyberspace knows no significant pauses or interruptions – networks and systems are ideally available 24/7, allowing users to interact at any time of the day or night. 24/7 adds complexity to regulating online behaviour, as a breach or dangerous action can be taken at any time and from anywhere in the world.

As for the real-time regulation of digital events, given the rapidity with which incidents (e.g. cyber-attacks, dissemination of fake news, or manipulation of information) can occur, cyberspace regulation must allow for rapid interventions. States and international organisations must adopt intervention procedures that can respond in a short timeframe to prevent major damage.

The cyber time component also influences legal issues related to the statute of limitations – i.e. the period of time in which legal actions can be brought. In cyberspace, these periods can be different from those in traditional law, due to the continuous nature of information flows and the possibility of withdrawing or modifying data in a way that can lengthen or shorten the limitation period. Cyber time actually has a specific feature in setting legal time limits for litigation and in regulating how legal actions can be enforced. Actions and interactions in cyberspace unfold rapidly; decisions taken in this context can have long-term effects. Data protection or online privacy regulations can affect the digital behaviours of individuals and organisations in the long term. Decisions by international institutions in the area of fundamental rights or cybersecurity may determine legal and technological trajectories that will shape the digital space for many years to come.

Some concrete discussions about cybertime were initiated in 2015.[8] Guy, without addressing a legal vision, considered that there are certain aspects of the functioning of cyberspace, in particular those related to the march of a time that could be attached to it: cybertime. He linked his analysis to the way people understand space and time, which are always associated, and tried to question the properties of cybertime. From a legal point of view, without being a jurist, Guy opened a debate which, if pursued multidisciplinary by a jurist, would have led to remarkable results. All this from a simple comparison of the functioning of cyberspace and cybertime, on the one hand, and that of space and time, on the other. 'We can speak of space and time in the case of cyberspace and cyberspace time; in some respects, the latter refer to concrete experiences, and their functioning defies even the excessive abstractions of our representations of space and time in physics. Like a supermicroscope, cyberspace seems to be a formidable revealer of hidden but very real things: social connections, knowledge, ideas… But in some ways, the correspondence with the words space and time doesn't work properly. We are faced with the anxiety of space and time that have been compressed, denied even in their elementary properties'.[9]

In the search for legal connections, we realise that time is closely linked to the legal norm. We know that the very formal sources of law, the material sources, lie in

[8] Bernard (2015).

[9] Ibid.

the factors of time and space and in social facts. Just one example could be the principle of the speed of legal liability, which is such as to ensure that the aims of legal liability are realised, because its application implies that liability must be incurred at the right time, in order to avoid the situation that, with the passage of time, there is no possibility of liability. It is not sufficient to regulate cyberspace without expressly dealing with cybertime. This is why separate and unambiguous legal provisions are so necessary. In law we cannot assume.

Like space, time takes on different characteristics because the internet has brought with it a new way of problematising time, embodied in human actions and social institutions, produced on a global scale, regardless of time zones. Just as specialists in other fields analyse the contours, content and unfolding of virtual time and the cyber-week that it makes possible, so too must legally treatment be given to.[10] All these features, such as the collapse of temporal boundaries, the compression of temporal distance and the differences between the cyber-week and the calendar week, are nowadays in need of appropriate regulation by international legal society.

Against this background another question arises: how are states spatialised? A striking example found in the literature is the biometric identification program in India that serves to temporalise the state (the Aadhaar initiative). Some voices argue that this project is meant to attribute the contemporary Indian state with the temporalising characteristics of innovation and speed through mobility, change and speed as motivating factors for the staff of the Unique Identification Authority of India (UIDAI). India is openly experimenting with cybertime.[11]

This international cyber time can therefore also be understood as the globalisation or internationalisation of the effects of actions in a digital context. A change in internet usage regulations or data protection policies in Europe may have immediate effects on users in Asia or America.[12] Similarly, regulations to combat cybercrime need to take into account the impact they may have on actors in different corners of the world, regardless of the specific hours of operation of each region.

2.1 *Timelessness, the Exception that Proves the Rule*

It is a challenging but also plausible concept, given the specific nature of this digital environment. Cyberspace, by its fundamental characteristics, is, anyway, seen as a space in which time is perceived and experienced differently from physical and geographical reality.

First of all, cyberspace is dominated by instantaneity and simultaneity, in which interactions, information processing and data exchange happen almost in real time,

---

[10] Laguerre (2004).

[11] Nair (2019). See also Munn (1992).

[12] See Balkin (2008) and Mathur (2015).

without significant delays. This feature of rapidity makes the perception of continuous 'time', in the traditional sense of the term, increasingly difficult to maintain. Seen from this angle, cyberspace appears timeless, as interactions are not governed by rigid temporal concepts (such as past, present and future) and are not constrained by the physical limits of the real world. Perhaps even this timelessness demands to be legally regulated in international documents. Perpetual access to information and the ability to interact at any moment with other digital actors suggests a form of 'continuous time' or even 'timelessness' in which there is no defined 'now'. Events and actions unfold in a constant flux and traditional temporal boundaries are not applicable in the same way. This has created an environment in which time seems to become diluted and notions such as 'delay' or 'delayed response' become less relevant.

In an attempt to find some examples, I stop at the metaverse, which can be seen as a vast virtual space, composed of both elements of physical reality and digital elements. Like cyberspace, the metaverse can be seen as a world in which the boundaries of time are less clear or even 'absent' in a traditional sense. Interactions in the metaverse are often almost instantaneous and simultaneous, and users may experience multiple events or activities in parallel without a clearly defined temporal structure, similar to the way they operate in digital networks. Here the concept of 'perpetual presentation' is central. People can browse continuously, change their avatars or participate in activities at any time, while their experiences are not limited by a clear beginning or end. To a certain extent, the metaverse becomes a world where users can experience simultaneously multiple 'realities' and 'times' in a fluid form, which can lead to a perception of timelessness. In the metaverse, the physical time of the real world becomes less relevant and the perception of it can be dissociated from geographical and biological reality.

Examples can continue with virtual reality (VR) and augmented reality (AR), which offer a hybrid experience where virtual elements are superimposed on physical reality and interactions take place in real time. VR is a computer-generated environment in which users can fully immerse themselves, usually with the aid of a VR headset or similar device. In VR, the user is surrounded by a virtual environment that replaces or completely alter-physical reality, and interactions are dictated by technology. Although AR does not create a completely separate world, as the metaverse does, it does alter and influence the perception of time, making it more fluid and 'subjective'. Users can experience virtual elements embedded in the real world, and these interactions are often immediate and simultaneous, even if they are only 'augmented' by technology. AR can also appear to be a technology that challenges traditional notions of time, as users can interact with 'information' from different time periods simultaneously, and present reality is constantly being altered by digital data streams. At the same time, AR enables interactions that may seem endless or without temporal clarity, and the time spent in these interactions may be perceived differently from real-world activities. Similar to the metaverse, AR can contribute to a form of 'fluidisation' of time, where the boundaries between past, present and future become blurred.

Both technologies – the metaverse and lifelike, mixed or augmented reality – further deepen the idea of timelessness in the digital realm. If the metaverse creates a complete virtual space where time seems suspended or diluted, augmented reality influences the way we experience time and events in the real world by adding a permanent digital layer. Both the metaverse and these types of realities represent a form of 'continuous time' that goes beyond traditional structures of temporal perception, bringing them into a zone of fluidity, simultaneity and connectivity without clear boundaries.

Because of these particularities, issues such as jurisdiction arise, which I will discuss in the next chapter. For the sake of the chances of finding good legal solutions, a multidisciplinary vision is needed.[13]

From a legal and moral point of view, the notions of time remain, or should remain, benchmarks, as we all know the relevance of time in law, especially in law enforcement. Atemporality should be seen as a danger to law enforcement. Regulations, rights and responsibilities are still governed by concepts of time, such as prescription and data protection. Therefore, how can we keep calendar time applied to the virtual world in the legal sphere? This is where we need to find the necessary safeguards to accommodate the maintenance of time. Although cyberspace may seem timeless, there remains a need for regulation that takes into account the continuous evolution of technologies and the behaviour of actors in this digital space. It is therefore advisable to treat timelessness in legal terms as a perception due to the fluid and rapid nature of cyber interactions rather than an objective reality.

In conclusion, international cyber time is not limited to the concept of 'time' as traditionally understood, but reflects essential characteristics of the digital space – instantaneity, continuity, global synchronisation and adaptability.

2.2 *The Tragedy of the Commons (Hardin) and Its Applicability in the Cyber Context*

The 'tragedy of the commons' is a theory developed by ecologist Garrett Hardin in 1968, which refers to the way in which common resources can be depleted or destroyed when individuals act in their own self-interest without considering the impact on the whole community. In the case of the commons, each user has unlimited access to available resources, and in the absence of effective regulation, they may overexploit those resources, leading to their gradual degradation. The 'tragedy' problem arises when resources are finite, but there is no effective coordination to protect and conserve them for the future. Effective coordination, in turn, cannot

[13] Popa Tache and Săraru (2024).

exist in the absence of knowledge and culture.[14] For this an inter, multi and transdisciplinary.[15]

The application of this theory in the cyber context becomes relevant due to the nature of digital resources that are common, accessible to all and yet susceptible to misuse. For example, in cyberspace, common resources include global digital infrastructure, such as communication networks, servers and data centres, as well as the data that flows over these networks. Without them, we cannot talk about the functioning of the internet and the entire digital ecosystem. From a legal point of view, there is a risk that individual actors or economic or even state entities will use them irresponsibly, without respecting the limits of their capacity or ensuring data protection and confidentiality.

A clear example of the re-emerging 'tragedy of the commons' in cyberspace is the overloading of internet networks through denial-of-service (DDoS) attacks or the misuse of cloud storage capacity. Many of these activities can reduce the efficiency and performance of the global digital infrastructure, affecting access and security for all users. The proliferation of harmful or illegal content on online platforms can be seen as another form of 'tragedy', where cyber resources are compromised by users exploiting these platforms for harmful purposes, such as hate speech or the distribution of false information, thus jeopardising the integrity of the entire digital ecosystem. All these intangible commons of the mind, including intellectual property, are now crying out for protection under international law. For Boyle, by way of example, empirical data, the role of the public domain and the commons are all elements that need to be taken into account. In some of his reflections on digital technology, the peer-to-peer revolution and the legislative responses and technological backlashes, Boyle believes that innovation and development will only continue to be encouraged by some lower intellectual property regimes and a larger public domain.[16] By this we can only infer that this 'larger' public domain is one subject to an international legal regime.

International cyber law and global regulation become indispensable to prevent this tragedy. Just as Hardin proposed solutions for regulation and control over shared resources to prevent their depletion, so in cyberspace an international system would be needed to limit the misuse of resources and promote responsible behaviour by all actors involved. Here is how, in search of theoretical models, we revisit

[14] Frow (2000).

[15] See Science and Tradition: Transdisciplinary Perspectives, Openings Towards the twenty-first Century.' Paris: UNESCO, December 2–6, 1991; Locarno, Switzerland. 1997. Statement and Recommendations: What University for Tomorrow? UNESCO and CIRET Congress, April 30 – May 2, 1997; The Venice Declaration: Final Communiqué of the Colloquium 'Science at the Frontiers of Knowledge: The Prologue of Our Cultural Past.' Venice, March 7, 1986; CIRET. The Charter of Transdisciplinarity, a document adopted at the First Congress of Transdisciplinarity held in Arrábida, Portugal, in 1994; and The Message from Vila Velha/Vitória: The Second World Congress of Transdisciplinarity September 6–12, 2005, Brasilia. All these documents are available in English here: https://ciret-transdisciplinarity.org/basicdocuments_en.php

[16] Boyle (2008). Also see Jones (2009).

Hardin[17] and reactivate Ostrom in the following. Our immediate goal is to identify infrastructure safeguards, strict regulations on data use and data privacy, and rules to ensure fair access to digital resources. International regulations should encourage collective responsibility in the use of cyber resources, given the impact that individual actions can have on the entire global digital ecosystem. Finally, the words of Hardin remain: 'The population problem has no technical solution; it requires a fundamental extension in morality,' calling for 'lifeboat ethics'.[18]

2.3 *Governance of Shared Resources (Ostrom) and Its Principles for Managing Cyberspace*

More practically, in contrast to Hardin's 'tragedy of the commons' theory, economist Elinor Ostrom has proposed an alternative view of how common pool resources can be managed sustainably. Ostrom has demonstrated through her research that common pool resources can be managed effectively by communities, even in the absence of centralised control or external authority, as long as there are clear rules, active community participation and self-regulatory mechanisms. It has identified a set of fundamental principles for the governance of common pool resources, which include clarifying property rights, establishing collectively accepted rules, monitoring and sanctioning irregular behaviour, and ensuring inclusive decision-making based on the participation of all relevant stakeholders.[19]

By testing the applicability of Ostrom's principles to cyberspace, we see how they can provide a useful model for the governance of global digital resources. First, the principle of clarifying property rights can be crucial to understanding who has control over digital infrastructure, data and online platforms. In cyberspace, many of these resources are controlled by private actors, such as companies that own data centres and telecommunications networks, which can lead to conflicts of interest and the exploitation of resources in a way that does not favour the collective good. One example is cloud data storage. Many states or organisations store data in centralised cloud infrastructure owned by private companies (such as Amazon, Google and Microsoft), and this control can create vulnerabilities to unauthorised access or foreign policy (e.g. foreign governments' access to stored data). The common data resource may therefore be under some form of centralised control, and managing it becomes a real challenge in terms of protecting sovereignty and individual rights.

The Ostrom principle can therefore be applied to establish clear rules on property rights over cyber resources in order to strike a balance between private control and public interest. In the case of cloud data storage, the danger is that without clear rules, controlled access and shared responsibility between states or users, data can

[17] Hardin (1968).

[18] Hardin (1974).

[19] See some comments relevant to this article in Earl and Potts (2011).

be exploited in a way that does not reflect the public or state interest. Thus, data can end up being managed irresponsibly, leading to a 'tragedy of the digital commons' – jeopardising national security and the rights of the individual.

Ostrom's second key principle is the establishment of collective rules. In the cyber domain, this can mean establishing international regulations on data use and protection, digital infrastructure security and fair access to online resources. For example, international regulations, such as the European Union's General Data Protection Regulation (GDPR), have been a first step towards establishing collective rules for the protection of personal data. More broadly, this principle could form the basis for the creation of international organisations to coordinate the management of cyber resources and monitor compliance with the rules set.[20]

The principle of monitoring and sanctioning is also essential in the governance of cyber resources. In cyberspacetime, users and entities managing digital infrastructure must be accountable for their behaviour, and failure to comply with the rules must attract appropriate sanctions. Monitoring in cyberspace refers to practices such as auditing internet traffic to detect illegal activities such as malware distribution or online harassing behaviour.

The solutions converge towards a democratic and fair system of governance of cyberspacetime. Ultimately, the common goods of humanity require transparency and broad participation so that all stakeholders can influence the regulations that govern cyberspacetime, a collaborative, consensus-based effort that respects the principles of equity and sustainability.

3 The Legality and Temporal Dimension of Cyberspace

Cyberspace, by its digital and global nature, poses significant challenges for international law, in particular with regard to the existing legal framework created for traditional domains, such as outer space or international seas. It is not a metric space, so the usual topological measurements are no longer sufficient. Probably measurements will now be made in ranges. The temporal dimension of this space does not align with the conventional rules of international law, which are designed for physical domains, where time and actions have a more structured and predictable rhythm. This character of cyberspace requires a reconfiguration of legal rules to keep pace with the speed and technological complexity of this environment. It raises questions of jurisdiction, the application of national laws and international regulation, as these digital environments can be considered as a *new territory*.

For example, whenever we discuss jurisdiction, we discuss personal jurisdiction and subject matter jurisdiction. With the online environment, the literature has discussed a third scope of jurisdiction, particularly important in today's society

[20] Some interesting details can be found in Schweik and Kitsing (2010).

dominated by constant, substantial and fluid online cross-border interaction.[21] We arrive, then, at the unit of measurement through the scope. The specific question is what are the limits of competence in cyberspace and time? There are as yet no definite answers. International law needs to adapt to regulate activities carried out in these virtual realities, including copyright, data protection and consumer protection in these environments. In practice, we will be able to add the prefix 'cyber' to any social, political, economic, civil, military, etc. activity.[22]

In the quest for cyber-jurisdiction, in virtual and augmented realities, users' personal data is collected and processed in a much more detailed way than in physical environments. Users are identified through their digital interactions, movements and behaviour, and this raises questions about the protection of fundamental rights, such as privacy and data security. International law, including regulations such as the European Union's General Data Protection Regulation (GDPR), needs to expand to encompass data protection in these global virtual spaces, ensuring that privacy rules are respected regardless of users' location: 'Jurisdictional domains are legal divisions of the Earth's surface commonly used in classification and search systems for location-based queries.' Cyberspace and time again become relevant to the subject of jurisdiction where we can analyse comparatively the population of spatio-temporal jurisdictional knowledge bases.[23] However, in this analysis, we will keep the focus in this analysis on identifying these jurisdictional issues and their relation to international law. Jurisdiction has traditionally been regarded as a matter exclusively for states, but over time it has been recognised that jurisdictional obligations may also fall to private parties, in particular through the development of the doctrines of denial of justice and access to justice. The concept of party autonomy, allowing parties to determine the jurisdiction of the courts and the applicable law, has also been widely accepted. These developments suggest the need for a new understanding of jurisdiction in international law to reflect today's complexity.[24]

Another argument is given by the particularities of conflicts and behaviours in virtual spaces. Virtual, augmented or mixed reality generates new forms of behaviour and interaction between users, including harassment, fraud, hacking or cybercrime. When such behaviour happens in an internationally accessible virtual space, questions of law enforcement, protection of rights and jurisdictional treatment become highly relevant. It would be preferable to rely on treaties containing specific clauses. International law is itself in a restart phase in order to be able to establish common rules for dealing with crimes committed in these environments and to regulate conflicts arising between states and private entities operating in virtual spaces.

The example of technologies enabling virtual and augmented realities demonstrates the dependence on global infrastructure, such as data centres, communication networks and online platforms. They are regulated nationally, but interactions

[21] Svantesson and Jerker (2016).

[22] Some details on EU cybergeopolitics can be found in Smith (2023).

[23] Lacasta et al. (2014).

[24] Mills (2014).

between users are global. International law needs to regulate these infrastructure, setting rules on accessibility, cybersecurity, net neutrality and collaboration between states to protect this critical infrastructure.

By way of example, in a scenario where virtual and augmented reality technologies are creating realities that are parallel to and, in many cases, in the business of states, the question arises as to whether the state can still fully control these new forms of interaction. Virtual reality can affect state sovereignty in unpredictable ways, by creating virtual territories and economies that do not respect a state's official borders. International law must master the regulation of 'virtual' domains in a way that protects national interests and sovereignty, but also promotes international collaboration in managing new technological realities.

The new 'spatiality' of international law raises the question of redefining the concept of 'space'. International law needs to reconceive space as much more than a limited physical domain, as virtual and augmented realities create a global 'new dimension' that requires transnational regulation and governance. A definition of the new spatiality means recognising that previously formally established borders and jurisdictions are no longer sufficient to understand and regulate modern interactions and conflicts.[25] The interdependence of states and non-state actors (such as international organisations and corporations) has transformed international law into a more decentralised and fluid system in which states are no longer the only authoritative entities.

Although States have at their disposal the possibility of using all instruments of international law, they remain responsible. Nor is the responsibility of states limited to their territorial domain, but extends to the regulation and protection of transnational cyber space-time. Part of this remains simply working together globally to prevent and respond to cyber threats, which can affect not only national security but also international stability.

In sum, throughout history, the 'maps' of international law have constantly been redrawn as the discipline revises its cohesion and sustains its effectiveness. Today, these dynamics are influenced by the new cyber-space-time, which seems to have eclipsed many of the previous discussions. The dominant hierarchies of scale and space that defined the traditional state-centred regulation of international law are now being challenged. Approaches that integrate the concept of space can help international law scholars to redraw the conceptual boundaries of the discipline and of research, expanding them to include new spaces within new conceptions of international law.[26]

In these circumstances, legal solutions to conflicts of jurisdiction in cyberspace need to be developed at the international level. One possible mechanism could be the creation of international conventions setting clear rules on jurisdiction in cyber-transnational cases. They could be complemented by dispute resolution mechanisms such as international arbitration or international courts specialised in cyberlaw.

---

[25] See some details in Sandvik (2015).

[26] Pearson (2008).

Today, cyberspacetime lacks a clearly regulated international legal framework, which makes the regulation and governance regime fragmented and often subjective.

Delimiting an international public domain or cybercommons would solve multiple problems related to resource management and protection of planetary interests. First, it would solve the problem of universal access to information and digital technologies, similar to the way large regimes of international law regulate common domains, such as international seas or outer space. Another argument would be to standardise regulations for an already de facto standardised field, such as cybernetics. Already the disciplines related to new technologies are not very different around the world but contain similar curricula. Therefore, the use and global circulation of data, which are now regulated differently in different countries, would have a chance, which makes its protection unequal.

4 Conclusions

The analysis of the proposal for the delimitation of an international public domain in cyberspacetime highlights the need for clearer and more effective international regulations to manage digital resources and to protect the fundamental rights of the individual. The importance of such a public domain cannot be underestimated given the interdependence of digital economies and societies.

To create an effective international governance regime in cyberspace, several initiatives and conscious approaches are needed. An important recommendation would be the creation of an international treaty similar to the Outer Space Treaty or the United Nations Convention on the Law of the Sea, defining the principles of cyberspacetime utilisation and setting clear obligations for signatory states. The establishment of an international forum (in or separate from the United Nations Organisation) for continuous dialogue and the development of an international regulatory mechanism that integrates the interests of the various parties and ensure that there is no monopoly of one actor or group of actors in defining digital regulations are not excluded.

Another important point is the creation of an international dispute settlement and sanctions system that responds quickly and effectively to abuses in cyberspace, such as cyber-attacks, the spread of disinformation or violations of fundamental rights.

The creation of an international regime will have to overcome the divergences between states and national barriers and harmonise laws to create a cohesive legal framework. A major benefit is to ensure universal data protection and fundamental rights in such a politically and culturally diverse context.

But how can international law regulate not only cyberspace but also cybertime? The concept of 'cyber time' is often overlooked in traditional legal discussions, but in digital reality it is becoming a crucial factor in the management and governance of digital resources. An innovative concept could be the development of an 'International Cyber Space-Time Law' (ICSTL), which will take into account both the physical dimensions of the internet and the continuous and non-existent temporal dimension of cyberspace interactions.

No other branch of law could have such possibilities. In cyberspace, an 'event' can be recorded in the continuous present, instantly accessible from anywhere in the world, and at the same time remain 'active' and have consequences for others indefinitely. Time, in the digital context, does not align with national timetables or internal laws. For example, a decision made in California may be instantly applicable in Europe or Asia without the national laws of those regions having any significant impact on the action. 'Cybertime' could be a public domain of international law – a universal concept that applies to all states and their citizens, regardless of borders or domestic laws. If in outer space and the international seas natural resources are considered common goods, then in cyberspace time and information in this 'cybertime' could be considered a global common good. International law can 'deal' with global policies for the management of data flows, the protection of personal time (e.g. records of an individual's digital life activities) and transparency in decision-making processes that impact on these time flows.

My proposal actually aims at a fusion between the classical concept of the public domain, cybercommons and a new type of legal regulation based on the simultaneity and permanence of time in cyberspace. As acts in cyberspace can have effects that extend beyond the immediate time limit of an incident or event, such a framework would allow, for example, international intervention to protect fundamental rights, such as data protection at any point in the digital future. A concrete example would be regulations related to 'digital tracking' or 'online financial transactions'. Illegal or harmful behaviour taking place in cyberspacetime can be 'recorded' and continuously reviewed, without time imposing strict limitations on its interpretation and resolution. Legal regulations should also address issues of limitation periods for legal or regulatory actions, which are not aligned with fixed time limits, as is the case in the national legal framework. In cyberspacetime, a violation of a right or cyber fraud can be detected and sanctioned long after the actual event has taken place, and international regulations should provide flexible mechanisms of action, without encouraging long-term impunity. Cyberspacetime, without the responsibility and conscious involvement of states, makes national sovereignty extremely fragile due to the transnational nature of the internet. Viewed in isolation, do states have the capacity to regulate, sanction and monitor activities carried out in a 'global cybertime' or not.

All these observations demonstrate the need for a radical new vision that can only be implemented through a reconstruction of international law.

References

Andrade P (2021) Mobile culture for tourism communication. In: Mehdi Khosrow-Pour DBA (ed) Encyclopedia of organizational knowledge, administration, and technology. IGI Global. https://doi.org/10.4018/978-1-7998-3473-1.ch112

Balkin J (2008) The constitution in the national surveillance state. Minn Law Rev 93(1):1–25
Bernard G (2015) À la recherche du cybertemps (reflections on cyberspace). hal—01175466. https://hal.science/hal-01175466/document
Boyle J (2008) The public domain: enclosing the commons of the mind. Yale University Press, London
CIRET-UNESCO Project: The Transdisciplinary Evolution of the University. Synthesis document, prepared by the International Center for Transdisciplinary Research and Studies (CIRET) in collaboration with UNESCO, 1997. Available at the international conference 'What kind of university for tomorrow? Towards a Transdisciplinary Evolution of the University,' Locarno, Switzerland, April 30–May 2, 1997. https://ciret-transdisciplinarity.org/bulletin/b12c8.php
Council of the European Union. Declaration on a Common Understanding of International Law in Cyberspace. 15,833/24, CYBER 334, COJUR 111, COPS 622. Brussels: General Secretariat of the Council, November 18, 2024. Text available here: https://data.consilium.europa.eu/doc/document/ST-15833-2024-INIT/en/pdf
Earl PE, Potts J (2011) A Nobel Prize for Governance and Institutions: Oliver Williamson and Elinor Ostrom. Rev Polit Econ 23(1):1–24. https://doi.org/10.1080/09538259.2011.526291
Frow J (2000) Public domain and the new world order in knowledge. Soc Semiot 10(2):173–185. https://doi.org/10.1080/10350330050009416
Hardin G (1968) The tragedy of the commons. Sci New Ser 162(3859):1243–1248. https://www.jstor.org/stable/1724745
Hardin G (1974) Commentary: living on a life boat. Science 24(10):561–568
Humphreys S (2022) Against future generations. Eur J Int Law 33(4):1061–1092. https://doi.org/10.1093/ejil/chac068
Jones R (2009) The public domain: enclosing the commons of the mind. Int Rev Law Comput Technol 23(3):255–257. https://doi.org/10.1080/13600860903265381
Lacasta J, Francisco Lopez-Pellicer FJ, Florczyk A, Zarazaga-Soria FJ, Nogueras-Iso J (2014) Population of a spatio-temporal knowledge base for jurisdictional domains. Int J Geogr Inf Sci 28(9):1964–1987. https://doi.org/10.1080/13658816.2014.911412
Laguerre M (2004) Virtual time. Inf Commun Soc 7(2):223–2247. https://doi.org/10.1080/1369118042000232666
Lawrence P (2023) International law must respond to the reality of future generations: a reply to Stephen Humphreys. Eur J Int Law 34(3):669–682. https://doi.org/10.1093/ejil/chad034
Mathur N (2015) Paper Tiger: law, bureaucracy and the developmental state in Himalayan India. Cambridge University Press, Cambridge
Mihalache A (2002) The cyber space-time continuum: meaning and metaphor. Inf Soc 18(4):293–301. https://doi.org/10.1080/01972240290075138
Mills A (2014) Rethinking jurisdiction in international law. Br Yearb Int Law 84(1):187–239. https://doi.org/10.1093/bybil/bru003
Munn ND (1992) The cultural anthropology of time: a critical essay. Annu Rev Anthropol 21:93–123
Nair V (2019) Governing India in cybertime: biometric ids, start-ups and the temporalized state. South Asia J South Asian Stud 42(3):519–536. https://doi.org/10.1080/00856401.2019.159812 2
Pearson Z (2008) Spaces of international law. Griffith Law Rev 17(2):489–514. https://doi.org/1 0.1080/10383621.2008.10854621
Popa Tache CE, Săraru CS (2024) Evaluating today's multi-dependencies in digital transformation, corporate governance and public international law triad. Cogent Soc Sci 10(1):45. https://doi.org/10.1080/23311886.2024.2024.23709
Sandvik KB (2015) The humanitarian cyberspace: shrinking space or an expanding frontier? Third World Q 37(1):17–32. https://doi.org/10.1080/01436597.2015.1043992
Schweik CM, Kitsing M (2010) Applying Elinor Ostrom's rule classification framework to the analysis of open source software commons. Transnatl Corp Rev 2(1):13–26. https://doi.org/1 0.1080/19186444.2010.11658219

Smith H (2023) The geopolitics of cyberspace and the European Union's changing identity. J Eur Integr 45(8):1219–1234. https://doi.org/10.1080/07036337.2023.2023.2277329
Strate L (1999) The Varieties of Cyberspace: Problems in Definition and Delimitation. West J Commun 63(3):382–412. https://doi.org/10.1080/10570319909374648
Svantesson D, Jerker B (2016) Jurisdiction in 3D – "scope of (remedial) jurisdiction" as a third dimension of jurisdiction. J Priv Int Law 12(1):60–76. https://doi.org/10.1080/17441048.2016.1144987
Wewerinke-Singh M, Garg A, Agarwalla S (2023) In defense of future generations: a reply to Stephen Humphreys. Eur J Int Law 34(3):651–668. https://doi.org/10.1093/ejil/chad033
Zalot MC (2013) Buying 'time' on eBay: cybertime, nostalgia, and currency in online auctions. Atl J Commun 21(1):17–28. https://doi.org/10.1080/15456870.2013.743317

Legal Foundations of the Digital Transformation of Administrative Proceedings

Vitalii Gordieiev, Oksana Melenko, Oleg Orlovskyi, and Pavlo Krainii

Abstract The digitalization of administrative justice is presented as a tool to reduce costs and speed up procedures, improve the quality of administrative justice, despite limited budgets. For litigants, it allows for better access to the law and jurisdiction, a possible general obligation to transfer a case to a judge for dematerialization and the development of videoconferencing may change the quality of justice for certain litigants. Digitalization also affects the operation of courts and the work of judges. Therefore, the evolution towards "administrative cyberjustice" will only guarantee quality if its implementation and consequences are carefully monitored. Digital tools seem to be particularly suited in law for a number of tasks, such as standardization and revision of certain acts, "advanced" legal research, client contact or dispute resolution through special platforms, or "quantitative" justice. All of these tools are aimed to increase the productivity of lawyers, just as spreadsheets made it possible for all professions to use numerical data. The issue of digital transformation in terms of online court hearings is poorly researched from a scientific point of view. Most aspects that reveal the mechanism of re-exercising the right to participate in court hearings online are covered in regulatory legal acts, namely laws, instructions, etc.

V. Gordieiev
Department of Procedural Law, Faculty of Law, Yuriy Fedkovych Chernivtsi National University, Chernivtsi, Ukraine
e-mail: v.gordieiev@chnu.edu.ua

O. Melenko · P. Krainii (✉)
Department of Public Law, Faculty of Law, Yuriy Fedkovych Chernivtsi National University, Chernivtsi, Ukraine
e-mail: o.melenko@chnu.edu.ua; p.krayniy@chnu.edu.ua

O. Orlovskyi
Department of Private Law, Faculty of Law, Yuriy Fedkovych Chernivtsi National University, Chernivtsi, Ukraine
e-mail: o.orlovskyy@chnu.edu.ua

C.-S. Săraru, C. E. Popa Tache (eds.), *AI, Sustainability and Solidarity in Advancing European Values in a Globalized Age*, European Union and its Neighbours in a Globalized World 28, https://doi.org/10.1007/978-3-032-06508-7_11

1 Introduction

One of the most important sectors is the administrative court, which plays a key role in reviewing administrative cases and protecting the rights of citizens in disputes with the authorities. The digital transformation of the administrative court has become relevant due to the growing volume of cases, changes in the requirements for the speed and quality of case consideration, as well as increased requirements for openness and accessibility of the judicial process. Therefore, the study of the legal aspects of the digital transformation of the administrative court is an extremely relevant and important task.

The modern world is experiencing unprecedented changes caused by the rapid development of information technology and the digital environment. Digital technologies are becoming an important tool in all sectors of society, including the legal system. Digital transformation offers enormous potential for improving the functioning of the state justice service. The introduction of digital tools has already enabled the development of legaltech companies operating in the judicial sector, which offer a wide range of new services. The success of e-justice is fundamentally dependent on the appropriation of technology by legal market players. E-justice should be seen as a way to improve the efficiency of justice for the benefit of litigants by rethinking the role of the judge and rethinking the role of technology and tools. The social utility should take precedence over the technology itself. The Dutch experience of online arbitration "e-courts" proves that the demand for justice is difficult to satisfy when parties are dealing with an algorithmic black box that does not motivate the decision-making process.

2 Theoretical Issues of Digitalisation of Administrative Justice and Public Administration

Currently almost all countries of the world are actively "digitalizing" the judicial system. Digital transformations that take place in the field of justice raise many problems for the solution of which some researchers propose building a conceptual model of the successful e-Justice system.[1] Other authors analyze the actions of the European Union aimed at the use of artificial intelligence in the field of justice in all its potential.[2] A comprehensive assessment of e-justice is being developed based on representing justice in the broad sense, e.g. not just as a set of services, but as a set of public values.[3] As a result of the analysis of foreign experience, we can conclude

[1] Jneid et al. (2019).
[2] De Abreu (2019).
[3] Lupo (2019).

that most of the existing acts are aimed at creating the most favorable conditions for innovation and research.[4]

The rapid advancement of digital technologies is now reaching into almost every aspect of human life. Administrative law scholars cannot separate themselves from this profound change, which prompts an intellectual and research challenge akin to that faced by administrative lawyers confronted with the growth of the welfare state, privatization, and other such paradigm shifts. As such, it may even require us—as transitions of similar scale have done—to call into question some of the foundations of the contemporary field.[5] The principal challenge is to identify the many interfaces between administrative law and the emerging digital world, seek to understand them, and search for answers to the questions that arise. Our aim in this chapter is to provide a provocation for administrative law scholars regarding the necessity of engaging with developments concerning digital technology. To this end, we explore a range of questions that are arising, by reference to a variety of examples from different common law countries, across three central domains of administrative law: judicial review of administrative action; administrative decision-making; and redress systems. The chapter is therefore broken down into three main parts, reflecting each of those domains.

Digitalization in the judiciary is a step that is important not only at the national level, but also, and above all, for cross-border cooperation in this area.

The main goal is to improve access to justice for citizens and companies, as well as to strengthen systems and make them more efficient, effective and resilient, helping them to face future challenges.

Some EU countries are already using digital tools in this area, allowing, among other things, the possibility of filing applications electronically and tracking the procedure online, an electronic document service or the use of video conferencing systems for hearings.

However, there is still considerable room for improvement in the digitalization of justice systems in the EU, as evidenced by the latest EU Justice Scoreboard 2023, prepared by the European Commission.

For example, in 25 Member States, it is possible to initiate proceedings or file a lawsuit online, which is a significant improvement compared to 2021 (the year when aspects related to the digitalization of justice began to be addressed in detail). However, one third of EU countries do not offer digital solutions, or where they do, they are very limited, for criminal cases.

The digitalization of justice aims to facilitate access to justice, increase overall efficiency and ensure the resilience of justice systems during crises such as the COVID-19 pandemic. The e-Codex system (e-justice through online data exchange) is a key digital technology tool for modernizing communications in the context of cross-border judicial communication.

[4] Lindgren et al. (2019).

[5] Daly et al. (2021).

It allows computer systems used by the judiciary to be interoperable. It allows different national e-justice systems to be interconnected to exchange data on civil and criminal cases.

The system has been under development for several years and is still managed by a consortium of member states and other organizations. The compromise aims to provide the system with a sustainable and long-term legal framework by entrusting its management to EU-LISA.

The Agency should take over responsibility for the e-CODEX system no later than 1 July 2023 and no later than 31 December 2023. The draft text introduces provisions protecting the independence of the judiciary, clarifying the governance and management structure of EU-LISA and allowing Member States to contribute to the development of the e-CODEX system.

Computerization began more than 40 years ago and continues to go beyond the equivalence between digital and paper. The potential of digital technology is increasingly being taken into account and we will soon be able to access a file online. For example, it is possible that a digital procedure will be created alongside oral and written procedures (or in the form of a written procedure without documents). It will no longer be characterized by a hearing, as in the case of oral proceedings, or by the exchange of written submissions, but by the structuring/fragmentation (digitization turns into tiny pixels) of the application, the completion of the hearing (except for videoconferencing), the immediate exchange of documents and submissions (by electronic communication at any time and systematically sent to all parties and the judge) and assistance in decision-making (through so-called predictive justice).[6]

With these caveats in mind, the development of a digital procedure is likely to facilitate access to law and justice, speed up procedures and increase the sense of fairness (to quote the Quebec academic J.F. Robert). It is not enough to say that we need a humanistic approach to the digitalization of justice (the position of my colleagues Cécile Chine or Nathalie Fritzero, for example) or to call for more rituals (suggested by Mr Garapon and Mr Lassegue). In addition, the fair trial will be increasingly digitized to enable automatic verification of reasons for impartiality and to ensure the principle of adversariality by making all documents available to the parties.

Digital technologies have the effect of accelerating and fragmenting: time through deadlines, facts through massive document processing, written opinions with structuring of claims, statements that are increasingly absent or limited in time to specific moments, judgements outside the scope or separate interpretation of judgements by so-called predictive justice tools. If care is not taken, this may undermine the autonomy of litigants and thus the principle of cooperation. However, it should be avoided that it leads to untimely acceleration of justice—when will the procedural principle of simultaneity be introduced?—, overloading with information or avoiding face-to-face meetings.

[6] Jeuland (2019).

The digitalization of proceedings is the first step: the exchange of arguments and the transfer of documents in a case now takes place electronically in most cases. It is conceivable that the chain of proceedings could be followed online and in the public domain, as we see in some judicial systems.

Castells' theory of the networked society provides an interesting basis for considering the issues of organizational performance from the technological side.[7] According to Castells, productivity growth in a market economy over the past 30 years has been the combined effect of new information technologies.

The doctrine of administrative law emphasizes the close connection between the methods of public administration and the forms of public administration. The scientific literature notes that methods are reflected in the forms of public administration. Methods are a complex and multifaceted construct that expresses the substantive essence of public administration. At the same time, the methods may be modified and their combination may vary. For example, legislation may introduce new types of administrative methods, while outdated ones may be cancelled.[8]

To achieve the research objective, various scientific methods and approaches are used: analysis of legal norms: study of various aspects of legal regulation of the administrative court in the context of digital transformation, including legislative acts, rules of procedural law, and others; comparative analysis: study of the experience of other countries in the field of digital transformation of judicial systems to identify best practices and lessons for Ukraine; statistical analysis: analysis of statistical data on the work of the administrative court and the effectiveness of digital transformation.

The use of these methods will allow for a comprehensive analysis and an objective assessment of the state of affairs in the field of digital transformation of the administrative court.

Digitalization of public services has long been a hot topic on the agenda of worldwide researchers, generating both consensus and debates. Most authors share the opinion that the digitalization of the public services changes the interaction between citizens and public servants,[9] claiming that digitalization requires new skills in order for citizens and public servants to interact more efficiently.[10] New digitalization opportunities emerge, as both citizens and public servants have voluntary as well as mandatory interactions with the government by means of technology and these interactions range from unstructured to highly structured one, based on the implemented technology or business processes.[11]

Digital transformation technologies in justice administration applied in civil and administrative cases are the research objects in both computer science and law. Data

[7] Kaifeng and Rho (2007).

[8] Melnyk (2009), p. 151.

[9] Lindgren et al. (2019), p. 427–436.

[10] Scholta and Lindgren (2019).

[11] Androutsopoulou (2019).

scientists[12] believe that the study of litigation using digital technologies is a borderline area between computer science, sociology, anthropology and law. A new approach to legal proceedings changes not only the civil procedure itself as a type of human activity, but also the science of data. The law acts not only as a behavioral regulator in the society, but also as a way of processing data sets. At the same time, a full trial is possible both with technology application and without it. Scientists question the possibility to transform the law so that machine learning, algorithmization and information processing will automatically replace part of the routine operations in the civil and administrative procedure.[13] And most importantly, is it applicable in democratic value systems based on the rule of law, humanism and equality of individuals.

The digitalization of litigation process raises a number of ethical and procedural problems. Thus, the dehumanization of justice deals with the aspect of its fairness a priori.[14] From the procedural paradigm view adopted in the Russian Federation, making decisions by a chat bot model as in China is not acceptable. However, the use of ASF can contribute to the further integration of justice systems in the world.[15]

Digitalization accelerates a shift in relations between people and the state that administrative justice scholars must take seriously. First, scholars must reconsider the internal perspective from which administrative justice theories assess an outcome's acceptability. Digitalization compels the development of new justice models centered on the values of system users within and outside of administrative institutions. Second, scholars must reassess administrative justice theory's procedural focus. In digitalized settings, 'administratively just' decision-making processes may generate substantively unjust outcomes.[16]

3 Digitalization of Administrative Services and Judicial Proceedings in Europe

Today, it is simply impossible to imagine our lives without information technology. A large number of modern human needs can be met thanks to the rapid development of digitalization. The needs of public administration are no exception. The introduction of e-governance is a manifestation of the digitalization of administrative services, and there is no doubt that it is necessary and relevant, as it is a requirement of the times and the next step in the development of social relations.

Digitalization is the next stage in the development of human civilization, its logical continuation. This process covers all areas of human life and aims to change

[12] Bagherian-Marandi et al. (2021).

[13] Murray and Fussey (2019).

[14] Wing et al. (2021).

[15] Velicogna et al. (2020).

[16] Raso (2021).

them for the better. The existing legal and socio-political reality is in a state of active change, which is one of the main components of the digitalization process.

Advanced digital technologies allow transforming existing and creating new business models, developing new products and services, increasing the efficiency and competitiveness of the economy, and contributing to broader social and economic development. In line with the green transition policy, they reduce the negative impact on the environment and promote sustainable development, resilience and energy efficiency.

Upon completion of the Digital Slovenia 2020 Strategy and the process of preparing the future strategy, in early 2020, a review of the implementation of the Digital Slovenia 2020 Strategy was prepared, and in March 2023, the Government of the Republic of Slovenia adopted the Digital Slovenia 2030 Strategy.

The Digital Slovenia 2030 is a response of the Government of the Republic of Slovenia to the challenges of digitalization and is intended for strategic planning to promote the digital transformation of Slovenia in the development period until 2030.

The structure of the Digital Slovenia 2030 Strategy is in line with the Digital Compass presented by the European Commission in March 2021, the relevant political program.

"The Road to the Digital Decade" until 2030, as well as the European Declaration of Digital Rights and the principles of the Digital Decade.

The National Strategic Roadmap for the Digital Decade defines the main policies, measures and activities that contribute to the achievement of the European digital goals for the next decade in Slovenia. National Strategic Roadmaps are prepared by all Member States of the European Union in order to implement the Political Agenda "The Road to the Digital Decade", which sets goals related to digital competences, digital infrastructure, digital transformation of the economy and digital public services. The roadmap also focuses on the topics of digital citizenship, empowerment, green transition and digital rights.

One of Slovenia's greatest strengths is its human capital. The knowledge required for digital transformation is already concentrated in the country. This is reflected in the high proportion of graduates in science, technology, engineering and mathematics and, in particular, in the large number of ICT start-ups (which exceeds the EU average). The Slovenian start-up community is extremely active and has close ties at the regional, European and global levels.

The Strategy for Digital Public Services until 2030 was adopted by the Government of the Republic of Slovenia in December 2022 with a vision of a digital public service focused on citizens and business entities, which ensures integrated, coordinated, secure and efficient interaction of citizens and businesses with the state. The goal is to provide convenient and easy-to-use digital services, data for better services and decision-making, and a safe, secure and inclusive digital environment.

The Informatics Development Council was established by the Government Decree at the end of January 2022 and acts as a governing body whose main objective is to promote digitalization and digital transformation in public administration and public administration-related e-services for the people of Slovenia and the economy of Slovenia. It coordinates public sector operations related to IT investments, standards, support systems and other technological developments where interoperability of systems is essential for their operation and maintenance.

The reform aims to create a legal basis for further digitalization of public services. Amendments were made to the Law on General Administrative Procedure and the Regulation on Administrative Operations, which expanded the scope of electronic procedures in administrative procedures.

The investment is aimed at improving access to justice for businesses and citizens. The investment will accelerate the further digitalization of services and the development of new IT solutions that will ensure the comprehensive exchange of information and legal documentation and facilitate the speedy resolution of court proceedings. Secure and high-quality audiovisual equipment will improve access for citizens and businesses. A system of distance learning and digitalisation of exams will be developed for the Judicial Training Centre.[17]

The target is expected to be achieved by 30 June 2026.

The Strategic Council for Digitalisation was established in April last year, and in June, it prepared the first package of measures for a modern and digital Slovenia. These are 40 very specific solutions for the digitalisation of public administration, healthcare, education, the economy and society as a whole. To implement these proposals as soon as possible, the Government Office for Digital Transformation was established in August.[18]

The Government Digital Transformation Office has also implemented other measures from the first package of the Strategic Digitalisation Council. These include an informative calculation of family benefits, a virtual box of administrative units, a mandatory electronic signature in public administration, and the promotion of co-ownership of employees of technology and other companies. We have also implemented measures to attract Slovenian and foreign experts to Slovenia, increase the coverage of ICT studies and actively co-create the European digital policy. In the healthcare sector, the first joint e-procurement, the eHealth mobile application and a public tender for e-care for the elderly were held.

To summarize, the main achievements in the digitalisation of the legal system in Romania come from: the intensive use of electronic signatures, the submission of applications to courts in electronic format, the use of electronic signatures, case studies can be scheduled online and even court hearings are held online.

Compared to other departments, such as HR, finance or IT, which have more easily adapted to change and implemented various technologies in their daily processes, transformation in the legal department is more difficult due to the sensitivity of activities and data, as well as the management of risks generated by change.

---

[17] Digitalna preobrazba javnega sektorja in javne uprave. At: https://www.gov.si/zbirke/projekti-in-programi/nacrt-za-okrevanje-in-odpornost/o-nacrtu-za-okrevanje-in-odpornost/digitalna-preobrazba/c2k7-digitalna-preobrazba-javnega-sektorja-in-javne-uprave/

[18] Digitalna preobrazba Slovenije – realiziranih več kot polovica ukrepov prvega paketa. At: https://www.gov.si/novice/2022-03-17-digitalna-preobrazba-slovenije-realiziranih-vec-kot-polovica-ukrepov-prvega-paketa/

However, we see steps and efforts by both lawyers and courts to improve this situation. In fact, according to the Consero 2020 Corporate Legal Operations report, 80% of legal leaders will focus their efforts on managing legal technology, 74% believe their current infrastructure is not up to par, and 79% expect to see increased costs when implementing specific technologies in the next 12 months.[19]

At the level of the system, for example, they resorted to sending subpoenas, other applications or documents to courts by e-mail, but only if they are accompanied by an electronic signature, according to the Decision of the HCJC No. 520/2019.

In this way, lawyers/petitioners can benefit from a tool that links their real identity to their electronic identity. Another example is the e-file, which has been introduced since the end of 2019 in most courts in major cities (e.g. Bucharest, Constanta, Iaşi, Alba Iulia, etc.). This application allows persons involved in a trial to view and download documents in electronic format from the file generated by the court. In addition, case studies can be scheduled online, and during the state of emergency, the Bucharest Court as well as the High Court of Cassation and Judicial Review took concrete steps towards digitalisation by hearing certain cases by video conference. The Romanian government has also adopted a draft law containing various measures in the field of justice, some of which are aimed at digitalizing certain activities carried out at the court level.

At the level of law firms, the technologies adopted include automation of billing and analysis of legal costs, automation of document creation, digitization of contracts, and automatic management of their terms and conditions.

A good example is the case of Deutsche Bank, which was fined $2.5 billion for manipulating the LIBOR index. The investigation involved collecting, filtering, analysing and reviewing tens of millions of electronic files, including documents, emails, chat and phone calls, to identify only the relevant evidence that was presented to the court. As the volume of electronic information grows exponentially (2.4 billion emails sent every second), digitization and partial automation of the evidence identification process is becoming a necessity, especially in criminal proceedings or as a result of Competition Council investigations.

E-discovery services are most commonly used in criminal actions or investigations conducted by authorities (Competition Council, DNA, DICOT, etc.), but they can be used in other litigation (e.g. commercial, civil) or arbitration proceedings to identify, organize and review evidence relevant to the litigation/arbitration.

The digitalisation of the Romanian judicial system covers several aspects, including both the adaptation of the system to new technologies and its users to a new way of working.[20]

For these new technologies to lead to greater efficiency, they must be accompanied by organizational change, high transparency in their use, and massive adoption of digital public services by citizens and businesses. In this area of digital administration, France already has assets with a large supply and a proactive open data policy.

---

[19] Barac and Toader (2020).

[20] Săraru (2019), p. 416.

First and foremost, and this is a key role for the state, it is important to continue efforts to make data open, comparable and accessible, while ensuring the protection of users who "provide" data. At the same time, we recommend increasing transparency in the use of these new tools and leaving room for the "crowd" to improve them. This should lead to a rethinking of the way public services are produced by encouraging the use of 'agile' methods and experimentation in public services, and by involving users in co-production through a participatory approach. Promoting a culture of experimentation should be accompanied by systematic evaluation of the economic and social performance of online services.[21]

France generally scores very well in international e-government rankings. In 2014, it was ranked first in Europe and fourth in the world (after South Korea, Australia and Singapore) according to the United Nations' E-Government Development Index (EGDI), which has been established since 2003 (E-Government Survey 2014). This composite index is based on a weighted average of standardized scores across three dimensions: the Online Services Index (OSI), digital infrastructure and human capital. France ranks first in the world in the supply component. However, this classification should be qualified, as the method of assessing dematerialized public services does not allow for the documentation of either their quality or actual use.[22]

The digitalisation of public services is a fundamental issue for the effectiveness of public action, the trust of citizens in institutions and the flexibility of administration. However, while legislation has largely developed the doctrine of digital data use in France, the burden remains and France is struggling to establish a clear legal and regulatory framework.

Digitalisation covers both the dematerialization of administrative procedures and acts, the management of citizens' digital data, and the relations between public authorities themselves.

Currently, each ministry proposes its own dematerialization program, which is sometimes not ambitious enough, especially given the proliferation of digital data in the public space. For example, as part of the Ministry of the Interior's Law on Orientation and Programming (Lopmi), the Ministry of the Interior approved the merger of the various departments within the ministry responsible for digital issues in order to optimize their work. Finally, the minister has repeatedly emphasized that half of the additional 15 billion euros allocated for Bovo Square will be spent on digitalisation of the ministry.

Just like the economic world, the legal world is undoubtedly in the process of transitioning to the digital age. The Ministry of Justice has embarked on an unprecedented digital transformation plan that will lead to profound changes in the way it operates. This transformation plan aims to make justice more accessible, faster, more efficient and more transparent. It will enable the total dematerialization of

[21] Algan et al. (2016).

[22] Cour des Comptes (2016): Relations aux usagers et modernisation de l'État: vers une généralisation des services publics numériques, janvier, https://www.ccomptes.fr/fr/publications/relations-aux-usagers-et-modernisation-de-letat.

civil and criminal proceedings. It will lead to profound changes in the information systems of penitentiary administration and judicial protection of youth.[23]

Thus, magistrates and judicial officers will have access to effective tools, exchange of views with legal professionals will be facilitated, litigants will be able to apply for legal aid and file cases online, follow their cases online, orientation of detainees will be facilitated, they will benefit from online services (canteen, education), their relatives will be able to conduct online procedures (request to visit the visiting room, send money). Minors under judicial protection of minors will be more effectively monitored.

Alongside the main projects of the Ministry (PORTALIS, Native Digital Criminal Procedure, ASTREA, DOT, NED, PARCOURS, SIVAC, etc.), other legal actors such as judges and civil servants and ministerial employees (lawyers, notaries, bailiffs, court representatives, etc.) and various private companies (legaltechs) are developing other innovative services (predictive justice or access to legal information).

All these projects use new tools, be it open data or artificial intelligence. Other concepts (GDPR, blockchain, smart contracts, etc.) that are not necessarily readily available are also emerging and are being introduced into the digital lexicon.

Finally, this digital transformation of justice and society raises various legal and societal issues, whether it is the law applicable to digital tools, the protection of fundamental rights (freedom of expression, freedom of enterprise, right to privacy, right to be forgotten, data ownership and use, copyright, etc.), or the redefinition of the judge's functions.

As of 4 January 2021, any party to a court proceeding can apply online from the justice.fr website to file applications for the protection of adults with a guardianship and civil acts judge by intervention, after having been notified to the victim.

A global program for the modernization and simplification of justice, the PORTALIS project—or justice.fr—is a vector for profound change in the organization and tools of the judicial chain.

Divided into six versions, each corresponding to a specific stage of development and an increase in the range of services, it leads to a gradual transformation of the civil chain, up to and including its end-to-end dematerialization.

Litigants can follow the progress of their civil and criminal proceedings online: they have direct access to the dates of hearings and the nature of the hearings (motion or pre-trial).

They can download various documents (summonses, notices of dismissal, notices, etc.) that were previously sent to them by simple letter.

As soon as a new notice or summons is posted online, the litigant automatically receives an email notification, and the email address does not contain any personal data. Similarly, they are reminded of hearing dates by SMS.

---

[23] La transformation numérique du Ministère de la Justice. At: https://www.justice. gouv.fr/actualites/espace-presse/plan-transformation-numerique-du-ministere-justice.

It is potentially unfair and possibly even inefficient to leave control of ODR (Online Dispute Resolution) to private companies such as Legaltechs, even if they are certified (Article 4.7 of Law No. 2019-222 of 23 March 2019 on the programming and reform of the justice system for 2018–2022). Private management is better than public management when the public interest is at stake. However, in North America, all ODR platforms failed and eventually closed, with the exception of Domain Name Dispute Processing (ICANN) and the Ebay dispute resolution site. However, according to Nicolas Vermeijs, a cyber justice specialist from Quebec, Ebay has introduced a form of guarantee that should gradually deprive the ODR platform of its interests. Private ODR platforms fail for two reasons: you cannot force a party to use them if they do not want to, and even if they agree to participate in such a settlement, they cannot be forced to do so. Ebay settled 60 million disputes because parties who did not want to use its online payment platform risked being excluded from the Ebay community, which proved to be a sufficient incentive given the size of the community. Finally, Canada is developing ODR platforms that are supported by public authorities. Parties may be required to negotiate and mediate on these platforms. Most likely, an arbitration option will be added to these functions. Approval of an online transaction can also be obtained in front of a judge. Again, it is the support of public authorities that guarantees the implementation.[24]

Administrative jurisdiction has undergone a major reform since 1953 and the establishment of administrative courts, but especially since 1987 with the creation of administrative courts of appeal and the subsequent transformation of the State Council into a true supreme court. The concomitant evolution of the way courts and tribunals are governed has fostered a global reflection on the goals of the administrative court and the way it operates. Numerous projects have been launched to improve the speed and reliability of procedures, the transparency of the administrative process and the role of the parties. All these changes have led to an improvement in the quality of administrative proceedings. Not all of them are complete. For this reason, further reforms are underway to make further progress towards the overall quality and efficiency of procedures and administrative justice in general.

One idea would be to centralize court proceedings that contain evidence in digital format, for example by creating a joint software exchange platform between the Ministry of Justice and the Ministry of Internal Affairs. One of the direct benefits of such an initiative would be the speed of processing court cases containing video evidence highlighting flagrante delicto, as evidenced by the above-mentioned study. Another direct benefit relates to the statistics of disc recording and USB storage budgets of different police stations.

Derived from Skipper, a file management application, cce allows parties to administrative proceedings to "view most of the information contained in their case online and thus know at what stage of the investigation their case is". Since 2004, this application "allows applicants and their lawyers to follow the progress of their

[24] Jeuland (2019), p. 193–199.

cases online"[25] using an access code provided at the time of registration of the application. Thus, it is a case history that is freely accessible, even to parties who are not represented by a lawyer. Although it is not possible to read the content of the documents, all events are recorded in this application: registration of the application, communication of briefs, filing of documents, notification of public hearings, transfer of the case to the cassation judge, etc.

The first effect of this program is to make the parties to the trial observers—or even censors—of the proceedings. They will be able to find out about any delays and address the court. Secondly, the application allows the parties to consult the content of the public reporter's findings. Thus, even if the parties do not know the exact content of the submissions before the hearing, consultation with Sagace allows them to prepare to respond to those submissions orally during the public hearing or in a written "notes during the discussion".

From the case law of the Council of State and the Constitutional Council, it is clear that the aims of economy and efficiency sought by the legislature and contributing to the "proper administration of justice and the proper use of public funds" are legitimate, provided that equality between applicants and the constituent elements of a fair trial are ensured.[26] However, in criminal cases, the European Court of Human Rights (ECtHR) requires that videoconference hearings meet a legitimate aim under the Convention (including "the protection of public order, the prevention of crime, the protection of the rights to life, liberty and security of witnesses and victims of crime, and the requirement of a 'reasonable time' for the trial", as long as "the manner in which they are carried out respects the rights of the defence".[27]

There are two criticisms of audiovisual hearings, at least in immigration disputes, and especially in asylum disputes. On the one hand, the asylum seeker remains in detention instead of going to court. This means that the asylum seeker is not in a neutral territory. On the other hand, videoconferencing does not allow people to face the unconscious elements of communication that only a physical meeting allows. As the former President of the Administrative Court of Appeal, Mr Patrick Mindou, has noted, "dematerialization carries the risk of dehumanizing administrative proceedings, a risk already highlighted by the written nature of the administrative procedure".

In terms of security, the administrative justice system has chosen a flexible approach. Thus, an electronic certificate is not mandatory for filing a court action. Similarly, the author of the litigation verifies the authentication of his request through a simple username and password system, and the electronic signature is difficult to use. The Administrative Court has also adopted a general position of easy access, with login and password only. There are plans to gradually increase the

[25] Stoker (2006).

[26] Conseil d'État, 23 septembre 2013, Syndicat des avocats de France, n° 360070.

[27] Conseil constitutionnel, n° 2003-484 DC, 20 novembre 2003, Loi relative à la maîtrise de l'immigration, au séjour des étrangers en France et à la nationalité, Conseil constitutionnel, n° 2011-631 DC, 9 juin 2011, Loi relative à l'immigration, à l'intégration et à la nationalité.

security of the data exchanged when using the Télérecours and Sagace applications. Nevertheless, this low level of authentication is appreciated for its simplicity.

The deployment of ICT has implications for human relations in administrative jurisdiction, initially between magistrates, but also between lawyers and court reporters. Any dematerialization leads to a modification or even loss of human relationships. For example, Teleregrey has weakened lawyers' ties with the judiciary, as opportunities to travel to court to present evidence are becoming increasingly rare. Likewise, magistrates have fewer opportunities to meet in the court library to discuss their deliberations. Information technology can create isolation for judges and a sense that they are increasingly an integrated tool, or even self-sufficient, as all the information and functions needed for the judicial function are on the desk. Similarly, some regret that Sagace can discourage lawyers from physically attending public hearings when the public rapporteur's findings go in their direction, damaging the quality of adversarial debate at the hearings.

There is a well-established idea among administrators that it is necessary to exercise the powers of public administration subjects through administrative procedures, i.e. in a procedural form. At the same time, the procedural form should hardly be considered as a category with an independent meaningful load.[28] In today's public administration, the establishment of the circumstances necessary to resolve a particular issue is simplified due to new technical capabilities for obtaining, storing and transmitting information as a result of the introduction of digital technologies (digitalisation). For example, due to the possibility of providing public administration entities with prompt access to a significant amount of data from numerous public electronic registers, and the possibility of automatic exchange of information between such registers. This leads not only to the simplification of many administrative procedures, but also to the possibility of obtaining the necessary information and resolving the relevant issue immediately upon the request of the interested person, without the participation of other entities (due to the absence of the need to contact them to establish certain circumstances) or even automatically—using software tools of information and communication systems, without human intervention.[29]

In Ukraine, the challenges of digitalization of public management and administration are reflected in a number of normative legal acts of the Cabinet of Ministers of Ukraine: in the orders "Some issues of reforming the state administration of Ukraine" dated June 24, 2016 No. 474-r, "On the approval of the Concept of the development of the electronic services system in Ukraine" dated November 16, 2016 No. 918, "On the approval of the Concept for the development of e-government in Ukraine" dated September 20, 2017 No. 649, "On the approval of the plan of measures for the implementation of the Concept for the development of the electronic services system in Ukraine for 2017–2018." dated June 14, 2017 No. 394-r, "On the approval of the Concept for the Development of the Digital Economy and

[28] Kivalov (2022).

[29] Ibid, p. 10.

Society of Ukraine for 2018–2020 and approval of the plan of measures for its implementation" dated January 17, 2018 No. 67-r; Resolutions "On approval of the Regulation on data sets subject to publication in the form of open data" dated October 21, 2015 No. 835, "Some issues of electronic interaction of state electronic information resources" dated September 8, 2016 No. 606, "Some issues of documenting management activities" dated January 17, 2018 No. 55, "Some issues of digital development" dated January 30, 2019 No. 56.[30]

The Law of Ukraine "On Amendments to Certain Legislative Acts of Ukraine Aimed at Providing Additional Social and Economic Guarantees in Connection with the Spread of Coronavirus Disease (COVID-19)"[31] of 30.03.2020 amended the procedural codes to allow court hearings to be held using the parties' own technical means outside the courtroom.

Thanks to these changes, for more than a year now, litigants have been able to participate in court hearings from the comfort of their own homes and using their own technical means. Such a procedure for holding court hearings not only allows not to violate the quarantine and self-isolation regime, but also significantly saves time for the parties to the cases, eliminates the need for business trips to other cities of Ukraine, and reduces financial costs.

On 10 March 2023, the Cabinet of Ministers submitted to the Verkhovna Rada of Ukraine Draft Law No. 9090 on Amendments to Certain Legislative Acts on Digitalisation of Court Proceedings and Improvement of the Order Proceedings in Civil Proceedings (hereinafter—Draft Law No. 9090). According to the legislator, the purpose of the amendments is to improve the system of remote proceedings and introduce new means of administering justice. In particular, the amendments relate to the possibility for judges and clerks to hold court hearings remotely outside the courtroom, as well as the possibility of questioning witnesses and experts and giving evidence online. At first glance, it does look progressive, but will the innovations be successfully implemented in practice? Let's try to understand certain aspects of the new draft law.

Draft Law No. 9090 also proposes to draft and sign court decisions, in the event of a videoconference outside the courtroom, exclusively in electronic form, without a paper copy.

We believe that the parties will not be restricted in their right to receive a paper copy of the decision if necessary. It is also interesting to note that the case may be transferred to another court in case of an appeal. We believe that we will learn these details if this draft law is adopted and these changes are implemented in practice.

An electronic cabinet is a personal cabinet (web service or other user interface) in a subsystem (module) of the Unified Judicial Information and Telecommunication System, which provides a person who has passed electronic identification with

[30] Nikolina (2020).

[31] The Law of Ukraine "On Amendments to Certain Legislative Acts of Ukraine Regarding Mandatory Registration and Use of Electronic Offices in the Unified Judicial Information and Telecommunication System or its Separate Subsystem (Module) Enabling Document Exchange". https://zakon.rada.gov.ua/laws/show/3200-20#Text.

access to information and services of the Unified Judicial Information and Telecommunication System or its separate subsystems (modules), including the possibility of exchanging (sending and receiving) documents (including procedural documents, written and electronic evidence, etc.) between the court and participants in court proceedings. Electronic identification of a person is carried out with the use of a qualified electronic signature or other means of electronic identification that allow to unambiguously identify a person (The Law of Ukraine).

Article 18 of the Code of Administrative Procedure of Ukraine stipulates that administrative courts operate the Unified Judicial Information and Telecommunication System, which ensures the exchange of documents (sending and receiving documents) in electronic form between courts, between the court and litigants, as well as recording of the court proceedings and participation of litigants in court hearings via video conference. The court sends court decisions and other procedural documents to the parties to the court proceedings to their official e-mail addresses, performs other procedural actions in electronic form using the UJITS in accordance with the procedure established by this Code, the Regulation on the Unified Judicial Information and Telecommunication System and/or provisions defining the procedure for the functioning of its individual subsystems (modules). Persons who have registered official e-mail addresses in the UJITS shall be served by the court with any documents in cases in which such persons participate exclusively in electronic form by sending them to the official e-mail addresses of such persons, which does not deprive them of the right to receive a copy of the court decision in paper form upon a separate application.

At the same time, there is still an insufficient level of detail of certain elements in the field of electronic administrative justice at the regulatory level, as well as the functioning of the "electronic court" in practice. In this regard, there is a need for further development, improvement and creation of a coherent system of legal provisions that would properly regulate all the specifics of the e-court functioning in the administrative proceedings of Ukraine.

The quintessence of the impact of digital transformations on the nature of public administration is the concept of Digital Era Governance (hereinafter—DEG), which is the successor to New Public Management and provides for more modern "digital" governance with an emphasis on "customer-oriented" integrity and digitalisation.[32] The era of digital governance means that public sector entities reflect the current challenges and rapid changes in information technology and information systems.[33]

The main problems that need to be addressed for the digitalisation process to develop and achieve its goal are: the growth of cybercrime in the context of an increase in the number of information systems that use personal data; the lack of secure exchange of identification data of individuals and legal entities processed in information systems of public authorities and the private sector, the lack of

[32] Razumei and Razumei (2020).

[33] Dunleavy et al. (2006), p. 189 et seq.

confirmation of identification data; and the use of information in registration and access control systems.

On 29 July 2019, the Verkhovna Rada established the Committee on Digital Transformation. The Committee is tasked with organizing and overseeing work in the following areas: creating a digital society in Ukraine, functioning and use of the Internet, development of programs on digital cooperation, distribution of electronic services, cybersecurity, etc. Subsequently, on 2 September 2019, the Cabinet of Ministers established the Ministry of Digital Transformation of Ukraine, which coordinates the optimization of the digitalisation system and the relevant work of public authorities. And after the Regulations on this Ministry were approved, the implementation of our country's entire state policy in the field of digitalisation began, that is, the formation of digital innovations, the economy, etc. So, to speak, the IT industry in Ukraine has begun.

The government sees digitalisation as one of the ways to fight corruption.[34] To this end, the government plans to provide citizens with the opportunity to receive 100% of public services online by 2024. The government is confident that digitalisation will be a means of restoring trust in state institutions. "Digital technologies are the basis of Ukraine's sustainable prosperity; a new world with new opportunities; a sphere that significantly affects the country's transformations to improve the lives, work, creativity, education and recreation of Ukrainians.

The accelerating digitalisation of public administration has necessarily led to the use of digital identification, which is already used by 77% of internet users to make some type of request, process or administrative management, and this percentage rises to almost 87% when it comes to people aged 24–35.

In recent years, more than 90% of Spanish public administrations have chosen corporate digitalisation projects in their departments. According to the Digital Economy and Society Index (DESI) 2020, in digital public services, Spain ranks second among the 28 countries of the European Union, two points above the 2019 index and well above the average thanks to the digital strategy implemented by the central government. It also stands out for its good results in the communications sector, ranking fifth. On the other hand, it is below the EU average in terms of human capital.

Recent legislative reforms on digitalisation, such as Law 39/2015 of 1 October on the Unified Administrative Procedure of Public Administrations and Law 40/2015 of 1 October on the Legal Regime of the Public Sector, have given impetus to the renewal of digital processes in public administration, which has reduced unit costs and processing times.

Taking into account the analyzed data, it can be said that Spain has a good starting position for the promotion of digital administration.

Digital transformation is a springboard for achieving transparency, proximity, efficiency and effectiveness of administrative procedures for citizens using the Administration's digital public services. The main goal is to bring these services to

---

[34] Cherednichenko (2021).

citizens and companies through their mobile devices with usability and accessibility features.

The evolution of society in the context of technological progress should go hand in hand with the increasing digitalisation of public administration. There are still digital procedures and public authority procedures with difficulties of access, efficiency and flexibility that do not meet the requirements and digital experience desired by users. The efficiency or digital flexibility needed to overcome the complex processes that exist today must be integrated into internal operations, in addition to external citizen operations.

4 Conclusions

In general, given the progress made, it is necessary to update regulations in the context of European integration, which involves unification of norms, consideration of the legal positions of the European Court of Human Rights and implementation of positive experience in public administration. Digitalisation of management processes creates a great potential for socio-economic development for any country. However, to fully realize this potential, it is not enough to solve the technical problems of digitalisation; instead, it is necessary to simultaneously improve the culture of doing and administering business, public administration, and overcoming corruption.

Digitalisation is an essential element of organizations in the modern world. Every year, it gives impetus to economic development, allows for the formation of a more democratic society, mechanisms to improve governance functions, make education, banking, healthcare, public services, etc. more accessible. Digitalisation is the basis for achieving prosperity in the country, improving and at the same time making life easier for citizens. However, it should be remembered that without sustainable socio-economic growth, it will be more difficult to control the digital space and avoid risks or problems. That is, first of all, information security still needs to be created and ensured.

The emergence of digital technologies and virtual space is a natural consequence of scientific and technological achievements of mankind. Today digital technologies are actively used in the field of law, in particular in law enforcement. Digital technologies and changes in social life have affected the types and forms of on the types and forms of administration of justice. Judicial proceedings as a process of administration of justice in in the context of digital culture and forced quarantine measures has responded to the challenges of by creating an electronic court and the application and use of artificial intelligence.

References

Algan Y, Bacache-Beauvallet M, Perrot A (2016) Administration numérique. Notes du conseil d'analyse économique 7(34):1–12. https://www.cairn.info/revue-notes-du-conseil-d-analyse-economique-2016-7-page-1.htm

Androutsopoulou AN (2019) Transforming the communication between citizens and government through AI-guided chatbots. Gov Inf Q 36(2):358–367

Bagherian-Marandi N, Ravanshadnia M, Akbarzadeh T (2021) Two-layered fuzzy logic-based model for predicting court decisions in construction contract disputes. Artif Intell Law 29(4):453–484. https://doi.org/10.1007/s10506-021-09281-9

Barac A, Toader O (2020) Nevoia de digitalizare în sistemul judiciar din România. Universul Juridic. https://www.universuljuridic.ro/

Cherednichenko NS (2021) Digitalisation of public administration. https://conf.ztu.edu.ua/wp-content/uploads/2021/01/354.pdf

Cour des Comptes (2016) Relations aux usagers et modernisation de l'État: vers une généralisation des services publics numériques, janvier. https://www.ccomptes.fr/fr/publications/relations-aux-usagers-et-modernisation-de-letat

Daly P, Raso J, Tomlinson J (2021) Administrative Law in the Digital World. Forthcoming in Harlow C (ed) Research Handbook on Administrative Law. Edward Elgar, Aldershot. Available at SSRN: https://ssrn.com/abstract=4008531

De Abreu JC (2019) The role of artificial intelligence in the European e-justice paradigm – Suiting effective judicial protection demands. PoLaR Portuguese Law J 2(1):3–48

Digitalna preobrazba javnega sektorja in javne uprave. https://www.gov.si/zbirke/projekti-in-programi/nacrt-za-okrevanje-in-odpornost/o-nacrtu-za-okrevanje-in-odpornost/digitalna-preobrazba/c2k7-digitalna-preobrazba-javnega-se ktorja-in-jav ne-uprave/

Digitalna preobrazba Slovenije – realiziranih več kot polovica ukrepov prvega paketa. https://www.gov.si/novice/2022-03-17-digitalna-preobrazba-slovenije-realiziranih-vec-kot-polovica-ukrepov-prvega-paketa/

Dunleavy P, Margetts H, Bastow S, Tinkler J (2006) Digital era governance: IT corporations, the state and e-government. Oxford University Press, Oxford

Jeuland E (2019) Justice numérique, justice inique? Les Cahiers de la Justice 2(2):193–199

Jneid M, Saleh I, Fakhoury R (2019) Digital transformation in justice: discussion of challenges and a conceptual model for e-justice success. In: Kaya T (ed) Proceedings of the European Conference on e-Government. Cyprus International University, pp 35–42

Kaifeng Y, Rho S-Y (2007) E-government for better performance: promises, realities, and challenges. Int J Public Adm 30(11):1197–1217. https://doi.org/10.1080/01900690701225556

Kivalov SV (2022) Regarding the systematicity of administrative and legal thinking in the conditions of the development of digitalization vectors of governance [Shchodo systemnosti administratyvno-pravovoho myslennia v umovakh rozvytku tsyfrovizatsiinykh vektoriv vriaduvannia]. In: Kivalov SV, Bila-Tiunova LR, Latkovska TA et al (eds) Administrative science in conditions of digitalization: theory, legal regulation, practice [Administratyvistyka v umovakh tsyfrovizatsii: teoriia, pravove rehuliuvannia, praktyka]. Helvetyka, Odesa, pp 5–42

La transformation numérique du Ministère de la Justice. https://www.justice. gouv.fr/actualites/espace-presse/plan-transformation-numerique-du-ministere-justice

Lindgren I, Østergaard Madsen C, Hofmannc S, Melin U (2019) Close encounters of the digital kind: a research agenda for the digitalization of public services. Gov Inf Q 36(3):427–436

Lupo G (2019) Assessing e-justice smartness: a new framework for e-justice evaluation through public values. In: Rodriguez BM (ed) Setting foundations for the creation of public value in smart cities. Public Administration and Information Technology, vol 35. Springer, pp 77–113

Melnyk AF (2009) Public administration: textbook. Znannya, Kyiv

Murray D, Fussey P (2019) Bulk surveillance in the digital age: Rethinking the Human Rights Law approach to bulk monitoring of communications data. Israel Law Rev 52(1):31–60. https://doi.org/10.1017/S0021223718000304

Nikolina II (2020) Analysing the trend of digital transformation of public management and administration in Ukraine. http://www.pag-journal.iei.od.ua/archives/2020/19-2020/12.pdf
Raso J (2021) Implementing digitalization in an administrative justice context. Oxford Handbook of Administrative Justice. Available at SSRN: https://ssrn.com/abstract=3821117
Razumei HY, Razumei MM (2020) Digitalisation of public administration as a component of digital transformation of Ukraine. Public Adm Custom Adm 2(25):139–145
Săraru CS (2019) Contenciosul administrativ român. CH Beck, Bucharest
Scholta H, Lindgren I (2019) The long and winding road of digital public services – one next step: proactivity. Fortieth International Conference on Information Systems, Munich. https://www.researchgate.net/publication/338775455_The_Long_and_Winding_Road_of_Digital_Public_Services-One_Next_Step_Proactivity
Stoker G (2006) Public value management: a new narrative for networked governance? Am Rev Public Adm 36(1):41–57
The Law of Ukraine "On Amendments to Certain Legislative Acts of Ukraine Regarding Mandatory Registration and Use of Electronic Offices in the Unified Judicial Information and Telecommunication System or its Separate Subsystem (Module) Enabling Document Exchange". https://zakon.rada.gov.ua/laws/show/3200-20#Text
Velicogna M, Steigenga E, Taal S, Schmidt A (2020) Connecting EU jurisdictions: exploring how to open justice across member states through ICT. Soc Sci Comput Rev 38(3):274–294. https://doi.org/10.1177/0894439318786
Wing L, Martinez J, Katsh E, Rule C (2021) Designing ethical online dispute resolution systems: the rise of the fourth party. Negot J 37(1):49–64. https://doi.org/10.1111/nejo.12350

Human Resources and Cooperative Structures in the Global Economy

The Power of Scale: How European Large Corporations' HR Practices Drive Global Workforce Standards

Dana Volosevici

Abstract The study aims to explore the potential of major European corporations to establish a global minimum standard for employee rights, thereby enhancing employee protection and promoting European values related to labour rights and human dignity. In the initial stage, the research identifies the key pillars of employee protection as defined by European legislation and policies, with a focus on the most relevant legal provisions and principles. The second stage involves a detailed analysis of the sustainability reports published by major European corporations, with an emphasis on identifying global initiatives that establish minimum employee protection standards, regardless of the national legal frameworks governing these employees. By comparing the findings from these two stages, the study evaluates the extent to which these corporations influence the global promotion of essential labour rights. The research highlights how corporate social responsibility and sustainability practices enable European corporations to contribute to the creation of safer, more equitable work environments. In doing so, these corporations play a pivotal role in aligning global labour practices with European values, including respect for human dignity, equity, and transparency, demonstrating the potential for European principles to shape labour standards worldwide.

1 Introduction

The overall development of society, combined with the growing commitment of companies to social responsibility and sustainable development, has resulted in a decreasing tolerance for inequalities in general and, more specifically, those that

D. Volosevici (✉)
Petroleum Gas University of Ploiesti, Ploiesti, Romania
e-mail: dana.volosevici@upg-ploiesti.ro

C.-S. Săraru, C. E. Popa Tache (eds.), *AI, Sustainability and Solidarity in Advancing European Values in a Globalized Age*, European Union and its Neighbours in a Globalized World 28, https://doi.org/10.1007/978-3-032-06508-7_12

characterize employment relationships.[1] These employment-related inequalities manifest both within organizations, among different categories of workers, and externally, at local and global scales, particularly when a company operates with a complex structure comprising various divisions and/or subsidiaries.[2] In such cases, the causes of inequality are multifaceted and primarily relate to national legislation, the historical development characteristics of the state or region in question, and local traditions. Differences in the legal framework and quality of life among various workers worldwide have become increasingly visible due to the trend toward regional unification of employee status, creating broad areas of status uniformity where countries develop along similar principles and timelines for implementing reforms. For instance, within the European Union, social policy—primarily based on Articles 151-161 of the TFEU,[3] as well as Title IV "Solidarity" of the Charter of Fundamental Rights of the European Union[4]—promotes high employment levels, adequate protection of working conditions, equal opportunities and treatment for men and women, and the fight against social exclusion. EU Member States develop their national labor relations policies under the influence of European social policy, or, in some areas under EU competence, in accordance with European regulations. Thus, Europe, with its 27 Member States, becomes a geographic space with shared social values, influencing how companies, particularly large ones, shape their actions in relation to society and its components.[5]

Regarding companies' approach to non-commercial or non-profit aspects of their activities, after a period during which corporate social responsibility (CSR) was primarily analysed theoretically,[6] companies began, from the 1980s onwards, to integrate CSR into operational management[7] to address the needs and interests of specific groups with whom they maintained close relationships—such as shareholders, employees, and consumers—collectively referred to as 'stakeholders'. The 1990s, characterized by the globalization of corporate operations, introduced new dimensions to the concept of CSR. During this period, companies, acting both as economic players and employers, operated in markets with diverse or poorly regulated legal frameworks, where the presence of a powerful economic actor could exert significant economic, social, and even political influence.[8] Over time, a body of literature on moral capitalism emerged, often critiquing efforts to incorporate

[1] For an in-depth analysis of social inequalities and their causes, see: Piketty (2014).

[2] Davies and Markusen (2021).

[3] Treaty on the Functioning of the European Union (TFEU). Official Journal of the European Union C 326, October 26, 2012.

[4] Charter of Fundamental Rights of the European Union. Official Journal of the European Union C 326, October 26, 2012.

[5] For specific analyses, see, for example: Ratti and Garcia-Muñoz (2022); Zaccaria (2020).

[6] For a detailed analysis of the chronological development, see: Latapí Agudelo et al. (2019).

[7] Jones (1980); Carroll (2008).

[8] Carroll (2015).

ethical considerations into managerial decisions that, undeniably, are primarily aimed at profit generation.[9]

A new phase in corporate responsibility emerged as sustainability became a key objective of public policy. The integration of sustainability into public policies gained global momentum following the 1992 United Nations Conference on Environment and Development in Rio de Janeiro, which underscored the importance of sustainable development and environmental protection as integral components of global economic and social policies.[10] Through Agenda 21, adopted in Rio, governments were encouraged to integrate sustainable development principles into all political decisions, emphasizing the importance of cooperation among the public and private sectors and civil society to achieve sustainable goals. Subsequent initiatives, including the United Nations Sustainable Development Goals (SDGs) adopted in 2015, have continued to encourage governments to integrate sustainability across all levels of governance and administration. These goals provide a global framework to address issues such as poverty, inequality, climate change, environmental degradation, prosperity, peace, and justice by 2030. The European Union has also been a leader in promoting sustainability legislation and policies, integrating environmental and social objectives into many of its economic and structural policies, exemplified by strategies such as the European Green Deal.

To address increasing social and environmental challenges, the EU adopted the Non-Financial Reporting Directive (NFR) in 2014, which established minimum legal requirements and sought to standardize non-financial reporting across Member States. Building on this foundation, the Corporate Sustainability Reporting Directive (Directive (EU) 2022/2464, or CSRD) represents a significant advancement, requiring companies to include detailed reports on environmental, social, and governance (ESG) aspects in their annual management reports. The directive mandates comprehensive disclosure, covering key EU environmental objectives, such as climate change mitigation and adaptation, sustainable water and marine resource management, the transition to a circular economy, pollution control, and biodiversity conservation. Reporting also addresses areas related to company strategy, due diligence practices, value chain management, and policies on human rights, working conditions, social dialogue, fair wages, health and safety standards, social protection, and other social issues.

By 2025, the CSRD will apply to all large limited liability companies in Europe, including those that are subsidiaries of non-EU entities. Reporting obligations will gradually expand to include listed small and medium-sized enterprises (SMEs) and non-EU companies with significant operations in the EU. Furthermore, voluntary standards are being developed for unlisted SMEs, reflecting the directive's comprehensive approach to promoting transparency and accountability in corporate sustainability practices across Europe.

---

[9] Boltanski and Chiapello (2011); Salmon (2009).

[10] For an in-depth analysis: Clémençon (2012); Mensah and Casadevall (2019).

Considering the evolution of public policies and the redefinition of corporate objectives to include social responsibility aspects, this study aims to examine whether firms headquartered in the European Union can contribute to establishing a minimum standard for employees worldwide, thereby enhancing employee protection and promoting the global dissemination of European values related to human and employee rights. The analysis will focus on three of the largest corporations based in the European Union:[11] Novo Nordisk, LVMH, and SAP.

In the first phase of the research, we will identify the primary axes of employee protection as established by EU legislation and soft law instruments. In the second phase, we will examine the sustainability reports of the selected corporations to identify actions undertaken on a global scale to establish, irrespective of national laws or practices, a minimum framework of protection for non-EU workers. Finally, by comparing the findings from these two phases, we aim to evaluate the role of corporations in extending and globalizing rights that, within the European Union, are considered fundamental at the current stage of labour relations regulation.

2 The Employee Protection Framework at the EU Level

The European Union's legislative intervention in employee protection is grounded in solid legal foundations, primarily outlined in the Treaty on the Functioning of the European Union (TFEU) and the Charter of Fundamental Rights of the European Union. Each provides distinct rationales and bases for the directives and regulations adopted. In the following, we will present a brief overview of EU competencies to highlight the complexity of this framework and the significance the EU attaches to this domain.[12]

A central pillar of the EU's legislative intervention is Article 153 TFEU, which grants the Union competence to support and supplement Member States' measures in areas such as improving working conditions, protecting workers' health and safety, and ensuring employee consultation and information. Based on Article 153, essential directives have been adopted, including Directive 2003/88/EC on the organization of working time, which limits working hours to 48 h/week and establishes the right to paid annual leave. Another key directive within this framework is Directive 89/391/EEC on occupational health and safety, which requires employers to conduct risk assessments and implement preventive measures to safeguard employees' safety and health. These directives underscore the EU's commitment to creating a fair and safe working environment as an essential element of its broader social objectives.

[11] Finance Charts, Biggest Companies in Europe by Market Cap for November 2024, available at: https://www.financecharts.com/screener/biggest-country-europe

[12] Barnard (2021).

Supporting this legislative approach is Article 151 TFEU, which establishes the Union's social objectives, including promoting employment, improving living and working conditions, and ensuring adequate social protection. Although Article 151 does not confer direct legislative competence, it provides a normative and political foundation for developing a coherent and uniform social regulatory framework across the Union. For example, Directive 2019/1158 on work-life balance for parents and carers, which promotes parental leave and similar rights, reflects the objectives outlined in Article 151 by supporting employees' professional integration without compromising family responsibilities.

Another significant dimension of EU labour legislation arises from Article 45 TFEU, which guarantees the free movement of workers within the Union. This provision grants the EU competence to adopt regulations ensuring the social rights of employees who move between Member States. Under this article, measures such as Regulation (EC) No 883/2004 on the coordination of social security systems have been enacted to guarantee the continuity of social security rights for mobile workers, ensuring their protection regardless of their place of employment. Thus, Article 45 not only facilitates labour mobility but also strengthens economic and social integration within the EU.

Although employment remains an area where the EU holds limited coordination competencies and cannot legislate for full harmonization, it provides a vital platform for improving labour standards governance. Article 148 TFEU outlines the framework for the European Employment Strategy, establishing steps for implementing an interactive strategy to support employment across the Union. Meanwhile, Article 149 TFEU allows the EU to adopt incentive measures, using the ordinary legislative procedure, to encourage Member State cooperation and support their employment initiatives.

In addition to treaty provisions, the Charter of Fundamental Rights of the European Union, which holds legal force equal to the treaties, offers further legislative support for employee protection. Article 31 of the Charter enshrines the right to fair and just working conditions, while Article 30 provides protection against unjustified dismissal. These provisions serve as a basis for legislative measures, such as Directive 98/59/EC on collective redundancies, which mandates prior consultation and notification in restructuring cases. Similarly, Directive 2008/94/EC on employee protection in the event of employer insolvency ensures the protection of employees when employers are unable to meet their financial obligations, thereby reinforcing fundamental rights.

The flexibility clause under Article 352 TFEU grants the Council the authority to adopt measures necessary for achieving the Union's objectives in cases where no explicit legal basis exists within the treaties. This clause has occasionally been used to implement additional social protections, extending worker rights when other treaty articles are insufficient. For instance, the Council Recommendation on access to social protection for workers and self-employed individuals,[13] urges Member States to provide adequate social protection and establish minimum standards for all workers and self-employed individuals.

The European Pillar of Social Rights, proclaimed in Gothenburg on November 17, 2017,[14] establishes essential principles and rights to support EU citizens in various professional and personal aspects of life. The document emphasizes working conditions, social protection, and inclusion while addressing contemporary challenges such as digitalization, demographic shifts, and the diversification of work forms. Although not directly legally enforceable, the European Pillar of Social Rights informs subsequent EU legislation and initiatives and integrates into the coordination and oversight processes of the European Semester, which monitors Member States' economic and social policies.

Under the competencies described above, the European Union has developed a comprehensive framework for employee rights protection, integrating various directives into the national legislations of Member States. This framework addresses key areas of workers' rights, ensuring uniform protection across the Union. One such area concerns transparency and predictability in working conditions. Directive (EU) 2019/1152[15] obliges employers to provide essential information about working conditions in a clear and understandable manner as soon as possible after hiring. This directive enhances workers' awareness of their rights and obligations, requiring disclosure of aspects such as probation periods, work schedules, remuneration, termination procedures, and employer-provided training. Furthermore, it establishes minimum standards to protect workers in atypical employment arrangements, thereby addressing their vulnerability.

The EU has also established standards for working conditions, including rules on maximum working hours, rest periods, and paid annual leave. Thus, the Working Time Directive[16] limits working hours to a maximum of 48 h/week, allows for reference periods, and mandates minimum rest periods. It also enshrines the right to paid annual leave, promoting employee well-being and enabling a balance between professional and personal life. To further promote work-life balance, the EU establishes minimum standards for key aspects such as maternity leave,[17] paternity leave, parental leave, and carers' leave, and establishes additional rights, such as the right

[13] Council Recommendation of 8 November 2019 on access to social protection for workers and the self-employed (2019/C 387/01). Official Journal of the European Union C 387/1, November 15, 2019.

[14] European Pillar of Social Rights, proclaimed in Gothenburg on November 17, 2017.

[15] Directive (EU) 2019/1152 of the European Parliament and of the Council of 20 June 2019 on transparent and predictable working conditions in the European Union. Official Journal of the European Union L 186/105, July 11, 2019.

[16] Directive 2003/88/EC of the European Parliament and of the Council of 4 November 2003 concerning certain aspects of the organization of working time. Official Journal of the European Union L 299, November 18, 2003, pp. 9–19.

[17] Council Directive 92/85/EEC of 19 October 1992 on the introduction of measures to encourage improvements in the safety and health at work of pregnant workers and workers who have recently given birth or are breastfeeding [tenth individual Directive within the meaning of Article 16(1) of

to request flexible work arrangements.[18] Furthermore, Directive 2006/54 ensures legal protection for employees on maternity, paternity, or adoption leave. These employees are entitled to return to their previous position or an equivalent one under conditions no less favourable than before their leave. They are also entitled to any improvements in working conditions that would have applied during their absence and are safeguarded against dismissal for reasons related to maternity, paternity, or adoption leave.

A cornerstone of the European Union's employee protection framework is its commitment to the principles of equality and non-discrimination. This commitment is reflected in two main categories of directives. The first encompasses directives on equal treatment, such as Directive 2000/78/EC,[19] which establishes a general framework for addressing discrimination in employment based on religion or belief, disability, age, or sexual orientation. The second category focuses on gender-specific directives, aimed at ensuring equitable conditions for men and women. Notably, Directive 2006/54/EC[20] governs equal opportunities and treatment between men and women in employment and working conditions, reinforcing the right to equal pay for equal work and safeguarding against gender-based discrimination.[21]

Ensuring health and safety at work is a fundamental pillar of the EU's employee protection framework, establishing minimum requirements to secure a safe and healthy working environment. This framework extends beyond physical safety to address mental health and ergonomic risks, requiring employers to adopt a comprehensive approach to employee well-being by tackling a broad spectrum of workplace hazards.

The EU's strategic action framework for health and safety focuses on three key transversal objectives: enhancing accident and disease prevention at work, anticipating and managing changes in the evolving workplace driven by green, digital, and demographic transitions, and strengthening preparedness for potential future health crises. A crucial element in achieving these objectives is social dialogue, which serves as a cornerstone for regulating labour relations at the European level and fostering cooperation between employers and workers.

Directive 89/391/EEC]. Official Journal of the European Union L 348, November 28, 1992, pp. 1–7.

[18] Directive (EU) 2019/1158 of the European Parliament and of the Council of 20 June 2019 on work-life balance for parents and carers and repealing Council Directive 2010/18/EU. Official Journal of the European Union L 188, July 12, 2019, pp. 79–93.

[19] Council Directive 2000/78/EC of 27 November 2000 establishing a general framework for equal treatment in employment and occupation. Official Journal of the European Union L 303, December 2, 2000, pp. 16–22.

[20] Directive 2006/54/EC of the European Parliament and of the Council of 5 July 2006 on the implementation of the principle of equal opportunities and equal treatment of men and women in matters of employment and occupation. Official Journal of the European Union L 204, July 26, 2006, pp. 23–36.

[21] For an analysis on the employment gender gap, see: Isbășoiu et al. (2024).

Directive 2002/14/EC[22] establishes the fundamental right of workers to be informed and consulted in all enterprises within the European Union, providing a general framework applicable regardless of an organization's size. The directive obliges employers to conduct consultations prior to implementing significant organizational changes, such as structural adjustments or economic restructuring. To enhance employee involvement in multinational enterprises, where decision-making is often complex due to organizational structures, Directive 2009/38/EC[23] stablishes mechanisms for transnational employee representation. It mandates the creation of European Works Councils in multinational companies, serving as bodies for consultation and information exchange. These councils ensure employees actively participate in strategic decision-making processes that have a substantial impact on the workforce, particularly in cross-border contexts. By fostering cooperation and transparency at the transnational level, this directive ensures employees are systematically informed and consulted on economic developments and the company's strategic decisions, reinforcing their role in shaping organizational outcomes.

Furthermore, procedures for information and consultation establish an equitable and stable legal framework for restructuring and termination of employment. Directive 98/59/EC,[24] concerning collective redundancies, requires employers to provide detailed information, including the reasons for redundancies, the number and categories of affected employees, the criteria used for selecting employees to be laid off, and the measures proposed to mitigate social consequences. The directive aims to ensure that employees can participate meaningfully in the decision-making process, thereby reducing the adverse impacts of redundancies on the workforce.

Supplementing this framework, Directive 2008/94/EC[25] on employee protection in the event of employer insolvency ensures the safeguarding of unpaid wages and outstanding benefits for employees affected by employer bankruptcy. The directive obliges Member States to establish guarantee institutions or funds to cover unpaid wages for a specified period, thereby shielding employees from financial losses that could adversely affect their quality of life.

[22] Directive 2002/14/EC of the European Parliament and of the Council of 11 March 2002 establishing a general framework for informing and consulting employees in the European Community. Official Journal of the European Union L 80, March 23, 2002, pp. 29–34.

[23] Directive 2009/38/EC of the European Parliament and of the Council of 6 May 2009 on the establishment of a European Works Council or a procedure in Community-scale undertakings and Community-scale groups of undertakings for the purposes of informing and consulting employees. Official Journal of the European Union L 122, May 16, 2009, pp. 28–44.

[24] Council Directive 98/59/EC of 20 July 1998 on the approximation of the laws of the Member States relating to collective redundancies. Official Journal of the European Union L 225, August 12, 1998, pp. 16–21.

[25] Directive 2008/94/EC of the European Parliament and of the Council of 22 October 2008 on the protection of employees in the event of the insolvency of their employer. Official Journal of the European Union L 283, October 28, 2008, pp. 36–42.

In the context of contemporary digital challenges, the employee protection system, as implemented through the GDPR[26] and AI Act,[27] plays a critical role. The GDPR mandates employers to adhere to principles of legality, transparency, and data minimization, restricting the collection and use of employee data to legitimate employment purposes. It also grants employees rights to access, request rectification, and seek deletion of their data, thereby enhancing their control over personal information and mitigating risks associated with excessive monitoring or unjustified data processing.

Building on these protections, the AI Act introduces additional safeguards for the use of artificial intelligence systems in the workplace. Adopting a risk-based approach, the AI Act classifies AI systems used in employment relationships as "high-risk" and imposes stringent requirements for transparency, accuracy, and reliability.

This framework aims to prevent the misuse of AI in monitoring, evaluation, or automated decision-making processes related to employee selection, assessment, and promotion—practices already subject to GDPR oversight.[28] By ensuring transparency and accountability in automated systems, the AI Act minimizes discrimination risks and guarantees fair treatment for employees in the context of advanced technologies.

This overview of the primary regulatory areas for the protection of European workers highlights the European Union's enduring commitment to fostering a legal framework that is both flexible and adaptable. Such a framework is designed to address evolving challenges in the labour market and respond to broader societal transformations. At its core, EU labour legislation seeks not only to safeguard the fundamental rights of workers but also to remain attuned to economic and technological developments. This dual objective ensures the creation of a labour market that is both competitive and inclusive.[29]

EU regulations strike a careful balance between protecting the rights of individual workers and addressing the operational needs of employers. They safeguard essential elements such as job security and wage rights, while simultaneously preserving labour market flexibility to accommodate the diverse economic realities of

[26] Regulation (EU) 2016/679 of the European Parliament and of the Council of 27 April 2016 on the protection of natural persons with regard to the processing of personal data and on the free movement of such data, and repealing Directive 95/46/EC (General Data Protection Regulation) (Text with EEA relevance). Official Journal of the European Union L 119, May 4, 2016, pp. 1–88.

[27] Regulation (EU) 2024/1689 of the European Parliament and of the Council of 13 June 2024 laying down harmonized rules on artificial intelligence and amending Regulations (EC) No 300/2008, (EU) No 167/2013, (EU) No 168/2013, (EU) 2018/858, (EU) 2018/1139 and (EU) 2019/2144, and Directives 2014/90/EU, (EU) 2016/797, and (EU) 2020/1828 (Artificial Intelligence Act) (Text with EEA relevance). Official Journal of the European Union L 2024/1689, July 12, 2024.

[28] See, for example, the case of Amazon and the fine imposed by the French data protection authority: https://www.cnil.fr/en/employee-monitoring-cnil-fined-amazon-france-logistique-eu32-million

[29] Garben (2020).

Member States. By doing so, the EU facilitates a labour market environment that is resilient yet fair, fostering equitable working conditions across its jurisdictions.

Moreover, these regulations embody the EU's broader goal of promoting upward social convergence—a process aimed at harmonizing labour standards and social protections at a high level across Member States. This convergence strengthens the EU's shared foundation of workers' rights, reducing disparities while ensuring that economic competitiveness does not come at the expense of social protections. By continually refining this legal framework, the EU underscores its dedication to fostering cohesion, equality, and a robust labour market capable of addressing future challenges.

3 Practices of EU Multinational Corporations and Employee Rights on a Global Scale

The most significant national corporations headquartered in the European Union include Novo Nordisk, LVMH, and SAP. Headquartered in Bagsværd, Denmark, Novo Nordisk[30] is a leading pharmaceutical company specializing in diabetes care. In 2023, Novo Nordisk surpassed LVMH to become Europe's most valuable company, highlighting its substantial economic impact.[31] Based in Paris, France, LVMH (Moët Hennessy Louis Vuitton)[32] is a multinational conglomerate specializing in luxury goods, including fashion, jewelry, and wines. It has been a dominant force in the luxury market, with a diverse portfolio of prestigious brands. Headquartered in Walldorf, Germany, SAP[33] is a global leader in enterprise software solutions, providing applications and services for business operations and customer relations. It has played a pivotal role in the digital transformation of businesses worldwide, offering innovative solutions that enhance operational efficiency. SAP's collaboration with companies like Novo Nordisk underscores its influence in the technology sector. These corporations not only represent significant economic entities within the EU but also have substantial global influence, making them pertinent subjects for analyzing corporate social responsibility and the establishment of global employment standards.

This analysis is not intended to be exhaustive; its primary objective is to examine how these corporations approach employee rights. Specifically, the aim is to determine whether the rights of employees in subsidiaries are strictly aligned with the national legislation applicable to each subsidiary or, alternatively, if minimum

---

[30] https://www.novonordisk.com

[31] For further financial information, see https://www.nasdaq.com/articles/novo-nordisk-surpasses-lvmh-to-claim-europes-most-valuable-company-title

[32] https://www.lvmh.com/en

[33] https://www.sap.com

protection standards are established at the corporate level and uniformly applied across all subsidiaries, irrespective of the legal framework in each country.

Novo Nordisk employs over 69,000 individuals worldwide, operating production facilities in nine countries: Algeria, Brazil, China, Denmark, France, Iran, Japan, Russia, and the United States. Additionally, the company maintains ten research and development centers across five countries: China, Denmark, India, the United Kingdom, and the United States.

Since 1996, Novo Nordisk has operated under 'The Novo Nordisk Way',[34] a set of core principles that function as both an ethical and managerial code, ensuring consistency in decision-making and actions across its global operations. Structured around 'The 10 Essentials', this framework encompasses critical aspects such as patient-centered care, a commitment to setting and achieving high standards, and accountability for financial, social, and environmental performance. It also prioritizes innovation and curiosity to benefit patients and society. The principles further emphasize building strong stakeholder relationships, respecting diversity, fostering a healthy work environment, and promoting agility and simplicity in operations. Additionally, Novo Nordisk maintains a steadfast focus on uncompromising quality and ethical conduct, which underpins its global approach to corporate responsibility.

The Labour Code of Conduct[35] serves as a practical extension of the principles outlined in 'The Novo Nordisk Way,' offering a concrete framework to establish a safe, fair, and ethical work environment. It translates the overarching values of 'The Novo Nordisk Way' into actionable policies and practices, ensuring that the company's principles are consistently applied across all aspects of employee relations.

The Code addresses a wide range of critical issues, including working hours and rest periods, wages, personal data protection, prevention of discrimination and harassment, the right to free association, and accessible grievance mechanisms. By operationalizing these principles, the Labour Code of Conduct reinforces Novo Nordisk's commitment to fostering equitable and respectful workplace conditions worldwide.

The Novo Nordisk Labour Code of Conduct embodies the company's voluntary commitment to providing a minimum standard of protection for employee rights, regardless of national legal requirements. Where discrepancies arise between national law and the Code, the higher standard is applied to ensure a consistent level of employee welfare.

In the area of working hours, the Code establishes a uniform corporate standard that limits regular working hours to 48 h/week, excluding overtime, in cases where no stricter national laws or collective agreements exist. Pre-agreed overtime is permitted up to a maximum of 12 additional hours per week, resulting in a total of 60 h. This limitation, aimed at safeguarding employees' health, is mandatory even in

---

[34] For more information, see: Morsing and Oswald D (2009); Dey and Burns (2010); Rendtorff (2018); Sarafinovska and Qiu (2021).

[35] Available at: https://www.novonordisk.com/content/dam/nncorp/global/en/sustainable-business/pdfs/esg-portal/labour-code-of-conduct-2023.pdf

jurisdictions where national legislation does not impose such restrictions. Additionally, the Code ensures that performance targets are achievable within standard working hours, thereby preventing undue pressure on employees to work overtime. This approach effectively harmonizes workload expectations across all subsidiaries, promoting equity in working conditions. Compensation for overtime is also guaranteed at a minimum of 125% of the base salary, except where national laws or collective agreements provide more favorable terms.

Parental leave represents another area where Novo Nordisk has committed to establishing uniform standards. All employees who give birth are entitled to at least 14 weeks of leave, while non-birthing parents receive a minimum of 8 weeks following the birth or adoption of a child. Both parents may request additional unpaid leave beyond the minimum period, subject to operational requirements. Aligning with Directive 2006/54, the Code prohibits terminating the employment of any employee during parental leave for reasons related to pregnancy, childbirth, adoption, or their consequences. Upon returning to work, employees must be reinstated in their previous or an equivalent position, with no reduction in salary or benefits.

In matters of personal data protection, the Code incorporates the principles of Article 5 of the GDPR, ensuring compliance with EU standards while respecting employees' rights as data subjects. Access to confidential management information is restricted and may vary depending on national legislation. Special categories of data, including union membership and health-related information, are treated with additional sensitivity, and practices such as pregnancy testing during recruitment or employment are expressly prohibited.

The principles of equality, harassment, and non-discrimination are central to the Code. It explicitly prohibits all forms of abuse or discrimination and underscores the company's commitment to fostering a respectful and inclusive workplace. This commitment extends to providing employees with adequate training and development opportunities, ensuring they have the skills and resources necessary to fulfill their roles effectively.

Social dialogue is also a fundamental aspect of the Code, recognizing the right of employees to engage in discussions about workplace issues, even in the absence of union representation. In jurisdictions where collective bargaining or freedom of association is restricted, the company commits to supporting alternative mechanisms for protecting labour rights and refrains from influencing or controlling such initiatives. This aligns with Article 27 of the Charter of Fundamental Rights of the European Union, which enshrines the right of workers to information and consultation, ensuring that this value is upheld across all Novo Nordisk operations.

However, the Code does defer to national regulations in certain areas, limiting the standardization of employee rights. Matters such as remuneration, annual leave, sick leave, family leave, public holidays, and occupational disease or injury provisions remain governed by national laws. Employee wages and benefits must, at a minimum, exceed the higher of the national living wage, statutory minimum wage, industry benchmarks, or collectively negotiated wages.

The Code demonstrates that Novo Nordisk employees benefit from a superior level of protection, voluntarily provided by the employer and aligned with the principles promoted by EU directives. This approach reflects a proactive commitment to fostering equitable and sustainable working conditions, transcending legal obligations and embedding European values into the company's global operations.

The question that arises is whether Novo Nordisk can be regarded as a representative model for European corporations in advancing values and practices consistent with EU directives on social responsibility, employee protection, and sustainability.

The answer to this question is nuanced. As will be demonstrated in the following analysis, the other two corporations examined—LVMH and SAP—while publishing extensive sustainability reports, have not voluntarily adopted a labour code of conduct or entered into a transnational labour contract. Although these corporations extend rights to their employees on a global scale, their approach appears less structured and systematic when compared to Novo Nordisk.

In 2023, LVMH reported a workforce of over 213,000 employees operating across 81 countries. While fully embracing global sustainability goals, the company's Code of Conduct[36] and 2023 Sustainability Report,[37] reveal a commitment that is primarily grounded in adherence to international standards, conventions, and initiatives, rather than the establishment of proprietary labour standards.

For example, in 2019, LVMH signed the United Nations Standards of Conduct for Business, demonstrating its dedication to combating discrimination against LGBTI+ individuals in the workplace. This commitment was further reinforced in 2021 when LVMH joined the International Labour Organization's (ILO) Global Business and Disability Network, signing its charter to advance workplace inclusion for individuals with disabilities. In February 2023, LVMH expanded its efforts by committing to the "Working with Cancer" initiative, the first global coalition of companies aimed at creating a supportive and inclusive workplace culture for employees affected by cancer. Launched by Publicis Groupe, this initiative seeks to eliminate the stigma and insecurity associated with cancer in the workplace, encouraging companies to foster environments where employees diagnosed with cancer feel supported and empowered during their recovery.

These actions highlight LVMH's alignment with prominent international standards, emphasizing inclusivity, diversity, and workplace dignity. However, its approach relies on external frameworks and global partnerships rather than the development of a comprehensive internal labour code tailored to its unique corporate identity.

Nevertheless, several LVMH programs contribute to advancing EU labour policies within the corporation. One prominent initiative is EllesVMH, launched in 2007 to promote gender equality and support the professional development of women across all organizational levels. This program aims to achieve equitable representation of women in leadership roles, with a target of 50% by 2025, while

[36] Available: https://www.lvmh.com/ethics-and-compliance/the-lvmh-code-of-conduct

[37] Available at: https://www.lvmh.com/investors/esg

also ensuring global pay equity. As part of its efforts, EllesVMH[38] has introduced the EllesVMH Collective, a digital mentoring platform that connects employees from different departments and regions to facilitate women's career advancement.

Despite these efforts, most of LVMH's actions in labour relations remain fragmented at the Maison level, lacking comprehensive group-wide policies. In critical areas such as the right to disconnect or flexible working arrangements, regulation is implemented primarily at the Maison level rather than across the entire group. For example, Kenzo has introduced a Disconnect Charter, while Celine implemented a collective labour agreement on January 1, 2023, addressing quality of life at work. This agreement includes a new process for monitoring working hours and ensuring employees' right to disconnect. Similarly, Moynat, another Maison within LVMH, signed a Remote Work Charter, providing additional guidelines for flexible working arrangements.

While these Maison-level initiatives reflect a commitment to improving working conditions, their localized nature underscores the absence of a unified labour policy across LVMH. This fragmented approach can be attributed to LVMH's complex structure and the presence of 75 prestigious brands operating across diverse sectors. To effectively manage this diversity, LVMH employs a decentralized organizational model that grants significant autonomy to each Maison. This structure allows individual brands to maintain their unique identities, heritage, and operational practices while benefiting from the shared resources, expertise, and strategic support of the larger group. However, it also results in variability in the implementation of labour policies and practices across the group, with certain initiatives being Maison-specific rather than uniformly applied at the group level.[39] While this approach aligns with LVMH's focus on brand individuality and sector-specific operations, it inherently limits the standardization of labour policies and employee protections across the conglomerate.

Founded in 1972, SAP SE (Societas Europaea) is a global leader in business applications and artificial intelligence, employing over 107,000 people in 157 countries.[40] Information regarding SAP's promotion of employee rights is primarily published in the SAP Integrated Report.[41] However, the language in the report is broad, with actions largely focused on human resource management rather than explicitly recognizing employee rights. For instance, SAP has committed to transforming its workforce's skills to meet evolving technological demands. The company has developed a unified skills library and is working to consolidate existing skills management tools into a single platform, SAP SuccessFactors, for use by all employees. According to SAP, this initiative aims to enhance transparency in workforce skills, enable data-driven workforce planning, and support intentional skills development.

[38] For a description of the program: https://www.lvmh.com/en/commitment-in-action/for-people/ellesvmh

[39] Fiorani et al. (2022).

[40] Data available at: https://www.sap.com/about/company.html

[41] Available at: https://www.sap.com/integrated-reports/2023/en.html?pdf-asset=5234b263-ad7e-0010-bca6-c68f7e60039b&page=1

Some initiatives directly impact employee rights. Through its pay equity program, SAP conducts annual global evaluations of salary ranges and pay equity to ensure fair compensation for all employees within established pay bands. This process includes centrally funded adjustments to address discrepancies, ensuring that salaries remain within acceptable ranges and that pay differences among peers are justified by role- and performance-related factors. Notably, SAP's approach is neutral regarding employees' personal characteristics, focusing exclusively on job-related criteria. This commitment has been recognized as market-leading in fair pay practices by The Josh Bersin Company.

Another significant initiative is the Own SAP program, which facilitates employee participation in the company's capital, regardless of their location. Through this program, employees can invest in company shares, aligning their interests with SAP's long-term performance and growth. In 2023, participation in the program reached 75%, with employees collectively investing in over 6.7 million shares.

Despite sharing a commitment to global employee protection driven by social responsibility and sustainability objectives, Novo Nordisk, LVMH, and SAP employ markedly different strategies to achieve this goal. The variation in their approaches reflects distinct corporate philosophies and organizational structures, shaping how each company addresses labour rights and workplace standards.

Novo Nordisk's Labour Code of Conduct exemplifies a highly structured and unified model. Functioning as a transnational collective labour agreement, it establishes standardized protections applicable across the company's global operations. This centralized approach ensures consistency in employee rights and workplace conditions, transcending local legal frameworks and creating a cohesive labour policy that aligns closely with EU values.

In contrast, LVMH and SAP adopt less standardized methods, relying on policies and programs articulated in their sustainability reports. These reports emphasize the companies' commitment to broader sustainability goals but lack the formalized, legally enforceable mechanisms seen in Novo Nordisk's Labour Code of Conduct. As a result, their approaches to employee rights are more fragmented and context-specific.

4 Discussions

The global operations of major European corporations significantly influence labour relations by combining national legislation applicable to each subsidiary with voluntary corporate actions developed under European values. While these corporate measures may not explicitly aim to advance EU legal standards, a comparison of corporate practices with EU labour regulations reveals important parallels. Both frameworks prioritize the protection of fundamental employee rights, the creation of fair and safe working environments, and the promotion of diversity and inclusion. For instance, corporate policies frequently align with EU principles by addressing equal opportunities and combating discrimination. Additionally, many corporations adopt environmental and social policies that meet EU sustainability goals, reflecting a shared commitment to sustainable development.

Although corporations may not deliberately seek to "export" EU values, their actions often result in a convergence between the protections promoted by EU regulations and the labour practices implemented globally. This alignment is particularly evident when multinational corporations standardize certain employee rights across all subsidiaries, irrespective of the country's legal framework. By doing so, they extend protections that are rooted in EU standards to employees worldwide. However, this standardization is not absolute. Financial constraints, market-specific conditions, local legal requirements, and strategic corporate choices often limit the extent to which uniform rights can be applied across different jurisdictions.

A closer examination of the sustainability reports of Novo Nordisk, LVMH, and SAP illustrates the diversity in corporate approaches to employee protection and labour relations globalization. Each company has developed its own priorities and strategies, shaped by its specific business focus and the social responsibility principles it supports. Novo Nordisk, for example, adopts a systematic and highly standardized approach, closely mirroring the structure of the EU regulatory framework. Its comprehensive Labour Code of Conduct ensures that labour protections are uniformly implemented across its global operations. On the other hand, SAP's pay equity program targets salary fairness, particularly benefiting employees in countries with lower living standards, addressing global economic disparities in a focused and impactful way. LVMH takes a more localized approach, delegating responsibility for labour rights to its Maisons, which allows for tailored measures but limits group-wide standardization.

This diversity in approaches underscores the fact that European corporations are not necessarily driven by a singular goal of "Europeanizing" the global labour relations system. Instead, the dissemination of European values often occurs indirectly, as a consequence of compliance with EU regulations at the parent company level. Corporations retain considerable autonomy in defining their global labour strategies, balancing adherence to European principles with the flexibility required to address local and international challenges effectively.

European corporations are pivotal in advancing global labour protections, yet their efforts should not be restricted to the wholesale replication of EU standards across all jurisdictions. Instead, they should have the freedom to craft innovative approaches that align with their unique operational realities and social responsibility objectives. By embracing flexibility, these corporations can address global inequalities and improve living and working conditions in a manner that is both meaningful and sustainable, while also respecting local values, traditions, and legal frameworks.[42]

Although ensuring employee rights is a universal imperative, the notion that the "European way" is the only correct approach risks undermining local traditions and

[42] For a critical analysis, see: Supiot (2007), p. 70 et seq.; Sen (2009), p. 85.

culturally specific understandings of work. Effective labour protections should balance the principles enshrined in European standards with sensitivity to the diverse economic, social, and cultural contexts in which corporations operate. This approach ensures that labour policies are not only equitable but also respectful of local identities and practices.

Such adaptability allows European corporations to act as catalysts for positive change, fostering a global labour environment that integrates universal rights with local nuances. It also highlights the importance of tailoring labour strategies to the specific needs and expectations of workers in different regions, avoiding the imposition of rigid frameworks that may be perceived as culturally insensitive or impractical.

5 Conclusions

In conclusion, European "moral capitalism" must transcend mere regulatory compliance, showcasing agility and adaptability to drive meaningful change at both local and global levels. While the influence of EU values is unmistakable in corporate practices, companies should harness their unique characteristics to develop reforms that genuinely reflect their commitment to sustainability, inclusivity, and employee well-being.

Such a balanced approach enables the advancement of labour rights and sustainability objectives while addressing the complexities of a globalized economy and respecting the diverse values, traditions, and legal frameworks of the regions in which they operate. By integrating universal principles with local sensitivities, European corporations can demonstrate that ethical capitalism is not only compatible with globalization but also a vital force for fostering equitable and sustainable development worldwide.

References

Barnard C (2021) EU 'social' policy from employment law to labour market reform. In: Craig P, Búrca G (eds) The evolution of EU law, 3rd edn. Oxford Academic, Oxford. https://doi.org/10.1093/oso/9780192846556.003.0021

Boltanski L, Chiapello E (2011) Le nouvel esprit du capitalisme, Gallimard, Collection Tel no. 380, Paris

Carroll AB (2008) A history of corporate social responsibility: concepts and practices. In: Crane A, Matten D, Moon J, Siegel D (eds) The Oxford handbook of corporate social responsibility. Oxford University Press, pp 19–46

Carroll AB (2015) Corporate social responsibility: the centrepiece of competing and complementary frameworks. Organ Dyn 44(2):87–96

Charter of Fundamental Rights of the European Union. Official Journal of the European Union C 326, October 26, 2012

Clémençon R (2012) Welcome to the anthropocene: Rio+20 and the meaning of sustainable development. J Environ Dev 21(3):311–338. https://doi.org/10.1177/1070496512457289

Council Directive 2000/78/EC of 27 November 2000 establishing a general framework for equal treatment in employment and occupation. Official Journal of the European Union L 303, December 2, 2000, pp. 16–22

Council Directive 92/85/EEC of 19 October 1992 on the introduction of measures to encourage improvements in the safety and health at work of pregnant workers and workers who have recently given birth or are breastfeeding [tenth individual Directive within the meaning of Article 16(1) of Directive 89/391/EEC]. Official Journal of the European Union L 348, November 28, 1992, pp. 1–7

Council Directive 98/59/EC of 20 July 1998 on the approximation of the laws of the Member States relating to collective redundancies. Official Journal of the European Union L 225, August 12, 1998, pp. 16–21

Council Recommendation of 8 November 2019 on access to social protection for workers and the self-employed (2019/C 387/01). Official Journal of the European Union C 387/1, November 15, 2019

Davies RB, Markusen JR (2021) What do multinationals do? The structure of multinational firms' international activities. World Econ 44(12):3444–3481

Dey C, Burns J (2010) Integrated reporting at Novo Nordisk. In: Hopwood A, Unerman J (eds) Accounting for sustainability, 1st edn. Routledge, Abingdon, p 18. https://doi.org/10.4324/9781849776332

Directive (EU) 2019/1152 of the European Parliament and of the Council of 20 June 2019 on transparent and predictable working conditions in the European Union. Official Journal of the European Union L 186/105, July 11, 2019

Directive (EU) 2019/1158 of the European Parliament and of the Council of 20 June 2019 on work-life balance for parents and carers and repealing Council Directive 2010/18/EU. Official Journal of the European Union L 188, July 12, 2019, pp. 79–93

Directive 2002/14/EC of the European Parliament and of the Council of 11 March 2002 establishing a general framework for informing and consulting employees in the European Community. Official Journal of the European Union L 80, March 23, 2002, pp. 29–34

Directive 2003/88/EC of the European Parliament and of the Council of 4 November 2003 concerning certain aspects of the organization of working time. Official Journal of the European Union L 299, November 18, 2003, pp. 9–19

Directive 2006/54/EC of the European Parliament and of the Council of 5 July 2006 on the implementation of the principle of equal opportunities and equal treatment of men and women in matters of employment and occupation. Official Journal of the European Union L 204, July 26, 2006, pp. 23–36

Directive 2008/94/EC of the European Parliament and of the Council of 22 October 2008 on the protection of employees in the event of the insolvency of their employer. Official Journal of the European Union L 283, October 28, 2008, pp. 36–42

Directive 2009/38/EC of the European Parliament and of the Council of 6 May 2009 on the establishment of a European Works Council or a procedure in Community-scale undertakings and Community-scale groups of undertakings for the purposes of informing and consulting employees. Official Journal of the European Union L 122, May 16, 2009, pp. 28–44

Finance Charts, Biggest Companies in Europe by Market Cap for November 2024. https://www.financecharts.com/screener/biggest-country-europe

Fiorani G, Bosco F, Gerio CD (2022) Measuring sustainability in the luxury fashion sector: a comparison between LVMH and Kering. Mod Econ 13:356–369. https://doi.org/10.4236/me.2022.133020

Garben S (2020) Balancing social and economic fundamental rights in the EU legal order. Eur Lab Law J 11(4):364–390. https://doi.org/10.1177/2031952520927128C

Isbăşoiu GD, Volosevici D, Grigorescu A (2024) Social challenges of the green transition: a focus on the employment gender gap in Romania. In: Vasile J, Grigorescu A (eds) Entrepreneurship

and development for a green resilient economy. Emerald Publishing, Leeds, pp 131–163. https://doi.org/10.1108/978-1-83797-088-920241005
Jones TM (1980) Corporate social responsibility revisited. Redefined Calif Manag Rev 22(3):59–67
Latapí Agudelo MA, Jóhannsdóttir L, Davídsdóttir B (2019) A literature review of the history and evolution of corporate social responsibility. Int J Corp Soc Responsib 4(1). https://doi.org/10.1186/s40991-018-0039-y
Mensah J, Casadevall SR (2019) Sustainable development: meaning, history, principles, pillars, and implications for human action: literature review. Cogent Soc Sci 5(1). https://doi.org/10.1080/23311886.2019.1653531
Morsing M, Oswald D (2009) Sustainable leadership: management control systems and organizational culture in Novo Nordisk A/S. Corp Gov 9(1):83–99. https://doi.org/10.1108/14720700910936083
Piketty T (2014) Capital in the twenty-first century, trans. Arthur Goldhammer. The Belknap Press of Harvard University Press, Cambridge, MA
Ratti L, García-Muñoz A (2022) EU law, in work poverty, and vulnerable workers. Eur Law Open 1(3):733–747. https://doi.org/10.1017/elo.2022.41
Regulation (EU) 2016/679 of the European Parliament and of the Council of 27 April 2016 on the protection of natural persons with regard to the processing of personal data and on the free movement of such data, and repealing Directive 95/46/EC (General Data Protection Regulation) (Text with EEA relevance). Official Journal of the European Union L 119, May 4, 2016, pp. 1–88
Regulation (EU) 2024/1689 of the European Parliament and of the Council of 13 June 2024 laying down harmonized rules on artificial intelligence and amending Regulations (EC) No 300/2008, (EU) No 167/2013, (EU) No 168/2013, (EU) 2018/858, (EU) 2018/1139 and (EU) 2019/2144, and Directives 2014/90/EU, (EU) 2016/797, and (EU) 2020/1828 (Artificial Intelligence Act) (Text with EEA relevance). Official Journal of the European Union L 2024/1689, July 12, 2024
Rendtorff JD (2018) The Danish model of corporate citizenship: the Novo group. In: O'Higgins E, Zsolnai L (eds) Progressive business models, Palgrave studies in sustainable business in association with future earth. Palgrave Macmillan, Cham. https://doi.org/10.1007/978-3-319-58804-9_10
Salmon A (2009) Moraliser le capitalisme. CNRS Éditions, Paris
Sarafinovska M, Qiu Y (2021) Chapter 30: Doing business the sustainable Novo Nordisk way. In: Markovic S, Sancha C, Lindgreen A (eds) Handbook of sustainability-driven business strategies in practice. Edward Elgar, Cheltenham. https://doi.org/10.4337/9781789908350.00047
Sen A (2009) The idea of justice. Penguin Books, London
Supiot A (2007) Critique du droit du travail, 2nd edn. Presses Universitaires de France, Paris
Treaty on the Functioning of the European Union (TFEU). Official Journal of the European Union C 326, October 26, 2012
Zaccaria ML (2020) The right to take collective action in EU law based on the European pillar of social rights and the recent case law of the CJEU. Pro Futuro 9(3):9–24. https://doi.org/10.26521/Profuturo/2019/3/5770

Opportunities of Digital Transformation in Local Autonomy: Successful Examples and Learnings

Cristian Dumitrescu

Abstract Digital transformation in local autonomy comes with promising opportunities, as well as with challenges related to adaptation, education and security. Success in digitalization requires a complex approach, based on collaboration, investments and a long-term oriented vision. The local authorities that have embraced these changes and learned from the experience of other governments have been able to bring significant benefits to their communities. The objectives of this study are: to analyze the opportunities created by digital transformation at local level, to assess the successful examples in digital governance at local level, to identify the challenges and limits of implementing technologies in local autonomy, to examine the lessons learned from the digital governance practices, to formulate recommendations for public policies and investments in local digitalization. Research will begin with a literature review and of the government documents, case studies and annual reports of local authorities that have adopted digital governance solutions. The goal is to understand the theoretical foundations and practical examples of digital transformation. The results and implications of the study will aim at: improving efficiency in local public administration, increasing transparency and citizen participation, local economic development, increasing data security and confidentiality, which are obstacles in the implementation of digitization.

1 Local Autonomy: Fundamental Principle of Organization and Operation of Public Administration in Romania

Addressing the European context of defining the concept of local autonomy took into account the fact that the Romanian constituent legislator from 1991 used as inspiration the European Charter for Local Autonomy, and as a consequence Law no. 215/2001 and currently the Administrative Code, along with the Constitution,

C. Dumitrescu (✉)
Faculty of Legal Sciences, Hyperion University, Bucharest, Romania

C.-S. Săraru, C. E. Popa Tache (eds.), *AI, Sustainability and Solidarity in Advancing European Values in a Globalized Age*, European Union and its Neighbours in a Globalized World 28, https://doi.org/10.1007/978-3-032-06508-7_13

bases the system of organization and operation of local public administration on this principle.

The local territorial collectivities[1] thus see their existence, competences and means stated and guaranteed at the highest internal normative level, through the constitutional pact, which also binds the state, under the angle of its authorities, starting with the legislative authority. The state thereby understands that at the highest internal level, the constitutional level, it guarantees the autonomy of local communities, whose existence it created or recognized and granted or recognized their autonomy.

The Romanian Constitution deals with the matter of local autonomy in Articles 120-123 listed in Title III 'Public Authorities'.[2] This constitutional regulation, considered from the point of view of the level of detail, is intermediate between the simple affirmation of the principle, without any development, and numerous and detailed rules regarding all important aspects related to local autonomy.

The systematic interception of the text does not reveal the idea of an inferiority of this principle to the fundamental principles that appear in Title I of the Constitution 'General Principles'.

These last principles have a higher legal force than those in the other titles, so local autonomy can only be interpreted and applied within the framework of the characteristics of the Romanian state, specified in article 1 of the Constitution, equally, article 120 of the Constitution cannot violate the regulations regarding the quality of the people as the holder of sovereignty (Article 2), the inalienable nature of the territory (Article 3), the unity of the Romanian people, the foundation of the state (Article 4).

Therefore, the term decentralization[3] provided by the Constitution also implies the notion of deconcentration.

The placement of Article 120 in the chapter on public administration means that both local autonomy and devolution have an exclusively administrative character. Autonomous administrative authorities, as well as decentralized public services, have only administrative, not legislative, governing or judicial powers. This, because only public administration is decentralized administratively, and not legislation, governance or justice.[4]

But this does not mean that local autonomy would have a technical character, of pure administration, relative to the efficiency of administrative activity. On the contrary, local autonomy is closely linked to politics and democracy. The extremely important purpose of local administration is revealed precisely by its political dimension and its democratic value, because it creates 'local democracies'.[5]

---

[1] Apostol Tofan (2023), p. 75.

[2] The Constitution of Romania of 1991 revised and republished in 2003 (Official Gazette no.767/2003).

[3] Iorgovan (2001), p. 87.

[4] Apostol Tofan (2023), p. 76.

[5] Alexandru (2012), p. 153.

Local autonomy constitutes a counterweight to the central authorities, thus integrating into a wider mechanism of the balance of authorities in the state.[6]

Local autonomy is the first and most important link of democracy, the basic link, as it concerns the direct and most frequent relationship between the citizen and the state.[7]

In the initial context of Law no. 215/2001, three elements of local autonomy can be distinguished and they logically define the content of the concept: the organizational element, the functional element and the management element.[8] In order to be in the presence of local autonomy, it is necessary to fulfill the condition of meeting all elements[9] cumulatively.

Organizational autonomy includes the self-organization capacity of local public administration authorities, which implies a new type of relationship established between them and other authorities, such as the prefect.

Functional autonomy entails consecration of full competence in solving problems of local interest. Managerial autonomy refers to the competence of local authorities arising from the legal personality of the territorial-administrative units that manage local heritage. The Administrative Code makes a specification regarding the nature of the principle of local autonomy: local autonomy is only administrative and financial, being exercised on the basis and within the limits provided by law,[10] thus expressly emphasizing that autonomy is a principle of an administrative nature and that its application excludes any political autonomy.

At the same time, the problem of the limits of local autonomy[11] is subject to analysis along with the recognition of the theoretical and practical value of the principle of local autonomy and its legislative stipulation, as the foundation of the organization and functioning of local public administration.

The principle of local autonomy, as it was stipulated by the Romanian legislator, is alien to any approach from an ethnic perspective, because the European legislations that served as a source of inspiration use the notion of local interest (local affairs), local community and not those of ethnic community.

This is an approach harmonized with European legislation, which treats local autonomy in terms of 'local interest' and 'local community', avoiding administrative separation based on ethnic criteria. Inspired by European models, Romanian legislation thus aims to promote unity and social cohesion, favoring the development of local communities based on the needs and interests of all citizens, regardless of ethnicity.

---

[6] Săraru (2018).

[7] Dincă (2018), p. 64.

[8] Article 4, paragraph 1 of the Local Public Administration Law no. 215/2001.

[9] Manda (2012), p. 89.

[10] Article 84 paragraph 3 of the Administrative Code.

[11] Podaru and Boariu (2023), p. 49.

This perspective supports the idea that local government must be centered on common development goals and the good of the community, rather than on cultural or ethnic differences, thus promoting inclusive and equitable governance.

At the same time, in order to protect local autonomy and guarantee its effective application, it is essential to have a direct legal action path, explicitly provided by law. This legal path would allow local authorities to defend their interests and challenge decisions that could affect their autonomy before administrative courts.

The recognition of such a judicial procedure would strengthen the capacity of local communities to function autonomously, allowing them to respond promptly to any external interference or decision of the central administration that might violate the principle of local autonomy.

Furthermore, such a legal path would ensure a clear and fast conflict resolution mechanism, contributing to the consolidation of a stable and independent local public administration, in accordance with the principles of the rule of law and decentralization.

2 Local Autonomy in the Digital Age

In an increasingly interconnected and digitized world,[12] local autonomy is redefining its role and function in modern governance.

With the advancement of technology and the growing adoption of digital solutions in public administration, local authorities face both ample opportunities and complex challenges in managing community businesses and services.[13]

In this digital age, local governance is becoming increasingly dependent on technology to provide more efficient, transparent and personalized services to citizens.

Digitalization is transforming the way local authorities interact with citizens and manage public affairs.

This provides opportunities for streamlining administrative processes, increasing transparency and involving citizens in decision-making.

Digitalization[14] offers local authorities' new tools and technologies to streamline and improve public services, facilitating communication and interaction with citizens.

These new technologies include:

- online platforms and municipal portals where local authorities can develop and manage online platforms or municipal portals where citizens can access information about available public services,[15] make online appointments or submit various demands and requests.

[12] Stoica (2023), p. 87.

[13] See about the evolution and features of public services: Săraru (2016, 2023).

[14] Apostol Tofan (2023), p. 77.

[15] Clipa (2024), p. 95.

- development of mobile applications that allow citizens to access public services directly from their mobile devices, offering them a convenient and fast way to interact with local authorities.
- implementation of citizen relationship management systems that allow local authorities to more effectively manage interactions with citizens, monitor and quickly respond to their requests and complaints.
- online payment services. In this sense, digitalization facilitates the introduction of online payment services for various local taxes and fees, allowing citizens to make payments quickly and safely, without the need to go to physical counters.
- digitally collected data that helps local authorities to better understand the needs and preferences of citizens, to anticipate demands and to make more informed decisions in the management of public services.

These tools and technologies are just a few examples of ways in which digitalization can contribute to the effectiveness and improvement of public services at local level.

Through online platforms (such as mobile applications and other digital solutions), citizens can more easily access information about available public services, communicate more quickly and effectively with local authorities and perform various administrative operations online, without having to physically go to the institution's headquarters.

Thus, digitalization contributes to increasing transparency, responsibility and participation of citizens in the decision-making process, at the same time strengthening the efficiency and performance of local public administration.

By using online platforms,[16] mobile applications and other digital tools, citizens can more easily access information about administrative decisions, monitor the activity of local authorities and interact more directly with the latter.

Furthermore, by implementing citizen relationship management systems and by collecting and analyzing digital data, local public administration can respond more quickly and efficiently to citizens' requests and needs. Thereby, citizens feel more involved in the decision-making process and have more confidence in public administration.[17]

In addition to these aspects, digitalization also contributes to increasing the effectiveness and performance of local public administration, by reducing bureaucracy, optimizing internal processes and using available resources more effectively. As a result, public administration can offer higher quality services to citizens more transparently and responsibly.

Nevertheless, there are also challenges such as cybersecurity, personal data protection and uneven digitalization that require innovative approaches and locally adopted solutions.

Cybersecurity is one of the biggest concerns in the context of digitalization, because with the transfer and storage of sensitive data online, there is a risk that it will be exposed to cyberattacks or IT security breaches. It is essential that local

[16] Stoica (2023), p. 88.

[17] Apostol Tofan (2023), p. 79.

authorities implement appropriate data protection measures and develop strong cybersecurity skills to prevent and manage potential threats.

Personal data protection is another major concern, especially in the context of the General Data Protection Regulation (GDPR) in the European Union. Local authorities must comply with personal data protection rules and standards when collecting, processing and using citizens' information.

Uneven digitalization is another issue, as not all citizens have equal access to technology and digital infrastructure.[18]

There is a risk that certain groups or communities are excluded or left behind in terms of the benefits of digitalization.[19]

Local authorities must therefore be aware of these disparities and take steps to ensure equitable access to technology and support the digital inclusion of all citizens.

Addressing these challenges requires innovation and collaboration between the public sector, the private sector and civil society, to develop solutions adapted to the specifics of each local community.[20]

It is also important that local authorities involve citizens in decision-making and are transparent about how they use technology and personal data for the benefit of the community.[21]

3 Digital Transformation Success Stories

Digital transformation offers multiple opportunities for strengthening local autonomy, improving the efficiency, transparency and accessibility of public services. In this sense, Romania can consider some examples of success from other countries, which have used digital transformation to support local autonomy and make public administration more productive:

3.1 Estonia: The E-Governance System

The first country I am talking about in particular is Estonia. It is recognized for its advanced e-governance system, which allows citizens to access almost all public services online.[22] With a single digital ID,[23] Estonians can vote, pay taxes, access

[18] Vedinas (2023), p. 165.

[19] Stoica (2023), p. 89.

[20] Vedinas (2023), p. 166.

[21] Clipa (2024), p. 96.

[22] Antoine Barde (2024), p. 78.

[23] Ebers et al. (2023).

medical records and other essential services.[24] This system supports local autonomy by reducing bureaucracy and giving local governments more time and resources for other community activities.

Estonia is a global example of digital governance, having one of the most integrated and advanced e-governance systems.

Since the 2000s, Estonia has implemented a national e-governance system that allows citizens to access almost all government services online, significantly contributing to the productivity of administration and strengthening local autonomy. The key elements of the e-Governance system in Estonia are:[25]

- Digital Identity (Digital ID). Every Estonian citizen has a unique digital identity, which they can use to access online services. The digital ID allows Estonians to authenticate themselves in a secure and simple way, providing quick access to all public services, from paying taxes and accessing medical records to electronic voting.[26]
- X-Road[27] System for Interoperability. X-Road is the backbone of Estonian e-governance. This platform enables the secure data exchange between different IT systems, both in the public and private sectors. Each public institution can access the necessary data without requesting additional information from citizens, thus reducing bureaucracy and the time needed to process documents.
- Electronic Voting (e-Voting). Estonia was the first country in the world to implement electronic voting at national level. Citizens can vote online in national and local elections using their digital ID. This option has increased accessibility and enabled wider participation, giving citizens more autonomy in the election process.
- Electronic Medical Records. Estonia has integrated electronic medical records into its e-governance system, allowing citizens to access their medical history, prescriptions and consultations online. This functionality simplifies access to essential information and improves efficiency in the health system, giving citizens greater autonomy in managing their own health.
- e-Residency. Estonia also offers an e-Residency program, which allows people from outside the country to obtain an Estonian digital identity, thereby gaining access to digital services and facilities offered by the Estonian government. Although not the equivalent of citizenship, e-Residency allows digital residents to open and manage online businesses in Estonia, thereby attracting international entrepreneurs and investment.

The implementation of e-governance[28] has given local authorities in Estonia more resources and more time to focus on community needs, unencumbered by traditional

[24] Sikkut (2022), p. 85.

[25] Ibid, p. 86.

[26] Ebers et al. (2023), p. 10.

[27] Antoine Barde (2024), p. 79.

[28] Baltac (2024), p. 87.

bureaucracy.[29] Local services have become more accessible and the interaction between citizens and local administrations has been simplified. Moreover, local governments have the opportunity to develop their own digital initiatives and collaborate effectively with central government in an integrated and secure way.

Thus, Estonia's e-governance system[30] is a reference model for other countries that want to adopt digital transformation in the public sector, illustrating how technology can support local autonomy,[31] increase productivity and improve the relationship between citizens and administration.

The development of an interoperability infrastructure[32] in Romania, similar to X-Road, could facilitate cooperation between local and central administrations. The implementation of a secure digital identity system could allow easy access to online public services, reducing the bureaucracy tape and improving the relationship between citizens and authorities.

These initiatives would transform the Romanian administration, making it more transparent, accessible and oriented to the citizens' needs, thus supporting the development of a modern and efficient local governance.

3.2 Spain: Decidim

Participatory Budgeting Platform. In Spain, cities such as Barcelona have implemented the digital platform Decidim,[33] a free Open-Source tool that facilitates citizen participation in local government decision-making processes. Decidim, which in Catalan means 'We decide', allows residents to propose and vote on investment projects in their community, thus promoting transparency and the direct involvement of citizens in the allocation of public resources.

The implementation of Decidim in Barcelona had a significant impact on the way public resources are managed and on the involvement of citizens in the decision-making process.[34] For instance, in the second edition of the participatory budgets, citizens had the opportunity to decide on the allocation of 30 million euros from the municipal budget for 2024–2027. The process, carried out through the Decidim platform, included stages of proposal collection, technical assessment and public voting, ensuring broad community involvement in local investment decisions.

Similarly, Romania could benefit from the implementation of a platform similar to Decidim to encourage citizens' participation in the budgeting process at local level. This could lead to a more effective allocation of resources, increase

[29] Sikkut (2022), p. 86.

[30] Antoine Barde (2024), p. 79.

[31] Ebers et al. (2023), p. 11.

[32] Stoica (2023), p. 90.

[33] Barandiaran et al. (2024), p. 70 et seq.

[34] Idem.

transparency and strengthen trust between citizens and local governments. Adopting such a tool could support the development of local communities[35] and promote more open and participatory governance.

3.3 France: Digital Portals for Local Services

In France, the digitalization of local government[36] has become a priority in recent years and many municipalities have developed digital portals that provide centralized access to a wide range of local public services. These digital portals facilitate interaction between citizens and local governments, reducing bureaucracy and time needed to obtain essential documents and information.

Citizens can request documents, report problems and access local information through these portals, simplifying interaction with the administration. These platforms support local autonomy by improving efficiency and providing a centralized experience for residents.

Romania could definitely be inspired by this model to develop digital platforms[37] at the level of local administrations, which could integrate similar functionalities. These portals could help local governments manage resources more effectively, respond promptly to citizens' needs and improve transparency.[38] Adopting this model would allow Romanian citizens to more easily access local services, increasing the autonomy and efficiency of public administrations in Romania.

3.4 Finland: Digital Health at Local Level

In terms of people's health, an example to follow is Finland, which is a global leader in the digitalization of health services,[39] offering citizens access to a well-integrated e-health system that facilitates fast and effective access to medical care at local level. This digital system is designed to connect citizens, health professionals and local governments, thereby improving the quality and accessibility of medical services.

In the Finnish health system we can note: unified electronic medical records (dme), kanta.fi—the national health portal, telemedicine and online consultations, electronic prescriptions and digital pharmacies, big data analysis and predictability in health.

[35] Stoica (2023), p. 91.

[36] Picon (2015), p. 47 et seq.

[37] Stoica (2023), p. 91.

[38] Picon (2015), p. 48.

[39] Olla and Tan (2022), p. 70 et seq.

In Finland, each citizen has a unique electronic medical record accessible to both patients and healthcare professionals.[40] This centralized record can be accessed by doctors, nurses and pharmacies across the country, facilitating effective collaboration between different institutions and providing a complete picture of the patient's medical history. Citizens can also consult their own record online, increasing their degree of control over their own medical information.

The implementation of a digital health system has enabled local governments in Finland to better manage resources and provide citizens with affordable and high-quality medical services. This system reduces the workload of doctors and medical staff, allows faster consultations and reduces waiting time for patients.

It would be extremely useful for Romania to have a medical system with a unified electronic record and a national digital health platform, to promote access to quality medical services and to improve the efficiency of the health sector at local level. Investments in telemedicine could also reduce disparities in access to care between urban and rural areas by providing online consultations for patients in remote areas.

Adopting such a model would substantially improve the health system in Romania, reducing costs, optimizing resources and increasing the quality of services offered at local level.

3.5 Germany: Infrastructure and Energy Management Systems at Local Level

If we refer to energy infrastructure management, the best example to follow would be Germany, which has implemented digital monitoring systems of local infrastructure and energy consumption.[41] These systems enable local authorities to monitor and manage resources effectively, optimizing energy use and reducing operating costs. Therefore, local administrations can develop their own sustainable and ecological policies, strengthening their autonomy and aligning themselves with environmental objectives.

Smart energy monitoring and management systems allow communities to optimize their resources, reducing costs and contributing to sustainability goals. Additionally, the use of real-time data and big data analysis helps in preventive planning and quick interventions in case of breakdowns.[42]

Likewise, if such a system were to be implemented in Romania, the management of infrastructure and energy resources at local level would be optimized. Monitoring platforms for urban infrastructure such as roads and water networks could improve safety and especially reduce maintenance costs by preventing problems. The

[40] Idem.

[41] Unnerstall (2017), p. 90.

[42] Idem.

implementation of smart energy networks and adaptive public lighting would help reduce energy consumption and support the transition to renewable sources.

3.6 The Netherlands: Intelligent Mobility Systems

Local governments in the Netherlands have implemented smart mobility systems, including platforms for traffic monitoring and optimization of public transport. These systems use real-time data to improve local mobility and reduce congestion. Local autonomy is thus strengthened by developing its own mobility solutions, adapted to the specific needs of local communities.[43]

The Netherlands has invested significantly in urban mobility solutions that optimize public transport, reduce congestion and promote green transport.[44] These intelligent mobility systems are applied both in large cities and in less congested areas, supporting local autonomy and adapting to the needs of communities.

Intelligent mobility systems in the Netherlands include:[45]

- Intelligent Traffic Light Systems. In the Netherlands, smart traffic lights are used, connected to networks of sensors and vehicles in traffic, which automatically adjust waiting times to reduce congestion. These priority traffic lights for cyclists and public transport allow them to pass more quickly, reducing congestion and waiting times. Likewise, in cities such as Amsterdam and Rotterdam, smart traffic lights are interconnected and synchronized to optimize traffic flow.
- Car Sharing and Ride Sharing Platforms. Car sharing and ride sharing are popular in the Netherlands, with digital platforms facilitating shared use of electric and hybrid vehicles. This not only reduces the number of cars on the road, but also promotes the use of clean vehicles. Dutch municipalities collaborate with ride sharing companies to expand local mobility options, thereby promoting a sustainable and affordable form of mobility.
- Charging Stations for Electric Vehicles. This country has one of the largest networks of charging stations for electric vehicles in the world. Charging stations are widely distributed and users can locate and book stations through mobile apps. Dutch cities have developed smart charging networks that adjust energy consumption according to demand, ensuring an optimal balance in the network and reducing the impact on the energy infrastructure.
- Smart Bike Lanes and Facilities for Cyclists. The Netherlands is famous for its bike lanes and some cities have integrated smart mobility technologies for cyclists. In Utrecht, for example, cycle lanes are equipped with sensors that monitor cycle traffic and optimize traffic lights to reduce waiting times. In addition,

[43] Jeekel (2016), p. 87.

[44] Wee et al. (2013), p. 94.

[45] Jeekel (2016), p. 88.

mobile apps for cyclists provide optimized routes, GPS guidance and information about available bicycle parking spaces.

– Intelligent Public Transport and Data Integration. Public transport in the Netherlands is integrated into a digital system that allows monitoring and optimizing the flow of passengers. Citizens can access information about the routes and arrival times of trains, trams and buses in real time through mobile applications and digital boards in stations. The data collected helps authorities adjust services according to needs and reduce congestion during peak hours.

If the Dutch model[46] of mobility systems were to be followed, Romania would improve its urban transport infrastructure and support the transition to sustainable mobility. Options include implementing smart traffic lights in large cities, since this is actually a major challenge facing Romania today. At the same time, networks of charging stations for electric vehicles would be created, including on highways, expand facilities for cyclists and integrating real-time public transport apps.

These measures would contribute substantially to more efficient citizen mobility, thus using public transport much more and reducing the negative impact of urban traffic, supporting the development of a modern and sustainable transport infrastructure.

4 Lessons for a Successful Digital Public System

A first lesson would be that it is essential that digital platforms[47] are intuitive and accessible for all age groups and that authorities invest in information campaigns to increase the rate of use.

The second lesson concerns citizen participation platforms that increase transparency and improve the relationship between citizens and administration, but must be managed skillfully and transparently to avoid misinformation and public skepticism.

Another lesson to bear in mind is that implementing smart city technologies[48] requires careful planning and a solid core infrastructure, without forgetting that success depends on collaboration between the public and private sectors.

Particularly important is the lesson on cybersecurity, which is fundamental in any digitalization process, considering that without adequate protection digitalization can expose administrations to major risks.

The final lesson to keep in mind is that without an investment in employee training, any digital initiative runs the risk of being underutilized or inadequately implemented. Trained personnel are a strategic resource in the success of digitalization.

---

[46] Androniceanu (2015), p. 85 et seq.

[47] Stoica (2023), p. 91.

[48] Baltac (2024), p. 74.

5 Conclusions

As digitalization and interconnectivity continue to rapidly evolve, local authorities must adapt their strategies and redefine how they operate to meet the changing needs of their communities.

Local autonomy[49] thus becomes an essential pillar of modern governance, having an increasing importance in ensuring an effective, transparent and responsible management of public affairs at local level.

This involves not only using technology to improve services and communication with citizens, but also developing the necessary capacities and skills to face new challenges and opportunities in a sustainable and innovative manner.

Thereby, the government's involvement in promoting local autonomy in the digital age is essential for creating a favorable framework for technological development at local level. Digital transformation can contribute to more efficient administration with less bureaucracy, allowing employees to focus on activities that bring value to the community.

But perhaps the most relevant thing is that reducing bureaucracy supports the development of communities and improves the relationship between administration and citizens.

References

Alexandru I (2012) Public administration. Theories. Realities. Perspectives, 3rd edn. Lumina Lex, Bucharest

Androniceanu A (2015) Sisteme administrative din state ale Uniunii Europene. Universitara, Bucharest

Antoine Barde SR (2024) The art of digitalization: a dive into e-Estonia. Asian Productivity Organ 10.61145/IINI4552

Apostol Tofan D (2023) Administrative law, vol 1, 5th edn. C. H. Beck, Bucharest

Baltac V (2024) E-government. The digital transformation of public administration. Pro Universitaria, Bucharest

Barandiaran XE, Calleja-López A, Monterde A, Romero C (2024) Decidim, a technopolitical network for participatory democracy. Springer

Clipa C (2024) Fundamentele ideologice ale dreptului administrativ. Vol II, Tome 2, 2nd edn. Hamangiu, Bucharest

Constitution of Romania of 1991 revised and republished in 2003 (Official Gazette no.767/2003).

Dincă D (2018) Local public services - case studies and exercises. Politeia Publishing House, Bucharest

Ebers M, Krõõt Tupay P, Juksaar J, Kohv K (2023) The promise and perils of AI and ML in public administration. In: Ebers M, Krõõt Tupay P (eds) Artificial intelligence and machine learning powered public service delivery in Estonia. Springer, pp 7–33

Iorgovan A (2001) Treatise of administrative law, vol I, 3rd edn. All Beck, Bucharest

[49] Vedinas (2023), p. 126.

Jeekel H (2016) Smart mobility and societal challenges: an implementation perspective. Tue Publishing House
Manda C (2012) Drept administrativ. Lumina lex, Bucharest
Olla P, Tan J (2022) Digital health care: perspectives, applications, and cases. Jones & Bartlett Learning
Picon A (2015) Smart cities. Wiley
Podaru O, Boariu A (2023) Drept administrativ. Administrația publică. Actul administrativ, 2nd edn. Hamangiu, Bucharest
Săraru CS (2016) Considerations on the public services in the XXI century. Juridical Tribune - Tribuna Juridica 6(Special Issue):160–166
Săraru CS (2023) Regulation of public services in the administrative code of Romania: challenges and limitations. Access to Justice in Eastern Europe 1(18):69–83. https://doi.org/10.33327/AJEE-18-6.1-a000110
Săraru CS (2018) Considerations about administrative decentralization and local autonomy in Romania. Juridical Tribune - Tribuna Juridica 8(2):596–607
Sikkut S (2022) Digital government excellence lessons from effective digital leaders. Wiley
Stoica A (2023) Digitalization of law and public administration in the current pandemic context. Universul Juridic, Bucharest
Unnerstall T (2017) The German energy transition. Design, implementation, cost and lessons. Springer
Vedinas V (2023) Drept administrativ, 13th edn, revised and supplemented. Universul Juridic, Bucharest
Wee B, Annema JA, Banister D (2013) The transport system and transport policy. Edward Elgar

European Cooperative Society in Creating a Community: A Current Issue

Arcadia Hinescu

Abstract Although the European Cooperative Society with Limited Liability is a legal form established at the level of the European Union by EU Regulation no. 1435/2003 is little used in practice. Through this study, we aim to highlight the functional legal benefits of the European Cooperative Society with Limited Liability for cooperative members, mainly by referring to the cooperatives regulated by Romanian Law no. 1/2005 regarding the organization and operation of the cooperative, as well as its ability to develop a community that operates in a certain field (e.g. energy), using as an example a Romanian company that activates in such a legal form. In developing the study, we used inductive, hermeneutic and comparative research methods. The result of the study is that this legal form is actually very topical given that in all fields of activity the creation of communities is pursued, the social interest becoming stronger than the individual one, both at the national and international level.

1 Introduction

This study aims to demonstrate the fact that the way in which the European Society is regulated compared to the cooperative company regulated by Romanian Law no. 1/2005 regarding the organization and operation of the cooperation, the first legal form is more favorable, for the establishment and operation of a community in a certain field. I am writing on this subject following several professional experiences related to the establishment and operation of European cooperative societies, but also

A. Hinescu (✉)
Bucharest Bar Association, National Institute for the Training and Improvement of Lawyers, Bucharest, Romania
e-mail: arcadia.hinescu@hinescu.ro

C.-S. Săraru, C. E. Popa Tache (eds.), *AI, Sustainability and Solidarity in Advancing European Values in a Globalized Age*, European Union and its Neighbours in a Globalized World 28, https://doi.org/10.1007/978-3-032-06508-7_14

a personal experience as a founding member and still a member of such a cooperative in Romania.[1]

There are extremely few studies at the national and European level related to the European cooperative society and especially to the approach of this legal form from the perspective of a community, which places the study on a new topic in the doctrinal landscape.

The paper begins with the identification of the legal framework of the European Society, after which we point the particular elements of a cooperative in general, in order to highlight all the strengths of the European Cooperative Society to create a community at the expense of the national cooperative.

Regarding the research methods used, they were: the inductive method, because in the analysis of the institution of cooperatives we specifically extrapolated to the case of European Cooperative Society, the hermeneutic method because, starting from the legal provisions found in various normative acts, we sought to understand the intention legislator in the legal text and to interpret them in a creative but at the same time pragmatic way, with constructive legal effects, and the comparative method, by comparing the legal regulations of the European Cooperative Society with the cooperative regulated by Law no. 1/2005.

The study ends with conclusions related to the limited and unrealistic provisions of Law no. 1/2005 and the proposal to amend the provisions of this law so that the national cooperative also becomes a properly regulated and functional legal form and not ultimately suitable for the creation of communities in various fields.

2 Legal Frame of European Cooperative Society

The legal form of a company as a European Cooperative Society (hereinafter referred to as SCE) is a little familiar in Romania, but even in the European Union, as there are few European Cooperative Societies, as it results from the studies and reports carried out at European level.[2]

---

[1] For the relevance of the topic see United Nations, 2025 UN International Year of Cooperatives, United Nations, https://2025.coop/.

[2] Study on the implementation of the Statute for a European Cooperative Society: Executive Summary and Synthesis and Comparative Report: https://eur-lex.europa.eu/legal-content/EN/TXT/?uri=CELEX:52012DC0072. Study on the implementation of the Statute for a European Cooperative Society: National Reports. https://ec.europa.eu/docsroom/documents/39568/attachments/1/translations/. Report from the Commission to the European Parliament, the Council, the European Economic and Social Committee and the Committee of The Regions: The application of Council Regulation (EC) No. 1435/2003 of 22 July 2003 on the Statute for a European Cooperative Society (SCE)/COM/2012/072 final. https://op.europa.eu/en/publication-detail/-/publication/494bb15b-c34d-4bdf-8518-75d6bde38cbb. Report of CooPilot—Guidelines regarding the improvement of the cooperative system at the local and European level a project co-financed by DG Internal Market, Industry, Entrepreneurship and SMEs of the European Commission, https://www.coopilot-project.eu/wp-content/uploads/2018/04/LG_ALDA_RO.pdf.

By Regulation CE no. 1435/2003 on the Statute for a European Cooperative Society (SCE)[3] (hereinafter referred to as Regulation 1435/2003) was created the legal frame for the set-up and functioning of the European Cooperative Society (hereinafter referred to as SCE). The European regulation has direct applicability at the level of Romanian legislation but requires complementary legislation at the national level of each Member State of the European Union. Moreover, Art. 78 of the Regulation requires that Member States adopt all appropriate provisions to ensure the effective implementation of the Regulation and designate the competent national authorities with powers regarding this type of company.

Therefore, in Romania, an internal legal framework was created for applying the provisions of Regulation 1435/2003. Presently, there are several regulations that Romanian legislation referring to SCE, and among them first place and of interest for this article is Law no. 265/2022 on the register of commerce and for the amendment of other laws with incidence on registration in the register of commerce.[4] According to this law, the register of commerce is the public service of general interest that ensures the registration and publicity of European Cooperative Societies (art. 4), it owns a special register for the registration of cooperatives and European Cooperative Societies with their main headquarters in Romania, their branches and, as the case may be, of branches of cooperative or European Cooperative Societies with their main headquarters abroad (art. 7). Also, there are legal provisions for the implementation of Regulation 1435/2003 in the Methodological Norms regarding keeping the register of commerce, making records and issuing information, Methodological Norms that were approved by Order of the Ministry of Justice no. 2594/2008 and amended by Order of the Ministry of Justice no. 6974/C/2020.

On the other hand, even in the context of internal legislation dedicated to this type of company, Regulation 1435/2003 provides in Art. 8, which is in fact the legislation applicable to an SCE as far as the hierarchy of its application. Thus, according to this article, an SCE is regulated primarily by Regulation 1435/2003, and then by the provisions of the SCE's constitutive deed if the regulation so provides so. On the other hand, when Regulation 1435/2003 does not regulate a certain subject or it is partially regulated by it, the nation provisions adopted in the application of the European provisions of the regulation, which regulate that subject, will be applied gradually. If they do not have provisions on the respective subject, then the provisions of the national

[3] Regulation CE no. 1435/2003 on the Statute for a European Cooperative Society published in Official Journal of the European Union no. 207 as of 18 August 2003 and Rectification published in Official Journal of the European Union no. 49 as of 17 February 2007.

[4] Law no. 265/2022 on the register of commerce and for the amendment of other laws with incidence on registration in the register of commerce published in the Official Gazette no. 750/26.07.2022. Until its adoption, the provisions regarding the registration of European cooperative societies were found in Law no. 26/1990 regarding register of commerce following its amendment by the Government Emergency Ordinance no. 52/2008 for the amendment and completion of Companies Law no. 31/1990 and to supplement Law no. 26/1990 regarding register of commerce.

law that apply to a cooperative with its registered office in Romania will apply.[5] And if they do not contain provisions on the respective subject, the provisions of the SCE's constitutive deed will apply, under the same conditions that apply to a cooperative established in accordance with Romanian legislation. On the other hand, to the extent that the national legislation provides specific rules and/or restrictions related to the nature of the activities exercised by an SCE or a form of control exercised by a supervisory authority, that legislation is fully applied to the SCE.

In addition, the mandatory common law provisions of Romanian law will be applicable in as regards the companies whose basis is Chapter VII of the Company Contract of the Civil Code, art. 1881 et seq. Among these, we note the provisions of art. 1887 according to which the provisions of the respective chapter represent the common law for companies, the law being able to regulate different types of companies in consideration of the form, nature or object of activity, as well as of art. 1888 regarding the forms of companies among which cooperatives are also listed.

Although apparently the provisions of Regulation 1435/2003 are complemented by those of the national legislation regarding cooperative societies, upon a careful reading of the text of the regulation we will find that there are certain subjects treated by it first through the lens of the national legislation regarding joint-stock companies, among which the most representative act is the Companies Law no. 31/1990.[6] Thus, in the case of SCE according to Regulation no. 1435/2003, the provisions of the national law regarding joint stock companies are relevant on several subjects, on the one hand, regarding the appointment of experts and the evaluation of contributions to the share capital of the EC, other than those in cash (art. 4 para. 6) and on the other hand in several topics related to the establishment of the SCE, namely: the SCE is registered in a register designated in accordance with the legislation applicable to joint stock companies, the requirements of publicity of national joint stock companies also applies to SCE (art. 11 par. 1 in conjunction with par. 5), the preventive control of a joint-stock company during the establishment stage, applies by analogy to the control of the establishment of SCE (art. 5 para. 3). Also, the acts regarding the SCE that are subject to publicity according to the Regulation will follow the legal publicity rules established by the legislation on joint stock companies (art. 12 paragraph 1). Regarding the mandatory mentions with which an SCE identifies itself to third parties, the provisions regarding joint-stock companies will also apply (art. 10 paragraph 1).

The referrals for legislative complementarity of the legal framework of the SCE with that of joint-stock companies are an exception, the rule being that in the lack of European provisions the national legislation regarding cooperative shall apply. However, as we will prove as it follows, the national legal provisions in the matter of cooperatives are restrictive and do not at all reflect those regarding SCE.

[5] For some details see Săraru and Popa-Tache (2024), pp. 61–74.

[6] Companies Law no. 31/1990 published in the Official Gazette no. 1066/18.11.2004.

The main law in Romania regarding cooperatives is Law no. 1/2005 on the organization and operation of the cooperation[7] (hereinafter referred to as Law 1/2005). Unfortunately, although this was published after the Regulation 1435/2003 it did not consider any provision regarding the European Cooperative Society, the context of the adoption of such a law being outside the scope of creating an internal legal framework regarding the SCE, which has consequences of cooperative to be suitable to have many members and to create a community.

3 Particularities of a Cooperative

Referring to both European and national provisions regarding cooperatives, we indicate in the following the main elements that characterize this form of society.

(a) company with legal personality—is based on a company contract concluded between its members, natural and/or legal persons based on their freely expressed consent
(b) the purpose is to promote the economic, social and cultural interests of the cooperative members (art. 7 of Law no. 1/2005), and therefore to satisfy the needs and/or develop the economic and social activities of its members, especially by concluding agreements with them, in order to provide goods or services or to carry out works within the activity exercised or controlled by the company (art. 1 para. 3 of Regulation no. 1435/2003). Moreover, the SCE may also aim to meet the needs of its members, encouraging, in the same way, their participation in economic activities in one or more SCEs and/or national cooperatives.
(c) is jointly owned and democratically controlled by its members—this means regardless of the social capital held, all members are equal and have the right to one vote.

The cooperative principles necessarily guide the company's activity (art. 7 of Law no. 1/2005), and these are:

1. the principle of voluntary and open association, according to which cooperatives are voluntary organizations that are established on the basis of free consent and are open to all persons capable of using their services and who agree to assume the responsibilities of cooperative membership, without any of discrimination based on criteria of nationality, ethnic origin, religion, political affiliation, social origin or gender;
2. the principle of democratic control of cooperative members, according to which cooperatives are democratic organizations that are controlled by cooperative members who participate in setting policies and adopting decisions. The persons

[7] Law no. 1/2005 on the organization and operation of the cooperation published on Official Gazette no. 368 as of 20 May 2014.

acting as elected representatives are accountable to the cooperative members. In cooperative societies of the 1st degree, members have equal voting rights, each having a single vote, regardless of the number of social shares owned;

3. the principle of economic participation of the cooperative members, according to which the members contribute equitably to the establishment of the property of the cooperative, exercising a democratic control over it. At least part of this property is indivisible. The cooperative members receive, as a rule, a limited compensation in money or in kind, from the profit established on the basis of the annual financial situation and the profit and loss account, proportional to the participation quota in the social capital. The cooperative members allocate from the net profit of the cooperative society the amounts necessary to achieve the following goals: the development of the cooperative society, rewarding the cooperative members in relation to the participation in the activity of the cooperative or supporting other activities approved by the cooperative members;
4. the principle of autonomy and independence of cooperative societies, according to which cooperatives are autonomous organizations based on self-help and are controlled by their members. Entering into legal relations with other natural or legal persons, including the Government, or attracting financing from external sources is done by ensuring the democratic control of cooperative members and maintaining the autonomy of cooperatives;
5. the principle of educating, training and informing cooperative members, according to which cooperative ensure the education and training of their members, elected representatives, executive directors or employees, so that they can effectively contribute to the development of the cooperatives they belong to. Cooperatives inform the public, especially youth and opinion leaders, about the nature and advantages of cooperation;
6. the principle of cooperation between cooperative societies, according to which cooperatives serve their members and strengthen the cooperative movement. Cooperative work together within local, national, regional and international structures;
7. the principle of concern for the community, according to which cooperative act for the sustainable development of the communities they belong to, through policies approved by their members.[8]

One essential characteristic of the principles of cooperatives must be taken into account, namely that they do not have a normative character. From the perspective of Law no. 1/2005, they are used in interpreting and applying the provisions of this law. Some of these principles are mentioned or result from the provisions of Regulation no. 1435/2003. To the extent that they are taken over in the constitutive act of the SCE, they would be directly applicable to the members. These principles are in fact guidelines in creating the best practices in the operation of a cooperative society.[9]

[8] More about it see in Lang and Novy (2014).

[9] For a comparative review regarding the best practices see Popa Tache and Săraru (2024).

Among the principles stated above, we note the last one, which is of interest in the current study, namely the principle of concern for the community, according to which cooperative act for the sustainable development of the communities they are part of, through policies approved by their members. We also approach from this perspective the definition of the word community, which has the general meaning of Group of people with common interests, beliefs or norms of life. At the legislative level, the term community is found in various compound forms such as energy community, community of a certain ethnicity, local community, etc. but they all bring together these points of the basic definition.

4 The Legal Strengths of SCE for Creating a Community

Following a critical examination of the national provisions regarding cooperatives and especially regarding those of Law no. 1/2005 resulted that the way in which the Romanian legislator outlined the legal framework of such a company is very restrictive, with various legal oversights[10] that make impossible the use of such form of company for the communities with hundreds or thousands of members.

Among these, we highlight first the one related to social capital. This, due to the specificity of such a company, involves a variable social capital as well foreseen by the Romanian legislator in art. 9 para. 1 of Law no. 1/2005, after enunciating the minimum capital for the establishment of such a company. This fluctuation of social capital is normal considering the type of company, i.e. in which anyone can become a cooperative member, can increase/decrease his participation at any time, respecting certain statutory limits. Unfortunately, the subsequent provisions of the law regarding its amendment completely neutralize this notion of variable capital, mainly due to the fact that any change (increase or decrease) of capital is subject to the approval of the general meeting of members (art. 41 letters d) and e)) and registration to the register of commerce. Thus, if in the case of a cooperative, which would remain at the level of the five founding cooperative members, these changes would not be impossible to be approved, but would create a very bureaucratic process, due to the legal obligation to register these changes in the register of commerce, in the case of a cooperative with tens, hundreds or even thousands of members, these legislative provisions become prohibitive.

Another major barrier in the functioning of a cooperative is related to the quorum of the general meetings of the members. Thus, according to Art. 36 of Law no. 1/2005. *(1) At the first summoning the ordinary general meeting is legally reunited in the presence of half plus one of the number of cooperative members and can take valid decisions with the majority of the votes of the cooperative members present, and the extraordinary general meeting is legally reunited in the presence of three fourths of the number of members cooperative members and can take valid*

[10] For a very good critical analysis on this subject, Lupulescu (2014).

decisions with the majority of votes of the cooperative members present. (2) If the requirements set forth in paragraph (1) are not met, the ordinary general assembly that will meet at the second summon can deliberate on the issues listed on the agenda, provided that at least one third of the number of cooperating members is present, and can make valid decisions with the majority of votes of the cooperating members present. (3) If the conditions set forth in para. (1), the extraordinary general meeting that will meet at the second summon can deliberate on the issues listed on the agenda, provided that at least half of the cooperative members are present, and can make valid decisions with the majority of votes of the cooperative members present. (4) If the conditions set forth in para. (2) or (3), the ordinary or extraordinary general meeting will be reconvened until the conditions provided for in the two paragraphs are fulfilled, as the case may be.

This is a completely unrealistic regulation for the operation of any type of society and in particular the cooperative society, as is not allowed that at the general assembly of the cooperative members on the second summon to be hold the meeting regardless of the number of cooperative members that are present and make decisions with the vote of the majority of the members present, therefore such provision it has the ability to block any decision-making process at the level of society, which can even be "lethal" to it.[11]

Fortunately, the provisions of the European legislator regarding the European cooperative society are realistic and make it a currently feasible legal option in the creation of a community. Thus, with regard to the share capital of SCE, it should be noted that it is significantly higher than that of a Romanian cooperative society, namely 30,000 euros (an amount that we consider to be justified in the context of the scope of the activity of such a society and the fact that it necessarily involves members from another Member State). However, Regulation 1435/2003 does not require the approval of the general meeting of the cooperative members for any change in the capital and, it expressly provides that changes in the capital do not require changes to the articles of incorporation or publicity in case of any change in the capital. Thus, the capital can increase through successive contributions of members or the admission of new members and can decrease through the total or partial restitution of contributions, made subject to the maintenance of the minimum capital. The annual general meeting regarding the annual financial statements will determine the amount of the capital at the end of the year and its variation compared to the previous year (art. 4 paragraph 8).

Regarding the quorum required for the decision-making by the general meeting of cooperating members of an SCE, Regulation 1435/2003 in accordance with art. 61 provides that the SCE's constitutive deed provide for the requirements regarding the quorum and the majority applicable to the general meetings. Also, the general assembly decides with the majority of votes validly cast by the members present or represented. However, the general assembly called to rule on a decision that entails the amendment of the constitutive deed deliberates validly at the first convocation

[11] For a comparative view see Jamaluddin et al. (2023).

only if the members present or represented represent at least half of the total number of those registered on the date of the convocation; on the second convocation regarding the same agenda, no quorum condition is imposed. In the previously provided cases regarding the amendment of the constitutive deed, the general assembly decides with a majority of two thirds of the votes validly cast, except in cases where the legislation applicable to cooperatives in the member state on whose territory the SCE headquarters is located requires a larger majority.

From the way in which the European legislator decided to regulate the decision-making process of SCE, it follows that through the constitutive deed of this company it will be possible to provide the presence quorum and the voting quorum of the general assembly, following that the general assembly at the second convocation will take decisions regardless by the number of cooperative members present.

Personally I have carried out this attentive comparison of the legal framework of a Romanian cooperative established on the basis of Law no. 1/2005 and of a European cooperative society in 2019 the context of the establishment of an entity to create a renewable energy cooperative following the model of other cooperatives operating in such a field with hundreds or thousands of members, established in various local legal forms, but also later in another project related to the legal form of an energy community.[12] The result was the establishment in 2019 of an SCE, more precisely Cooperativadeenergie.ro Societate Cooperativa Europeana cu Raspundere Limitata, which from the 15 founding members (including the author of this study) has now reached almost a thousand cooperative members, representing the first and the largest renewable energy community in Romania[13] and the legal form of SCE allowed it to develop naturally. Unfortunately, in Romania there is still a very small number of European Cooperative Societies, respectively four such cooperatives, according to the information obtained from the National Trade Registry Office this year.

5 Conclusions

In the context where a community involves a group of several people, tens, hundreds or even thousands, although the common interest unites them, they would not be able to organize and function easily in the form of a cooperative established under Law no. 1/2005 due to the legal barriers exposed above, but it will be able to take the form of the European Society, which in the way it is regulated by the European legislator, after 20 years, remains as a current legal form in which a community working in a certain field.

We consider imperative to amend Law no. 1/2005 for it to become a functional framework for people who want to organize and operate in the form of a cooperative

[12] Hinescu (2023).

[13] www.cooperativadeenergie.ro.

and to be inspired by the legal framework of the SCE and also contain provisions regarding it. Changing the national legislation to the European one will have a major impact and will allow the use with greater frequency in practice of this type of society, which should then be suitable for the creation and support of a community in a any field of activity. Until then, the European Cooperative Society remains a current structure for community organization.

Documents

Companies Law no. 31/1990 published in the Official Gazette no. 1066/18.11.2004.

Law no. 1/2005 on the organization and operation of the cooperation published on Official Gazette no. 368 as of 20 May 2014.

Law no. 26/1990 regarding register of commerce following its amendment by the Government Emergency Ordinance no. 52/2008 for the amendment and completion of Companies Law no. 31/1990 and to supplement Law no. 26/1990 regarding register of commerce.

Law no. 265/2022 on the register of commerce and for the amendment of other laws with incidence on registration in the register of commerce published in the Official Gazette no. 750/26.07.2022.

Regulation CE no. 1435/2003 on the Statute for a European Cooperative Society published in Official Journal of the European Union no. 207 as of 18 August 2003 and Rectification published in Official Journal of the European Union no. 49 as of 17 February 2007.

Report from the Commission to the European Parliament, the Council, the European Economic and Social Committee and the Committee of The Regions: The application of Council Regulation (EC) No. 1435/2003 of 22 July 2003 on the Statute for a European Cooperative Society (SCE)/COM/2012/072 final. https://op.europa.eu/en/publication-detail/-/publication/494bb15b-c34d-4bdf-8518-75d6bde38cbb.

Report of CooPilot—Guidelines regarding the improvement of the cooperative system at the local and European level a project co-financed by DG Internal Market, Industry, Entrepreneurship and SMEs of the European Commission, https://www.coopilot-project.eu/wp-content/uploads/2018/04/LG_ALDA_RO.pdf.

Study on the implementation of the Statute for a European Cooperative Society: Executive Summary and Synthesis and Comparative Report: https://eur-lex.europa.eu/legal-content/EN/TXT/?uri=CELEX:52012DC0072.

Study on the implementation of the Statute for a European Cooperative Society: National Reports. https://ec.europa.eu/docsroom/documents/39568/attachments/1/translations/.

United Nations, 2025 UN International Year of Cooperatives, United Nations, https://2025.coop/.

References

Hinescu A (2023) Comunitățile de energie. O analiza a formelor juridice de organizare și funcționare. Greenpeace. https://www.greenpeace.org/static/planet4-romania-stateless/2023/03/9bfaa5ea-analiza-a-formelor-de-organizare.pdf?

Jamaluddin F, Saleh NM, Abdullah A, Hassan MS, Hamzah N, Jaffar R, Abdul Ghani Aziz SA, Embong Z (2023) Cooperative governance and cooperative performance: a systematic literature review. Sage Open 13(3). https://doi.org/10.1177/21582440231192944

Lang R, Novy A (2014) Cooperative housing and social cohesion: the role of linking social capital. Eur Plann Stud 22(8):1744–1764

Lupulescu AM (2014) Particularities concerning the cooperative companies. Perspect Bus Law J 3(1):232–238

Popa Tache CE, Săraru CS (2024) Evaluating today's multi-dependencies in digital transformation, corporate governance and public international law triad. Cogent Soc Sci 10(1). https://doi.org/10.1080/23311886.2024.2370945

Săraru CS, Popa-Tache CE (2024) An overview of certain tendencies in extending the concept of administrative litigation in the European Union and international law. J Knowl Dyn 1(1):61–74. https://doi.org/10.56082/jkd.2024.1.61

MIX
Papier aus verantwortungsvollen Quellen
Paper from responsible sources
FSC® C105338

If you have any concerns about our products,
you can contact us on
ProductSafety@springernature.com

In case Publisher is established outside the EU,
the EU authorized representative is:
Springer Nature Customer Service Center GmbH
Europaplatz 3, 69115 Heidelberg, Germany

Printed by Libri Plureos GmbH
in Hamburg, Germany